FAST
EDDIE

FAST EDDIE

IN 60 SECONDS HE GRABBED £1.2M. THE TRUE STORY OF THE CHEEKIEST HEIST EVER

MARK BULSTRODE AND GRANT SHERLOCK

JOHN BLAKE

Published by John Blake Publishing Ltd,
3 Bramber Court, 2 Bramber Road,
London W14 9PB, England

www.johnblakepublishing.co.uk

www.facebook.com/Johnblakepub facebook
twitter.com/johnblakepub twitter

First published in paperback in 2014

ISBN: 978 1 78219 747 8

British Library Cataloguing-in-Publication Data:

A catalogue record for this book is available from the British Library.

Design by www.envydesign.co.uk

Printed in Great Britain by CPI Group (UK) Ltd, Croydon, CR0 4YY

1 3 5 7 9 10 8 6 4 2

Papers used by John Blake Publishing are natural, recyclable
products made from wood grown in sustainable forests.
The manufacturing processes conform to the
environmental regulations of the country of origin.

Every attempt has been made to contact the relevant copyright-holders,
but some were unobtainable. We would be grateful if the
appropriate people could contact us.

ACKNOWLEDGEMENTS

This book would not have been possible without the people who knew Eddie Maher and his family being willing to share their stories.

We would like to thank all those who answered the knock at the door from two inquisitive reporters and were willing to delve into their memories from so many years ago.

In particular, we are grateful to Peter Bunn for sharing his experiences from the day of the theft.

It also could not have been done without the assistance of a host of valued friends and colleagues. Colin Adwent, a crime reporter in a class of his own, was invaluable in providing his expert knowledge of the case, as were Richard Cornwell and Brad Jones, and Dave Stewart in the USA.

We are equally grateful to Bob Graham for all his help in filling in the gaps of Maher's life in the USA.

We would also like to thank Paul Scothern of the CPS,

FAST EDDIE

and Suffolk Constabulary's Lisa Miller, John Barnett and David Giles.

Finally, thanks to our families for their support during the endless hours spent writing and researching this book.

CONTENTS

PROLOGUE

They left with as little fuss as when they arrived. Clutching clothing gathered in moments mixed with fear and adrenalin, they got into their SUV and drove away, expecting never to see their short-lived home again. They were the actions of a desperate criminal and his ceaselessly loyal family.

It was all the confirmation patrol officers keeping watch over the apartment in North 23rd Street needed to see to convince them they had their man. The balding man in his mid-fifties really was an international fugitive thought to have been responsible for one of Britain's most infamous crimes.

He was 'Fast Eddie' – the £1m thief whose crime earned him infamy in his homeland. And here he was, 10,000 miles across the Atlantic, climbing into a beat-up four-wheel-drive, grabbing as many clothes as he could lay his hands on.

The Ozark Police Department officers had been watching ever since an alert colleague spotted a likeness between the driver's licence photo of Michael Maher, a cable company technician who made $12.43 an hour, and the wanted picture of Edward Maher, the man behind one of the most daring thefts England had ever seen.

It was on 6 February 2012 that the Ozark, Missouri, Police Department had received the tip-off. They had been told that this seemingly respectable British man was harbouring a dark secret. The man known as Michael Maher, according to the police source, was in fact Eddie Maher, a fugitive wanted in England for 'stealing a large amount of cash while working as a security guard'.

The photographs certainly seemed to marry up. There was a striking likeness between the man known as Michael Maher and the British security guard wanted over the disappearance of 50 money bags that went missing from Felixstowe in Suffolk in 1993. It was enough for the police to begin their covert surveillance operation.

As the police delved deeper into Maher's background, more information came to light. But then the surveillance operation took a surprising turn.

Lee King was in trouble with the police and had been arrested on 6 February 2012 – the same day as the tip-off about Maher's true identity. Lee was being questioned on suspicion of a domestic violence offence. And, not for the first time, it was left to Maher to bail out his son. But to help Lee, Maher would have to come into direct contact with the police – something he had desperately avoided for nearly 7,000 days, ever since 22 January 1993.

As police officers watched, Maher arrived at Ozark Police Department – apparently oblivious to the scrutiny he was under

- to pay the 'bond' that would secure his son's release. He appeared calm and unnerved. But rather than pay the money and get out as quickly as possible, Maher had other ideas. He told the police he wanted to make a complaint, alleging that one of his guns had been stolen by his son's wife, Jessica King.

It was a sign of how relaxed he had become. Rather than hiding from the authorities, he was confident enough to go to a police station to report a crime. The fact it would prompt an inquiry that would result in the police visiting his house was of no apparent concern to him. That inquiry would involve King being interviewed – and Maher had learned three months earlier that she had discovered the truth about his past. He had threatened to kill her if she ever told anyone about his true identity. Not only that, he was now accusing her of stealing something he should not have had in his possession. As a non-US citizen – and an illegal one at that – Maher was banned from keeping guns under American law.

Maher, not for the first time in his life, had made a decision that came with massive risk. Undeterred, he went ahead with making the allegation, pointing the finger at his daughter-in-law. What happened next must have brought his world crashing down.

In the space of a few seconds, he heard the words he had always dreaded. Incredibly, a police officer told him that he knew Maher was a fugitive wanted in England … but could not arrest him. It was an admission that had the potential to derail the police investigation and surveillance operation. The officer had taken the decision to confront Maher without the knowledge of more senior detectives.

Lee overheard the conversation – and so did the police surveillance teams. Everything had suddenly changed; Maher had been caught off-guard and, for the first time since stealing £1m, was on the back foot. The official police report described his mood as 'irate'.

Jeffrey W Atwood, an FBI special agent, was watching Maher's every move and listening to his every word. True to form, Maher's instant reaction was to run. In his report, Atwood wrote, 'Maher told his son that they would have to leave again and threatened to kill the person who tipped off police about his identity.'

As Lee was interviewed by police, the covert surveillance operation continued at 5117 North 23rd Street. Maher, meanwhile, was panicking and preparing a quick exit.

Atwood said, 'During the interview, Maher called his son and told him that they had to leave immediately. Maher's son told Maher that he could not go with him. Shortly after the interview was concluded, OPD officers observed Maher, a white female and a juvenile leave the residence carrying some clothing.'

The female was his wife, Debbie Brett, and the juvenile his youngest son, Mark.

Just like in 1993, Maher was back on the run. But instead of an armoured security van, this time his getaway car was the battered SUV, with 250,000 miles on the clock. And unlike the first time round, this time he had not had a head start. Unbeknown to him, he was being followed all the way.

Atwood said, 'OPD officers and FBI agents continued to conduct surveillance on Maher and eventually followed him to a motel in Ozark, where he, the female and juvenile male checked in to a room.'

That night, the rundown motel became a hideout for Maher, Debbie and Mark. Their plan was to disappear the next morning.

But overnight, Maher seemingly had a change of heart. He decided that his days on the run were over. Lee contacted Atwood by telephone to tell him that Maher had called. Atwood remembers, 'Maher told his son that he had checked into the motel because he was afraid that the police were coming to his house to arrest him. Maher told his son that he had changed his mind about leaving the area and that if the police were coming to arrest him, he would not resist. Maher told his son that he was going back home. Surveillance confirmed that Maher went back to his residence.'

This time, the police wasted no time in pouncing on Maher and, when they arrived at his house, the fugitive was waiting. In a final attempt to disguise his true identity, he told police his name was Michael Maher and offered to produce a Missouri driver's licence bearing his name. But his cover had already been blown and he was taken into custody.

With Maher out of the picture, police turned their attention to his wife, who identified herself as Deborah Ann Brett. It was then that the story of the couple's time in America began to be revealed. Brett told police that Maher had used the alias of Stephen King and was primarily known as Michael Maher, using the false date of birth of 17 April 1951.

It was a story Maher would confirm when interviewed

after being taken to Ozark Police Station. And for the first time in nearly 20 years, he was answering to the name Edward John Maher.

1
GONE

The dark-blue Securicor van pulled up outside Lloyds Bank in Hamilton Road, Felixstowe, just after 9.30am on 22 January 1993. It was a Friday and the Edwardian town's main shopping street was already a hive of activity. Less than a month had passed since Christmas and the chill wind of the recession was being felt throughout the country.

Unemployment was high and the economic outlook was grim. It would be another three months before Conservative chancellor Norman Lamont would declare Britain finally to be out of recession. The country was in the midst of the longest period of negative growth since the 1930s, with the economy failing for more than two years. Just four months earlier, the British Government, led by Prime Minister John Major, had endured what became known as Black Wednesday as Mr Lamont was forced to spend billions in an attempt to prop up the rapidly falling value of the pound.

The start of the decade had seen inflation in double figures and interest rates hit highs of 15 per cent. As many battled against the threat of having their homes repossessed, it was a time when spending was being closely checked. Yet on this biting cold, but dry, January day there was a still a steady procession of shoppers out and about, some picking up the last of the sale bargains.

The town still had its own magistrates' court in the red-brick Town Hall building on Felixstowe seafront, just a few hundred yards from the end of Hamilton Road down the steep Bent Hill. Most defendants appearing before magistrates that day would have had to sign in by 9.30am ready for court to start at 10.00am sharp. Any later and they would face being prosecuted for breaching their bail conditions. It meant there were normally a few people hurrying along to make it in time. For high-profile cases, television camera crews and newspaper photographers would often be camped outside waiting for the target of that day's story to arrive.

Like most traditional British coastal resorts, Felixstowe was a town few tourists visited in the winter. In summer, it would be a different story as people arrived from all over the country, flocking to the beach and packing out the resort's cafés, amusement arcades and restaurants. But today, thoughts of sun-soaked sands and holidaymakers seemed a long way off.

The rush-hour traffic was beginning to ease when Eddie Maher, only a few months into his new job as a Securicor guard, manoeuvred the armoured vehicle into its regular parking spot. Maher, a 37-year-old former firefighter and pub landlord from east London, picked a prime slot to pull into, just outside the front door of the bank, at 33 Hamilton Road.

Positioned on a junction at the top of the main shopping

street, the branch was set in an impressive nineteenth-century building. The area was known locally as 'bank corner', with Lloyds on one side of the road and Barclays on the other. Waves crashing in from the North Sea could be seen and occasionally heard from this elevated vantage point, depending on the wind direction. Diagonally opposite the bank was an imposing Methodist church and next door was Tooks, a popular independent bakery that ensured the smell of fresh bread wafted through the sea air each morning.

With a population of about 25,000, Felixstowe was Suffolk's fourth-largest town. Although slightly dwarfed by its near-neighbour Ipswich in terms of size and number of shops, the resort had managed to maintain a busy high street despite the effects of the recession. Major chains like Woolworth's, Courts furnishers and Argos had branches in the town, mixed with a variety of smaller shops, including Coes menswear shop, Cole's chemist, Orchard House grocers, Phillips bookstore and newsagent, Jardins shoes and Foster's Menswear. Eastern Counties Newspapers Group, which printed the *Evening Star* and *East Anglian Daily Times*, also had a base in Hamilton Road, opposite the town's post office.

The *Star* was known as a punchy, campaigning, tabloid-driven newspaper that sought to hold those in power to account. Its focus was Ipswich and east Suffolk, while the *EADT* – often referred to as 'the *Anglian*' – covered a larger patch incorporating all of Suffolk as well as north Essex and was less likely to take a stance on an issue than its in-your-face sister title.

A large proportion of residents in the town were retired but there was also plenty to keep younger generations interested with various bars and pubs. When it came to jobs, the Port of Felixstowe was the main employer, either directly or indirectly through the many haulage and shipping-related businesses in the area.

The port was on its way to becoming one of the biggest in Europe and had already helped to bring about major road improvements. Its expansion helped pave the way for the £24m Orwell Bridge opening in Ipswich in December 1982, making it much easier for both hauliers and tourists to find their way into Felixstowe. The port had also become one of the biggest employers in Suffolk as a whole and was seen as being crucial to the county's economy. Its development saw the name 'Felixstowe' appear on road signs for miles around as lorry drivers were directed to the east coast, ensuring the town was familiar to those far beyond the county borders of Suffolk.

As well as its Edwardian architecture, the town had other attractions, including Landguard Fort – claimed to be the site of the last opposed seaborne invasion of England in 1667. The fort, rebuilt in the eighteenth century and then modified in the nineteenth century, also proudly proclaimed to be the venue of the first land battle of the Royal Marines.

The dozens of beach huts nestled either side of the town's pier, which was once one of the biggest in the country, were in keeping with the traditional appearance of a seaside resort. Amusement arcades and fairs interweaved with neatly presented gardens, bowling greens and tea rooms. But behind the veneer of the postcard attractions, stories about the failing economy were dominating the town, as they were the country as a whole. Both of Suffolk's daily newspapers had tales of economic woe splashed across their front pages on this January day. The *Evening Star* led with an article titled 'YOUR CASH BLOW': 'People in Ipswich now face steep increases in car parking charges on top of the bigger than expected council tax bills,' the story began. Parking charges would have to go up by 15 per cent to pay for £250,000 closed-circuit television cameras, the newspaper reported.

Council tax was due to come into force in April that year in place of the unpopular Community Charge – more commonly known as the poll tax. The levy, targeting individuals rather than properties, was condemned by many as unfair because it imposed potentially heavy burdens on homeowners regardless of their wealth. Its introduction sparked trouble around the UK, culminating with riots in London in March 1990. Three years on, as the new property-based council tax was set to be introduced, the country had yet to recover its financial footing.

The *EADT* front-page story on 22 January 1993 reflected the bleak outlook for the region: 'Unemployment in East Anglia has climbed to its highest level for seven years – casting gloom over hopes for an economic recovery,' the newspaper reported. Elsewhere, Bill Clinton had become American President three days earlier and was setting out his priorities, which were dealing with issues in Iraq and Bosnia, according to the page 2 story in the *Star* that day. The *EADT* report of 'hostilities between Saddam Hussein and the United States' as an American warplane bombed an Iraqi air defence site was likely to have dominated much of Clinton's thoughts at the time.

The back page of the *Star* was looking ahead to Premier

League Ipswich Town's FA Cup fourth-round tie against Division One side Tranmere Rovers. The headline of 'MINNOWS TO POSE BIG THREAT' was based on comments from the Suffolk side's team manager Mick McGiven. Other stories on the Suffolk media agenda that day included 'good news' about the Queen, who had 'shaken off a stomach bug' to attend a Women's Institute meeting in Sandringham, Norfolk. The arrest of a man from the Ipswich area over the murder of a sex worker from Norwich called Natalie Pearman also featured.

As far as Felixstowe was concerned, two stories appeared to be leading the agenda in that day's newspapers. Martin Hogg china shops, which had a branch in Felixstowe and four other nearby towns, had gone into liquidation. There was also apparent controversy over 'traffic calming' measures in the town's Grange Farm Avenue: 'Fears have been voiced that lives could be put at risk if a planned traffic reduction scheme slows fire crews on their way to an emergency at the resort's largest group of houses,' the *Evening Star* reported.

It was a sign of how relatively peaceful Felixstowe was. The town rarely dominated news headlines, even locally, and January, as people got back into their post-Christmas routines, was never normally the most 'newsy' of months. For many, the end of January could never come quickly enough, with the period just after Christmas always feeling like a struggle. But now the weekend was approaching and wage cheques were landing in people's bank accounts to help ease the post-festive season malaise.

Arriving at the bank on 22 January 1993 in the back of the

Securicor van was 'payday' and 'weekend shopping' cash, neatly stashed in dozens of bags waiting to be delivered. In total, just under £1.2m in coins and notes was inside the van.

The Felixstowe branch was the first call of the day for Maher and his colleague, Peter Bunn, 48, who was to act as 'leg man'. Maher had left his partner and young son at home in Essex that morning before heading out to work.

After joining the Army as a teenager, Maher was embarking on another new career in joining Securicor. From a large family raised in Ilford, east London, he had passed the various security checks to land his role as a cash-in-transit guard. In many ways, his new job had echoes of his past. Just like his time with the Royal Green Jackets infantry, Maher's role had a regimented feel to it. His route was set out for him and his task clearly defined. At each stop, Maher would wait inside the van while Bunn delivered the cash. And his route that day was due to take in various branches of Lloyds Bank and Ipswich's main Post Office. The van was carrying more cash than usual because of the post office stop, which was visited less frequently than the banks and therefore a higher value of cash was carried as a result.

Being on the 'Felixstowe run' meant Maher would be able to have an earlier finish than he would have done on other routes, which covered longer distances from the Securicor base over the Suffolk border in Essex. The Securicor van, with its distinctive livery and noisy diesel engine, was easily recognisable and would typically draw passing glances as it made its many drop-offs.

On this unremarkable January day, it arrived at its first stop shortly before the bank opened. As the van pulled up, an elderly man was already waiting outside the door of the bank. Passers-by noticed the vehicle parked outside as the guards waited for staff at the bank to let them in. After an initial pause, Bunn got out of the van and waited alongside the elderly man. Moments later, the door was opened and Bunn was able to get on with the delivery.

It was often the case at Securicor that staff would share the driving, with the roles normally being swapped after lunch. On this day, Maher had started off behind the wheel and, because it was such a short route, there would be no need for any switch. Following the normal routine, Maher would wait in the vehicle as his workmate went inside.

The clock had just ticked past 9.30am when Bunn was able to enter the building and hand over the first of his cash deliveries. There were two boxes to be delivered, each containing up to £25,000, but strict rules around security meant only one could be delivered at a time. A quick delivery, hand over the money, out and on to the next job – that was the routine.

There was always time for a quick chat and maybe a laugh and a joke with the bank staff but, once the paperwork was completed, there was no time to hang around. This Friday morning drop was no different to the thousands of others Maher and his colleagues had completed.

While inside the bank, Bunn learned that he also needed to collect cash as well. This would add time to the journey but he knew he would be able to tell Maher when he went back to collect his second delivery. After collecting a signature from the cashier to hand over the first cash deposit, Bunn strode back outside. He marched through the front door and approached the spot where the van had been parked. As he looked up he realised it was nowhere to be seen. The van had gone.

The following day's front pages were yet again set to be dominated by another money-related story … but this time it wouldn't be the economy grabbing everyone's attention.

2

THE OTHER GUARD

As security guard Peter Bunn walked out of the bank, he could barely believe the sight that greeted him. The Securicor van he had climbed out of only minutes earlier had disappeared. All he could see was an empty space where it had been parked.

After looking to his left and right, his first reaction was to grab his hand-held radio. He twice attempted to contact his colleague inside the van but both calls went unanswered. After a moment's pause, he spun around and went back into the bank to raise the alarm.

'I was thinking there's something wrong here,' he said. 'You wouldn't be able to print what I said. I stopped and I thought, "Where the hell have you gone?" I had a hand-held radio. I called him up on that with one or two more expletives and I got no reply. I then went straight back into the bank. I told the cashier that the van had gone and I needed a phone, which they supplied straight away. I phoned up my control room in

Chelmsford, told them the van had gone missing and told them to phone the necessary people.'

The reality of what had happened had yet to sink in. Could Maher have simply driven off with the money? Perhaps there could be an innocent explanation? Had he been kidnapped?

'My initial feeling was that I didn't think he had been with us that long. Maybe he's done a runner? Then I thought maybe some stroppy traffic warden had told him to move off and the idiot had done so. It had been known but happened very rarely.'

Carol, a Lloyds cashier working at the bank that day, remembers the delivery from Bunn – and then the initial confusion over the disappearance of the van. She also recalls thinking a traffic warden could have been responsible for the panic in the first few moments.

'We were waiting for it to come back round the block,' she said. 'The guard waited a while but there was nothing. He was still pretty relaxed at this point and joked, "He'd better come back … my packed lunch is in that van." But as the time passed, we knew something was up. We started to think the guard might have been kidnapped or something. Our manager dialled 999. People were worried about what had happened to the guard. We thought he might be in trouble.'

As the minutes ticked by, the chances of an innocent explanation were receding rapidly. By 9.38am, police were on their way.

Bunn and the cashiers had attempted to put a brave face on what had happened – and joke about it - but all they could do was wait. Bunn had an empty box by his side, which he had been due to refill with the second delivery of £25,000 the bank had been expecting. That £25,000 – along with the rest of the £1,174,600 – was now long gone. There was also little point in Bunn collecting the cash he had been due to pick up from the branch. He had no van to put it in.

An awkward silence settled over the bank staff as it gradually dawned on both the cashiers and Bunn what had happened. This was serious. A huge amount of money had gone missing. Everyone present knew they would have to give their account of what had happened in the inevitable major police investigation that would follow. But they knew there was little light they could shed on that morning's events. They simply had no idea what had happened.

For Bunn, time was now a blur and he was left to reflect on the events of the past few minutes. 'I just waited for the police with my box,' he said. 'Time had just come to a standstill. I was thinking, "I want to go home." I was annoyed at what had happened. Each day I just wanted to get the job done and get home in one piece. We all knew the risks that came with the job. That's why I never hung around. I knew pretty quickly that wasn't going to happen that day.'

Police officers soon arrived at the bank and surveyed the scene. They quickly identified Bunn in his Securicor uniform and helmet and had a brief conversation with him. Minutes passed as frantic calls were made between police officers trying to establish what had happened and those attempting to locate the van. The time had gone quickly and, by 10.15am, the van had been found in Micklegate Road.

Shortly after the discovery, police officers at the bank approached Bunn and asked him to get into a police van. Bunn might have assumed he was being taken in for questioning, but that would come later. The officers had a more pressing task for him – they wanted him to join them on the short trip to the spot where the Securicor van had been found abandoned. Officers were already there but were unsure whether Maher was still inside. Aware that it was a crime scene, they did not want to contaminate the vehicle with their fingerprints and destroy any potential evidence. Yet they needed swift answers and so they decided to ask Bunn to attend the site.

'They asked me to see if he was inside it but not to touch it,' Bunn said. 'I just looked in the windows. I knew all the nooks and crannies of the van and where to look. They wanted to know if he was tied up in there. I told them that he wasn't. I was able to tell them pretty quickly. At that stage, I was thinking to myself, "He's not in the van … he's gone." I guess in my mind I had concluded that he had done a runner ...'

The police were still unsure what had happened but it was crucial to them that they had established Maher was definitely not in the vehicle. That meant scenes of crime officers could begin work on trying to find potential clues hidden in the vehicle. Any fingerprints, DNA samples or fibres could prove to be crucial pieces of evidence in the subsequent inquiry, and the police were intent on securing the vehicle to prevent any passers-by tampering with it.

A quick check of the van revealed all the cash had been taken, aside from a few bags of coins totalling £2,100. Photographs also had to be taken, showing the van as it was discovered.

For Bunn, the next stop was Felixstowe Police Station. He

was fully aware of the seriousness of what had happened by now. For a man who had started work at 6.00am, he was facing the prospect of a long day ahead.

He would spend the next seven hours being questioned.

He remembers it as a 'friendly' interrogation, although it was clear police were unable to rule him out as a suspect at that stage. Bunn understood why and thought it was the logical conclusion anyone might come to. 'They took me to the nick and put me into what they call a "soft room",' he said. 'It had nicely coloured walls. I suppose they were trying to put me at ease. Then this very nice lady comes in with a massive great notepad and then a detective. Then I was questioned. It wasn't aggressive. They were quite nice and friendly actually. But I had the feeling that I was obviously a prime suspect. It could have been a set-up job and police might have thought I was involved. That's just the way the police minds work, which is the way they have to think. I just answered the questions they put to me.'

During the course of the questioning, Bunn was asked to piece together his day from the moment he arrived at the Securicor branch, on an industrial estate in Russell Way, Chelmsford. He started by describing how he had got to work at about 5.50am.

'I was normally an early bird. I remember he turned up at about five-to-six in the morning, just as I was parking up,' he said. 'We were both due to start at 6.00am.'

Preparations for the day ahead would then begin, involving collecting the van they would use, picking up the bags of cash and then signing paperwork to confirm they had received the load. Maher was the allocated driver and Bunn the leg man.

'When people first join it's sometimes easier for the person who's been there longest to be the leg man,' said Bunn, who got a job as a guard at Securicor in 1971 after 12 years in the Royal Navy as a submariner. 'The cashiers can be funny with handing over the cash if it's someone they don't know.'

Bunn went on to describe his day in detail, including the fact that Maher had arrived in a taxi that morning. It was not something that Bunn thought was unusual, although it would prove to be a key part in Maher's planning of the day. 'I didn't think it was odd as cars can break down,' he said. 'I didn't actually know where he lived. I saw him turn up in a taxi and didn't think anything of it.'

One of the first problems they had to deal with on the day was the fact that Bunn's usual van would not start. It had broken down, meaning they had to switch to a spare van. 'It wouldn't have mattered what van it was. They all had the same security. This was just the spare one. It was exactly the same as the one we would've gone in,' he said. 'It was just a bit more of a beaten up old truck.'

Police asked Bunn about Maher but he was unable to provide much help. He could not even recall working with him a week earlier. 'When they said I had been out with him before, I said, "Had I?" I just couldn't remember. He was just one of those people I never got to know,' said Bunn. 'It was a bit of a company thing at Securicor, really. There was such a high turnover of people. They would go out there with bags of money and then hear about all the hold-ups and they'd be off. You didn't get to know people until they'd been there six months. So many would leave before that.'

As far as Bunn was concerned, Maher still counted as a 'new boy', having only started five months earlier. But although Bunn had not had much time to strike up a relationship with Maher, his first impressions were not favourable. According to Bunn, the pair barely spoke on the way to Felixstowe that morning. He said, 'We had nothing to talk about. He didn't come across as an overly chatty person and didn't seem that friendly. I'd say the odd thing, maybe giving the odd direction, a few words about the weather, moaning about the fact we were going to work in the dark, that sort of thing. But that was it.'

Despite the regular, prolonged spells of silence, Bunn said there was nothing to suggest Maher was at all nervous. 'He didn't seem edgy - he just came to work and we went out. He is obviously a very good actor. I didn't notice anything nervy. His hand certainly wasn't shaking or anything obvious like that. I didn't take much notice. If it was a friend, I would have had a laugh and a joke but I had nothing to talk about with him. He didn't say anything.'

The account of Maher's demeanour was carefully noted down during the interview. Bunn was still coming to terms with the magnitude of what had happened that day, although there was time for one almost humorous moment. While waiting inside the bank for police to arrive, it dawned on him that, along with the huge amount of money, also missing was his flask, sandwiches, pipe and tobacco. 'That was the only funny thing about it actually,' he said. 'Not only were my sandwiches gone but also my pipe.'

It was something the police took into consideration while he was at the police station. 'Because I hadn't got my pipe, they went to get me some cigarettes, which weren't quite the same,' he said. 'They did make me some cups of tea as well.'

Bunn, who at the time was living with his wife in Great Baddow on the edge of Chelmsford, remembered the gruelling police interview. 'This lady was writing it all down,' he said, speaking in the front room of his comfortable, semi-detached home in Chelmsford in 2013. 'Then all of a sudden they'd ask me a question I'd already answered about three pages earlier. It became obvious they were seeing if my answers were always going to be the same. I didn't feel threatened or anything. They were just doing their job.

'I can't remember exactly what time I left the police station but I know it was dark when I went out. I think I must have been there, at a rough guess, from 10.30am. I'm sure it must have been about 5.00pm in the evening when I left.'

Bunn's story stacked up and he had remained consistent throughout the interview process. However, it would not be the last time he was the focus of police attention.

3

THE GETAWAY

It appeared to be the perfect crime. The supposedly impregnable, two-tonne armoured security van had been emptied and dumped close to Felixstowe seafront. Fifty bags of money, which included coins and notes ranging in value from £5 to £50, had gone. Each bag contained up to £25,000.

Eddie Maher, the seemingly respectable family man whose past careers with the Army and London Fire Brigade had helped land him the job as a cash-in-transit guard, had vanished with them. He had beaten the system and hit the jackpot. The value of his haul had been more than he could have hoped for since the post office drop in Ipswich had significantly increased the typical amount carried on the Securicor run.

No one had been hurt. It was a plan executed with expert precision and one that clinically exploited the initial confusion caused by his disappearance. When police arrived at the bank, Maher might well have already been unloading the cash into a second getaway car.

Detectives had the task of retracing his movements – step by step. They started at the bank, where officers were met with a confused scene. It was several minutes before it was realised the van was not coming back, and 45 minutes before police found it. And despite it having a tracking device, staff at the Securicor depot in Chelmsford had not been able to pinpoint its location.

In 1993, tracking technology was still relatively new. This had been one of its first major tests. Speaking in 2013, Peter Bunn said, 'We did have some sort of tracking device but it was early days and it didn't work. I think that's why they took so long to find the van.'

The failure of the technology was one of three pieces of good fortune Maher benefited from that morning in Felixstowe. The first came when he initially arrived at the bank, only to find it had yet to open. Bunn, the leg man, immediately clocked the fact that there was a man waiting outside. 'When someone is standing there the wheels start going round in your head,' he said. 'It's the nature of the job.'

Maher would have been anxious to put his plan into action and could not afford any delays. Bunn was equally as keen to get the job done as quickly as possible. To their relief, the main front doors were opened at 9.30am.

By now, Bunn was satisfied that the man who had been waiting outside posed no threat. 'I took a look at the guy, saw he was quite elderly and wasn't bothered.'

And for Maher, the coast was clear for the first part of his plan to be executed. After watching his colleague enter the bank, Maher made his getaway. It would not be until a few minutes later that Bunn realised he had gone. His failure to reach Maher on the hand-held radio they both used would not have been enough to provoke immediate concern – the guards knew the radio coverage was patchy and it was possible the technology had failed. Had it been more reliable, Bunn would have immediately known it was suspicious and probably would not have tried a second time to get an answer. In turn, he would have been able to raise the alarm a few minutes earlier.

They were fine margins but every second counted in Maher's escape plan. He had no time to waste. Coupled with the initial theory that there could possibly have been an innocent explanation for the van's disappearance, it bought Maher valuable minutes.

Before the first police officer had even arrived at the bank, Maher would have been able comfortably to cover the 1.3 miles between Hamilton Road and Micklegate Road. It is a journey that would normally take less than five minutes. In a rush, it could be completed much quicker.

When the Securicor van pulled up outside the bank that morning, it was pointing towards the sea, with the majority of the Hamilton Road shopping street behind it. Maher's escape route is likely to have seen him carry on along Hamilton Road, past Barclays Bank and Argos and a cluster of about 20 more shops. The van was heading towards the sea. Had the tracking device been working properly, it would have immediately flagged up that there were no banks or post offices in that direction. It was already a major diversion from the normal route, and the alarm could then have been raised much earlier.

Hamilton Road continued into the steep and winding Bent Hill, with its nightclub and bar on the left-hand side. With the weight of the vehicle and the sheer incline, it is likely Maher would have had to apply the brakes as he negotiated the short distance to the bottom of the hill. Once there, he would have been able to see North Sea waves crashing on to the beach straight ahead. Traffic is unlikely to have been a problem at that point. The Spa Pavilion was to his left and the pier to the right. He would have taken a right turn into Undercliff Road West.

It was at this point that Maher had another slice of luck. Unbeknown to him, there was a high-profile case being heard in the town's magistrates' court, less than 100 yards to his left. There were journalists inside the building and at least one camera crew and photographer outside. Fortunately for Maher, their lenses were focused on people walking into the court building rather than on any passing traffic.

As he manoeuvred into Undercliff Road West, he passed a succession of seafront businesses on his right, most of which would have been shut at that time of day. On the other side was the sea, with the carefully prepared flowerbeds and neat grass lawns providing a barrier between the road and the promenade.

Once on Undercliff Road West, Maher would have been able to put his foot down and pick up some speed, or as much as the van would allow. It had a sluggish diesel engine and could reach a top speed of about 70mph, once it got going. The van they were using that day was H-registered, making it three years old, but it had not aged well, according to Bunn.

'It was a slug to drive,' he said. 'It was a battered old truck, that one. It could get up to 70mph after a while but, like any old diesel, it wasn't exactly a racing car.'

Although cars would have been parked on either side of the road, there was still enough room for two vehicles to pass comfortably in opposite directions. Maher's only concern would have been getting stuck behind a slow vehicle. If that happened, he would have had to simply to follow behind, waiting patiently as he edged towards the drop-off point. Overtaking would have been risky as it would have drawn attention to the van.

Passing the town's war memorial, he would then have approached its swimming pool and pier. He then had a decision to make about which route to take next – and the choice he made showed he had done his homework. He could have turned left into Sea Road or have driven about 200 yards further along Undercliff Road West and join Langer Road at the Ordnance Roundabout.

Langer Road, lined with a mixture of bungalows, detached and semi-detached houses along with the Langer County Primary School, would have been far busier. The school holidays were over and the area would have still been busy with parents making their way home after dropping off their children. It was also a bus route with a succession of junctions on either side of the road. Local people generally tried to avoid the area at peak times.

The Sea Road option would have given Maher a long, wide and straight route to make progress along, with views far ahead giving him the opportunity to see any potential problems. In the peak summer season, the area would have been packed with tourists, and roads would have been congested with prying eyes at every turn. On this bleak January morning, though, it would have been deserted. It was known to be far quieter than Langer Road.

Maher would have reached the same conclusion on the dummy run he would almost certainly have embarked on before the snatch. So as he approached the turning for Sea Road, the likelihood is that he had already decided that that was the best option. In comparison to Undercliff Road West, Sea Road was slightly further from the beach and the rows of beach huts that lined it. And instead of businesses, the majority of buildings along the pavement were either private houses, guest houses or hotels, some of which would have been shut for the winter season. There was a boating lake and go-kart track on his left but neither was in use.

Micklegate Road was the eleventh turn on the right. On a clearer day, he might have almost been able to see the junction along the dead straight road. But as he was travelling towards it, he saw the first problem ahead. Temporary traffic lights had been installed as new pipes were being laid. The work had only begun in the past couple of days.

It is inconceivable that Maher would not have carefully planned the route, timing how long it would take and coming up with the best roads to travel along. If he had done it the previous week, the traffic lights would not have been there.
It presented Maher with a problem.

If he had taken a diversion down one of the side roads that came off Sea Road, he would have run the risk of driving through streets packed with houses, thereby increasing the chances of someone seeing the van and realising it was a long way from its normal route. There was also the possibility that he could get stuck behind traffic in one of the streets. If he had to reverse, the van's warning beeper would have sounded, attracting further attention. That was the last thing Maher wanted.

But with work now being carried out on the road, it was unavoidable that there would be a higher number of people in the area. Police would later receive witness statements from workmen on Sea Road stating that they had seen a blue van. Fortunately for Maher, the workmen did not pay him much attention. They had not noticed anything out of the ordinary.

An Anglian Water worker, who was laying pipes, told reporters, 'I saw a blue van drive past which could have been the Securicor vehicle. There was nothing unusual about it and it certainly didn't seem in any hurry.'

Once through the traffic lights, the road was clear for Maher and Micklegate Road was rapidly approaching on the right. The choice of location to abandon the van was far from random. Most parts of the seafront were packed with houses, hotels and businesses. This area was not. Although close to the beach, it was further from the busier promenade. Police described it as a quiet side street.

Maher had already passed the majority of the town's seafront attractions, such as the pier, Spa Pavilion theatre and restaurants. They were clustered about a mile further north. Unlike neighbouring streets, this one had just four houses. The semi-detached properties were tucked away at the top of the short street, which was straight, wide and with exits at either end. Maher would not need to drive to the point where the houses were. There was plenty of space for him to stop well before that.

Manning's Amusement Park backed on to the street with a 15ft wall lined with trees. There would be no chance of any prying eyes from that side. On the other side was a car park, which, on most cold January days, was virtually deserted.

With no parking restrictions in the area and a view of the sea just a few hundred yards away, it might have appeared to be a good spot to stop for a short break. And although obvious to anyone with any knowledge of security, most people might not have thought it odd to see a van parked in such a street. Maher had also established that the only chance of people passing the area would be staff going to work at the amusement arcade. But that would be later. The business generally did not get going until 10.00am.

For Maher, Micklegate Road represented the ideal place to carry out the next stage of his plan. The van stopped parallel with what was known as the Crazy House, an attraction on the adjoining amusement park. The front of the van was facing Langer Road, confirming it would have been driven into Micklegate Road via Sea Road. It seemed highly unlikely that Maher would have performed any reversing routine once in the street. His aim was simply to get the cash out of the van as quickly as possible and carry on with his escape.

He wanted to park the van and get on with what he had to do. Time was of the essence. The bags had to be unloaded and transferred as quickly as possible. He did not have long. He would have known about the vehicle's tracking device.

What he probably did not know was that it had failed that morning, forcing police to scour the area to find the vehicle. It was another slice of luck Maher could not have counted on in planning his escape.

But when the police did eventually arrive, it was the transfer of the cash that provided them with one of their first major clues early in the inquiry. The security systems in the van meant access could only be granted if the driver allowed it. He would have had to have pressed a button on the driver's side of the cab. Without that, the bolt that secured the outer door would remain in place. To get out of the vehicle, the guard would have to open the inside door, which led to an airlock. Once in the airlock, the door linking it with the driver's seat would have to be shut and locked.

Using the same key, the door on the other side of the airlock could then be opened, which led to the back of the van where the cash was stored.

The security system meant only one lock could be freed at any time, with the one key for the two locks. Once through, the guard would be able to get the cash and go back into the airlock. It was then up to the driver to press a button next to his seat to allow the guard to exit the vehicle via the outer door. The guard would then slam it shut, which would see the bolt automatically swing back, locking the outer door.

In short, this intricate system meant Maher would not have been able to carry out the theft alone. Bunn said it would not have taken long to collect all the cash and transfer it through the airlock. But he said it was likely Maher and his accomplice would have both been inside the airlock at the same time. 'All he had to do was press the button on the side of the van to let the accomplice in. That would release the bolt on the outer door, which is how he would have let me in. Then that person can get into the airlock.'

Importantly, Bunn said it was possible for two people to be inside the airlock at the same time. Another button that opened the side door was accessible from the confined space. 'They could've done it in one hit, with all the bags in one go,' he said. 'It would've been a tight squeeze but they could've done it. The bags they would've wanted were quite large sacks. You wouldn't need any more than two people. It wouldn't take much to grab the 50 bags. They would have bunged it straight into the getaway car.'

Bunn said it would not have been possible to fit any more than two people inside the airlock at the same time as the cash. It supported the police theory that two people had cleared the cash from the van.

If they became trapped in the airlock, one option would have been to exit via the escape hatch. However, that was alarmed and would have led to a loud shrieking noise, Bunn said. In any case, it had not been breached.

Bunn gave detailed explanations to detectives about how the security system on the van worked. His evidence proved crucial in shaping the early part of the inquiry. His insistence that it would have been 'impossible' for Maher to release the locks, get the cash and complete the getaway alone also meant police knew they were hunting more than one person.

Without anyone noticing, the bags were quickly unloaded from the Securicor van and transferred into a Toyota Previa Space Cruiser, which had been stolen two months before. The van was left on the roadside, about halfway up the street and next to a line of trees.

When 31-year-old Sue Jones walked across the nearby car park into Micklegate Road at 9.45am, she noticed the Securicor van. There were no signs of activity around it and she thought nothing of it. She was on her way to the amusement park where she worked as a cashier.

That day, she was walking with park mechanic Eddie Fowler, who was lodging with her and her husband at their home in Pretyman Road, two streets away. 'We were starting work at 10.00am and we were walking through Micklegate Road at about 9.45am,' she said. 'I walked across the car park. We saw the Securicor van nearly outside the gate of the park, next to the Crazy House. We didn't take much notice of it to be honest. Sometimes people do park there.

'We went into work and about 10 or 15 minutes after we started the police came in and wanted to know if we had seen anything. There was nothing we could tell them. I remember walking past the back doors. The van was facing towards Langer Road and the back doors were facing the sea. They were shut. It was just parked there but it's not odd to see a van parked there. It does happen. We thought the van was just there for a break. Sometimes vans and lorries would stop in the street. I've seen an ambulance near there before.'

Mrs Jones said she had not noticed any cars similar to the Toyota Previa parked nearby and not seen anyone on foot. 'There was nothing happening around the van,' she said. 'Thinking about it now, I wonder if he was still in the van at the time. Either that or he had just left. It's possible he was still in the van.'

Mrs Jones, who still works on the park, gave a statement to police confirming what she had seen. The timing of her arrival in Micklegate Road suggested that Maher and his accomplice had already unloaded the cash into the stolen Previa by 9.45am. The seven-seater car – which had been fitted with the false number plates J540 LMD – had been stolen in November from Stepney, east London. Within two days of the theft, it was being stored on an industrial estate in Rainham, south Essex. Police believe an accomplice then drove it the 80 miles to Felixstowe.

It was a respectable saloon popular with families – the sort of car many people in Felixstowe would drive. It was nothing out of the ordinary; nothing that would prompt a second glance.

Police did not receive any reports of the Toyota having been seen parked in Micklegate Road. It is likely it would have arrived in the street a short time before Maher, with an accomplice or accomplices ready to help unload. The entire transfer could have been done within a matter of minutes. It was confirmed later that a total of £1,172,500 had been removed, mostly in bags of about £25,000. The majority was in £10 and £20 notes.

From Micklegate Road, the next stop was a further 1.2 miles away. They were heading for Landguard Fort, which dated back to the time of Henry VII in the 1500s. Strategically positioned to offer a vantage point over the North Sea, it sits on a peninsula which looks out towards the Essex port town of Harwich. As well as being a popular tourist attraction in its own right, the area is commonly used by shipping enthusiasts as a viewing spot to watch container ships going to and from the Port of Felixstowe.

There were two ways Maher and his accomplice could have travelled to the isolated spot, depending on which way they had positioned their getaway vehicle. The quickest route would have involved driving back towards Sea Road, the street Maher had used when he arrived minutes earlier in the Securicor van. They could then continue along Sea Road into the built-up residential area around Orford Road and then join the busy Langer Road. Once there, they would pass industrial units, another row of houses and a holiday park. A few hundred metres later was the left turn into the narrow View Point Road, with holiday homes on the left and the bustling container port on the right. This route would see them pass Custom House, the base of HM Revenue & Customs in the town. Ironically, the people working in that building could have had no idea that hundreds of thousands of pounds that would be lost from the government's coffers in tax was being taken from under their noses, yards outside their front door.

As the road meanders towards the fort, it narrows in parts to allow only one vehicle to pass at a time. Eventually, the Toyota Previa would have arrived at the fort's gravel car park, where the next stage of the getaway would be carried out. Police believe Maher's 15-year-old battered T-reg car was waiting, ready to become the second getaway car. Hours earlier, he had told his Securicor colleague Bunn that the car had broken down, forcing him to get a taxi into work. Police became certain that Maher had lied about the car, saying that the real reason the car could not be driven to work from his South

Woodham Ferrers home that day was because it was 62 miles away in Felixstowe.

Maher had not gone unnoticed at the fort. Witnesses who were at the car park later recounted how they had seen two or possibly three vehicles parked very close together in an isolated area. One was a Toyota described by witnesses as a 'space cruiser'. The other was described variously as a brown Cavalier or Marina-type vehicle. The description was remarkably similar to that of Maher's ageing Opel Ascona.

The accounts from witnesses varied over the precise details of what was actually taking place, but each described seeing what they thought were sacks being transferred from the 'space cruiser' to the 'dark-brown estate car'. One witness said the person transferring the sacks was wearing a uniform. Another witness told police the uniformed person looked like an ambulance driver 'because of the patches on their shoulder'. Two epaulettes and a Securicor tie were recovered nearby by a member of the public.

Investigating officers were still trying to work out how many people had been involved in helping Maher. There were differing accounts from witnesses, two of whom said they saw one person with the man in the uniform, transferring the contents of one vehicle into the other. Another witness told officers he saw two people with the man, and they thought that one of them was a woman.

While there were discrepancies between what had happened and who did what, each witness agreed that the uniformed man was being assisted. The brown vehicle was then seen being driven out of the car park.

The Toyota Space Cruiser was left abandoned and empty. The key was still in the ignition when police recovered it later that day.

Maher was taking huge risks with his every turn, but one of the biggest was the decision to transfer the cash in View Point Road. If anyone had seen what was going on, there would have been no way out. Even on foot, the journey back to the main road would have been difficult, with a shingle beach and the boggy nature reserve on one side and Felixstowe Port, surrounded by fences, on the other.

The car park might have been chosen because it was remote but that did not mean it was quiet. Just a few yards further along was an area popular with shipping enthusiasts who would spend hours watching giant container vessels coming and going from the port. It was a busy area at all times of the year, despite being isolated. Felixstowe, in its position on the east coast, was supposed to be one of the least likely places to be targeted by criminals, according to security experts, for the simple reason that there was only one main road out – one police road block and there would be no way through.

But Maher had shown that morning that geography was no obstacle if you were quick enough. He raced up Beach Station Road and on to the A45 - now known as the A14. Once past Ipswich, which is 10 miles down the road, routes to the rest of the country would open up – the Midlands, London and the South-East were easily accessible.

For Maher and his possible accomplices, the first stage of the getaway had been executed to perfection.

4

THE MEDIA
FRENZY

Richard Cornwell had just returned from Felixstowe Magistrates' Court when the telephone rang. His morning's work had ensured he already had one good story in the bag. It had made the front page of that night's *Evening Star* and was ready to be used in the next day's *East Anglian Daily Times*. He worked for both titles as the Felixstowe correspondent, covering stories in the town and surrounding Suffolk coastal area.

For Cornwell, it had been a good end to the week. The morning had been spent listening to the case of a man who had been charged with living under a false identity, or doing a 'Reggie Perrin', as it would be termed in later reports of the case. It had been a good tale – the type likely to attract the attention of national media. The piece concerned a former Suffolk property developer who had been accused of swindling £200,000 from two security companies by faking his own death. The unemployed 66-year-old, who had been photographed coming out of Felixstowe Magistrates' Court that day, was charged with attempted fraud.

Cornwell, who was later tagged 'Mr Felixstowe' in his weekly newspaper column, had just finished writing it up. 'I remember coming from court at about lunchtime thinking I had a really good story,' he said. 'Then after lunch, it all kicked off.'

At about 2.00pm, the telephone rang on his desk at his Hamilton Road office. The call was not from the police, it was from a contact who asked if he knew what had happened at 'bank corner', where there was a lot of 'police activity' focused on Lloyds Bank. Cornwell immediately got on the telephone to the Suffolk Constabulary press office, which was based about 10 miles down the A45 in Martlesham Heath.

'The caller asked if I had heard what was happening down at Lloyds Bank. The person thought there had been some kind of theft,' said Cornwell. 'I called the Suffolk Police press office and they said they would look into it and call me back. We had to wait a short while … it took a few minutes. Then they said, "Yes, we can confirm there has been a theft from a Securicor van taken from outside Lloyds Bank in Felixstowe." There wasn't a lot to go on.'

The press office had been very guarded in its initial response. A decision had been taken not to publicise the theft while police attempted to work out exactly what had happened. There were concerns that Eddie Maher, the driver of the van, could have been harmed. It was for that reason, police claimed, that no information had been released to the media about the incident any earlier.

Cornwell's call meant the force had to confirm details

earlier than had been originally planned. His next task was to find out more. Any theft involving a security van was of interest but it was now early afternoon and the deadline had gone for that day's paper. It would need to be a major story to stop the presses.

Cornwell made further calls and it was then that the full scale of the theft became apparent. 'Off the record, I was being told the theft was worth about £1m,' he said. 'It was quite surprising that was being released, even off the record. It was being stressed to me that this really is a huge amount of money.'

With that phone call, Cornwell knew he had a massive story on his hands. He was the first journalist to be given the breaking news and he knew time was of the essence. The next call he made was to his news desk, based in the company's offices in Lower Brook Street in Ipswich. 'It really was one of those "hold the front page" moments,' said Cornwell.

As he was relaying the information to his news editor, plans were being made to produce a special edition. The print run for that day's newspaper had been completed but a story as big as this meant the presses were put back into action. It was a story that could sell hundreds, maybe thousands, of extra copies. Cornwell had to file his copy as quickly as possible, while a photographer was sent to get shots of the bank and the police activity nearby.

Within an hour-and-a-half of Cornwell receiving the tip, presses at the newspaper's Lower Brook Street offices were rolling once again. A new edition with a spectacular '£1M BANK RAID' front-page story had been printed, referring to a 'daylight security van heist'. Copies from the extra print run hit the streets by 4.00pm, both in Ipswich and Felixstowe. The theft was now the talk of the two towns; soon it would be the talk of the country.

After filing his initial story, Cornwell had wasted no time in trying to find out further details about what had happened. He knew that once other media became aware he would have competition in getting to speak to the people he needed to find. He also knew that any progress he could make before rival outlets threw their resources at the story would give him a huge advantage.

He was now working on a fuller version of the bank heist story for the next day's edition of the *East Anglian Daily Times*. His office was less than 500 yards from 'bank corner' so the obvious first reaction was to walk along the street to see what he could find out.

'I went to go down to the bank but no one there was talking. I did the standard vox pops in the street, asking people if they had seen or heard anything,' he said. 'It was the usual story – they were surprised about what we were telling them. No one seemed to know anything about it.'

Further conversations with the police revealed they were just as keen to get to the facts of exactly what had happened. 'At that stage, the police were still getting things together,' Cornwell said. 'They said they hadn't released anything earlier because they were checking if he [Maher] had been harmed or whether he had been involved.'

Soon after Cornwell had confirmed the incident, a press release on headed Suffolk Constabulary paper was faxed out to local media. It was sketchy in detail and did not include any figure in relation to the amount of money involved in the theft. Securicor, realising the potential reputational damage the theft would cause, had been initially reluctant for the figure to be publicised. At that stage, the police were happy to agree to the request.

The first press release issued read:

Police are investigating the theft of money from a Securicor van in Felixstowe this morning. The incident began when Securicor made a delivery to Lloyds Bank, in Hamilton Road, Felixstowe, at 9.30am.

One guard made a delivery to the bank and returned to find the van and driver missing. The empty Securicor van was later found abandoned in Manwick Road, Felixstowe.

No value is being given for the money taken from the van. The driver has not yet been located, and extensive enquiries are being made to trace him. No identification for the driver will be released at present.

Detective Superintendent David Moss, quoted in the press release, said, 'Details of the incident remain unclear. However, we are obviously very anxious to trace the driver or hear from anyone who may have information about this theft.'

In the rush to get the information out, police had mistakenly said the van was found in Manwick Road, which was actually three streets away from the location where the vehicle was discarded in Micklegate Road.

The comments of the detective superintendent in the press release summed up much of the initial chaos that followed the theft. So much of what had happened was 'unclear'. The press release ended with a plea for witnesses to contact an incident room that had been set up at the force's headquarters in Martlesham Heath.

It was at that point freelance national newspaper correspondent Andrew Young, then aged 30, became aware of the story. The former Fleet Street reporter had set up his own news agency – East Anglia News Service – two years earlier and was regarded as one of the main national press reporters in the region. He also worked for ITV's *About Anglia* news programme.

Ironically, he had been in Felixstowe that morning covering the 'Reggie Perrin' court case for ITV and had heard 'whispers' of an incident involving a Securicor van. But at that stage it seemed much more likely to be a story of only local interest. Stories of security van drivers having their cash boxes snatched were sadly fairly common and not the type of crime that would find its way into a national newspaper.

He recalled, 'I remember being quite engrossed by the "Reggie Perrin" court case. The cameraman was outside. He picked up a whisper that there might be an incident involving a Securicor van or some kind of robbery. It was in the days before mobile phones. I had a pager. I remember the cameraman paging me like mad, saying there had been some sort of incident. Initially, I didn't reply because I was so engrossed in this case. I thought it was an everyday, local type of story. I don't think the police were giving too much away. We didn't really know what happened.'

After filing details of the court case to various media outlets, Young returned to his office at his home in Ipswich. 'It was only later in the day that the police put out exactly what had happened,' he said. 'I'm pretty sure they put it on their voicebank that journalists could dial in to listen to. Whereas the local paper would've picked that up instantly, I wasn't checking it as regularly as I obviously had a much bigger patch to cover.

'I was then faced with a bit of a rush job, trying to cobble together whatever I could over the phone very quickly. I didn't go to Felixstowe immediately. I sent the story to everyone. It made a splash in the *Mail* and the *Sun*. They used virtually all of my copy.'

Young had received an indication that at least £700,000 had been stolen and cited that figure in his first story. He also managed to track down a road worker in Felixstowe who thought he had seen the Securicor van drive past. With the story breaking so late in the day, and on a Friday, Young's concern was to get the information filed as quickly as possible.

In most newsrooms, the majority of planning for the next day's newspapers happens in the morning. By late afternoon, the majority of stories would normally have been allocated to a page. Using his Amstrad desktop computer, he sent the information out via a service known as Newslink, a news wire used by trusted correspondents such as Young. News travelled much slower back in 1993, which was still a time before 24-hour rolling news channels and up-to-the-minute websites.

Most of the national media found out about the story through Young. As soon as his copy landed on the wire, newsrooms in Fleet Street were buzzing with the story. Early drafts of the next day's editions were being torn up. The theft was a major story in almost every national newspaper the next day: 'GUARD DOES A RUNNER WITH £1M' blasted the *Sun* headline; the *Daily Mail*'s front page simply said: 'MISSING WITH A MILLION POUNDS'. It told how 'empty van at port sparks hunt for security guard'. The newspaper was already speculating about how Maher might have the fled the country, pointing out there were ferry services between Felixstowe and Belgium, Sweden, Germany, Holland and Norway.

An unnamed police officer told the *Mail*, 'It looks as if he has hit the jackpot, packed his Bermuda shorts and is off.' The article went on to say that police had not ruled out the possibility that the driver's wife and child had been taken hostage but officers had yet to find anyone who had seen a robbery or 'anything out of the ordinary'. It quoted a Securicor spokesman, who described the reaction of the guard who had been left behind: 'It is fair to say he was fairly stunned when he returned,' the spokesman said.

The story was leading the national news agenda and the theft was already being likened in various reports to the case of 'Florida Phil' Wells, a security guard who had disappeared with more than £900,000 from Heathrow Airport in 1989.

Local reporter Cornwell, eager to find a follow-up to his original story, found little extra information in any rival publications to feed off, so it was a case of seeing what more he could find out to keep ahead of the rest of the press pack. 'A lot more stuff started coming out over the weekend,' he said. 'I worked on the Saturday in order to produce new copy for that night's *Star*.'

After the initial press release on the day, the media was

now being flooded with additional information. On 23 January, Eddie Maher was named as the security guard who had gone missing. A photograph had also been rushed out in time for that day's evening newspapers. It would be a new line on the story for the national Sunday press, keeping the story on the front pages. The next day's *Mail on Sunday* had the headline 'FIRST PICTURE OF MAN WHO WENT MISSING WITH £1M' on page one. 'Detectives believe Maher's disappearance was part of a daring and meticulous plot,' the paper said.

The Press Association newswire, trusted by media outlets around the UK and beyond, was carrying the story on the Saturday, focusing on a £50,000 reward that had been put forward by Securicor for information about the case. The United Press International news agency had also sent out details to its customers around the world.

As with any major national story, the Fleet Street press were keen to outdo one another in finding new information about the story. The *News of the World* did just that. It reported claims that Maher had been involved in another raid three years earlier. The story seemed to be a spectacular exclusive and was used by the *Sunday Times* for their later editions, credited to the *News of the World*, but no evidence ever emerged to verify the claim. The *Sunday Times* concluded that Maher was thought to be 'hiding abroad' with his common-law wife and son.

Meanwhile, Cornwell and photographer Jerry Turner continued to look for new angles on the story back in Suffolk. On the Saturday morning, they came up with the idea of recreating the likely route the Securicor van would have taken after being driven off from Hamilton Road. In a story for that night's *Evening Star*, they estimated the 1.7-mile journey between Hamilton Road and View Point Road would have taken about 15 minutes to complete, taking into account the stop-offs and unloading of the cash at the two points.

Cornwell said, 'We would drive to each street, spend a couple of minutes there to allow the time we thought it would have taken to unload the money, and then carry on. It was all a bit of guesswork really. We worked out that he could have done it in about 15 minutes. If I remember rightly, I think that I wrote "it was 15 minutes of cool, calm and calculated villainy" in that night's *Star*.'

In the days that followed, every aspect of Maher's life would be raked over by journalists keen to find new stories. But unlike many newsworthy events, where the focus of attention is in one place, this story saw the press pack split between various locations. There was the obvious link to Felixstowe but there were other places reporters were sent 'door knocking'.

Young, who was busy filing stories to national newspapers for several days, said, 'It had happened in Felixstowe but, apart from that, it wasn't really a local story. There was little else for me to do in Felixstowe … he had nothing to do with Felixstowe. He had just chosen Felixstowe. It was a crime done out of sight of witnesses. The emphasis of the story once his name came out was switched elsewhere. All of the emphasis was on him. Reporters were digging into his background. I remember the facts coming out in dribs and drabs.'

In South Woodham Ferrers, in Essex, where Maher and his family lived, journalists arrived en masse. One of Maher's brothers, David, lived just around the corner and had camera crews and photographers camped outside his house for several days.

On 25 January, three days after the heist, David was quoted in the *Daily Mail* saying his brother was 'not the big villain he is pumped up to be'. He told the newspaper, 'Obviously we'd like to speak to Eddie but we don't know where he is. I saw him last week and he seemed the same as ever. He was an everyday sort of chap, no different from the average neighbour and certainly not the miserable sod they made him out to be. I have absolutely no idea where he has gone. Although we would like him to get in touch, it does not seem likely.'

In another statement, given to a television station, David insisted, 'I do not know where my brother is … I only know what police have told me. The whole thing is upsetting for the family.'

Maher's first wife, Sandra, and son, Terry, then in his early twenties, also became a focus of attention for the media. And since Maher had 11 siblings, there was plenty of research being done by investigative journalists to track down addresses for reporters to go to. Margaret Francis, one of Maher's sisters, was among those whose home received repeated visits from the media. She was living in Abridge, south Essex, with her husband, Alan, at the time. On 26 January 1993, she was quoted in national newspapers defending her brother, saying he was of good character and had not been in any trouble apart from 'a few fights as a lad in east London'. Tearfully, she added, 'We have lost a brother in all of this.'

As well as coming to terms with the shock of the audacious

theft carried out by Maher, his friends and family were now having to deal with the massive media interest in the story. In some cases, they were also dealing with questions over whether they had any knowledge of what Maher had obviously been planning for some time.

Aside from the occasional snatched quote, Maher's family and friends were largely remaining tight-lipped. They were co-operating with the police investigation but refusing to speak to the media in any depth. In many respects, the refusal to talk fuelled the journalists' hunger for information. But much to the media's disappointment, Maher's family was emphatic in their refusal to give interviews in the first few days after the theft. But with the possibility that any one of those family members might change their mind, editors in the London newsrooms knew they had to continue staffing the story to avoid missing out on any potentially exclusive new leads.

In turn, the continued fascination from Fleet Street meant there was plenty of money available to be thrown at the story. There was always a chance that a large cheque would persuade someone to talk. The result was that Maher's family and friends faced days of journalists being camped out in their streets and a constant stream of questions.

While leads were proving hard to come by from those closest to Maher, people who had known him in Kent, where he had previously run the Gardener's Arms in Higham, were happy to talk. From there, further details emerged that would fuel a succession of other stories. Brian Covington, the landlord who took over from Maher in 1992, said, 'They struck me as an ordinary couple. I could not believe it when I opened up the papers and saw the photograph.'

He also told reporters how Maher had spoken of his wish to move to America and had at one point received application forms to learn to fly at a US aviation school. 'While he was here, he told all the locals he was going to America with Debbie,' said Covington, then aged 42. 'They said they wanted to start a new life in the sunshine to get away from Britain for good. We have got no way of knowing if that is what he did. They could certainly afford to go now.'

That prompted inevitable speculation that Maher had fled to the States, although police were refusing to comment on the suggestion. One headline in the *Daily Mirror* posed the question, 'HAS FAST EDDIE FLED TO FLORIDA WITH £1M?'

On 26 January, the *Daily Mail*'s page 14 headline read: 'UP, UP AND AWAY!' 'Missing Securicor guard dreamed of running a flying school in America ...' it went on.

The disclosure that Maher had talked about his dream of a new life across the Atlantic 'heightened suspicions' that Maher had the fled the UK, according to the newspaper. But despite a succession of stories linking Maher with America, including some suggesting Suffolk detectives had flown out in pursuit of the guard, police were refusing to be drawn. A story in the *Evening Star* on 8 February 1993 began, 'Police have refused to comment on reports that detectives had flown to the United States to find security guard Eddie Maher.' The police spokesman quoted in the newspaper refused to confirm or deny the reports for 'operational' reasons.

For readers, it was an insight into the increasingly strained relationship between the police and sections of the media. In any case where a high-profile crime goes unsolved for a significant length of time, challenging questions are inevitably asked of the police officers leading the investigation. And by the time police conducted an anniversary appeal a week on from the theft, signs of a growing tension between the police and the media surfaced again. In an interview with the BBC's *Look East* programme, broadcast on 29 January, DS Moss was asked if he was confident of catching Maher. 'I'm not going to answer that,' he responded.

Police at the time believed they knew the answer to the major question surrounding the case – that Eddie Maher was responsible for the theft. Beyond that, they could only speculate on the various other unanswered questions: Where was Maher? How had the theft been carried out? Who had helped him?

The list was endless.

But there were no signs the media interest in the story was about to end. As facts emerged, there was plenty to keep the story in the national spotlight. The background of Maher's partner, Deborah Brett, proved to be another interesting aspect of the story, particularly after it was revealed she had previously worked for Essex Police as a call handler. '£1M SECURITY WIFE HAD POLICE 999 JOB' was one *Daily Mirror* headline.

Maher's background as a former firefighter was another interesting detail, as was the confirmation from police that Maher had completed a training course to be a locksmith months before the theft. The page 3 headline in the *Daily Mail* on 27 January read: 'LOCKSMITH LEAD IN £1M ROBBERY'.

A day earlier, reporter Teilo Colley had written a story for the Press Association revealing that police were investigating leads that Maher was a 'trained locksmith'. Reports also surfaced that Maher had built up 'gambling debts', offering a possible motive for the theft. Police confirmed they were investigating the claim.

Within a week of the theft, a new tag had been coined for 'super thief' Maher. He was regularly being referred to in some newspaper reports, mainly tabloid, as 'Fast Eddie' – it was a soubriquet that had previously been given to guitarist Edward Clarke, a member of British heavy metal bands Fastway and Motorhead, who became the original Fast Eddie. It suited Maher nicely – and was one that stuck with him.

By then, it was not just in the UK that the theft was becoming a major talking point - people around the world were speculating about how Maher might have done it. Jack Slipper, the retired Metropolitan Police chief superintendent who investigated the Great Train Robbery of 1963, told BBC radio, 'He seems to be a cool-headed individual. I think he would possibly go to ground for six weeks or two months in this country in a house until the fuss dies down. Then he could make his way out of the country to a place which is popular with tourists, where he could fit in. Perhaps the Costa del Sol? He could stay there for months.'

The scale of the theft had gained Maher notoriety and respect from within the criminal underworld. The news even travelled as far as Brazil, where Great British Train Robber Ronnie Biggs was hiding. He told national newspapers that he was 'delighted' to hear of the crime. 'I hope he gets away with it and I'm sure most of the British people would be behind him,' Biggs said.

In all the media reports that followed the theft, there were no comments from the general public condemning what Maher was suspected of doing. On the contrary, he had a great deal of public support and the nickname 'Fast Eddie' had endeared him to many.

As the reporter for Felixstowe, Cornwell spoke to numerous people about the crime. It was the biggest news story to happen in the town since a ferry disaster off the coast more than 10 years earlier, when six people were killed in December 1982 when the *European Gateway* capsized after colliding with a cargo ferry.

The Securicor van theft and the ferry disaster were completely different stories yet there were parallels in the amount of media coverage they received. In 1993, there was no cause for sadness or grief. In fact, many people were calling Fast Eddie's antics 'heroic'; he had taken on the Establishment and had seemingly won.

It was a perception that became a source of great frustration among the officers investigating the case. Cornwell said, 'Like a lot of people, I didn't particularly want him to get caught. It was too romantic. It was a massive story, so intriguing. It was one of those strange stories. He didn't come from here. Why us? How did he do it? Those vans were supposed to be impregnable. He must have had some inside knowledge to get round it. I used to sit and dream on weekend shifts that maybe he would ring up one Saturday and tell me how he did it.'

Young said there was a sense that it 'didn't really count as a proper crime'. 'Nobody seemed to have been hurt and the victim was a bank and a huge security company,' he said. 'It was in the days before the lottery. People were having a laugh saying it was like he'd won the Pools. Every reporter who ever had anything to do with it was always wondering what had happened to him.'

5

WHO IS
FAST EDDIE?

Eddie Maher had already led what most people would consider to be an eventful life by the time he reached his mid-thirties. One of 12 children born to a family of Irish descent, he was brought up on a tough east London estate. His mother Elsie and father Jimmy made their home in Ilford, Essex, after marrying in the town in 1951. Jimmy worked for the local council and Elsie was a housewife. Both had been married previously and had had children from those relationships; Elsie had two and Jimmy had three.

Jimmy's first wife, Rose Brown, died at the end of the Second World War – on VE Day. They went on to have seven children together. Eddie Maher was the fourth, with Margaret and Michael among his older siblings.

The family home was a large house in Leyswood Drive, Ilford. There was an age gap of more than 20 years between the youngest and oldest of the siblings, meaning they never all lived there at the same time.

The family was well known in the area. Jimmy, who worked for Redbridge Council in the civil engineering department, was a regular at the estate pub, The Avenue, less than half a mile from his home. As with many east London estates in the 1950s and 1960s, the local pub was the heart of the community. Next to the A12 road into central London, it was conveniently placed on Eastern Avenue, opposite Newbury Park Tube station, making it a popular stop with commuters.

It was a time of rapid growth as housing boomed in the post-war years. By 1965, Ilford had been swallowed up by the capital's growth and became part of Greater London. Leyswood Drive was on one of those typical post-war developments. The Mahers' home was a comfortable, end-of-terrace property, yards from open playing fields. By east London standards, it would have been a good place to bring up a family.

Henry Maher, 73, remembers the family well. He still lives on the closely-packed estate where they lived. And although he shares the Maher name, he is not related to the family. But he was good friends with Jimmy, who died in 1990 aged 78.

'They were a typical working-class family,' he remembers. 'Jimmy was a man that worked. He could certainly have a drink. He was from Tipperary and was typically Irish. He was a tiny little man with a Trilby hat. We used to talk about horses, or whatever. He was well-known and liked.'

Growing up in a large family, Eddie Maher followed in the footsteps of most young lads in the area when it came to deciding which football team to support. West Ham United was the local team and an obvious choice. It was an era when the likes of England World Cup winners Bobby Moore, Martin Peters and Geoff Hurst were the star names at the Upton Park club.

After attending Bovingers School in Forest Gate, east London, he left at the age of 16 and took on an apprenticeship at British Gas. Although from a 'good family', by his early teenage years he had already found himself in trouble with the authorities. At 2.30am on 23 March 1969, a jewellers' shop window was smashed and items were stolen by a group of youths. Maher, aged just 13, was arrested nearly two months later. Appearing at Stratford Juvenile Court on 6 May 1969, he pleaded guilty to handling stolen goods and was placed on probation for three years. He had denied an offence of burglary and prosecutors offered no evidence.

Then, on 29 August 1969, he was back before a court. It was two months after his 14th birthday. Maher was accused of stealing a British Railways stamp, a date stamp and an inking pad from Ilford Railway on 5 July 1969. He admitted the fraudulent use of railway stamps – he had probably thought they would get him free train rides – and handling the stolen goods. But he denied the theft. As before, he was placed on probation for three years but faced no separate punishment for breaching the previous order.

For Maher, the court appearances represented his first brush with the wrong side of the law. But having been convicted of the two sets of offences within five months, he ran the risk of being criminalised while still at school. It was a potentially slippery slope, but for the next two years he managed to keep his nose clean.

The convictions did not stand in the way of his future career as he earned a place in the Army. He was following in a proud family tradition when he joined the Royal Green Jackets, based in Darlington. Three of his brothers had already served in the same regiment, and he started his army career with two tours of Northern Ireland, along with a spell in Cyprus.

But while the young Maher was living a highly disciplined army life, with a blemish-free record, his time away from the barracks was far less regimented. The teenager had found himself landed with some big responsibilities. He had started a relationship with a girl a year older than him. Her name was Sandra Kidd, from Stepney in east London. The romance quickly blossomed and she fell pregnant.

At that time, the idea of having children outside of wedlock was very much frowned upon, particularly at such a young age, and the couple quickly decided to tie the knot. A hastily arranged marriage, in Redbridge, east London, in March 1972, ensured they avoided the potential embarrassment of having an illegitimate child. On the one hand, Maher was displaying a maturity beyond his years as he seemingly faced up to his responsibilities as a father-to-be. But in other ways he was showing he still had plenty of growing up to do. In the same month as the wedding, he found himself in trouble once again.

This time he had stolen a moped and swapped the number plates, and he had also stolen a friend's driving licence. It was not a sophisticated crime – the number plates had been switched for a set of cardboard replacements written in black ink.

Appearing at Stratford Juvenile Court on 10 March 1972, he

admitted the theft of the vehicle and the driving licence. He also pleaded guilty to having no insurance and driving licence. Again, he was put on a three-year probation order; all previous orders were cancelled.

At the age of 16, Maher had three youth court convictions, was married and had a child on the way. Sandra had moved to live with him in married quarters in Darlington. Then, in the late summer of 1972, their son Terry was born.

After two years in the Army, Maher decided to leave and went looking for a new career. He tried his hand at various jobs in the months that followed, including working as a market trader for a short spell. Then, a month before his 18th birthday, Maher was in court accused of his most serious offence to date. On 8 March 1973, a year after getting married and with a baby of just a few months old, he was alleged to have climbed a fire escape behind a business in High Road, Ilford, removed sealing tape from a skylight and attempted to break in.

He was arrested on 30 April 1973 and appeared at Barking Magistrates' Court three days later. He pleaded not guilty and the case was dropped.

It was clear that Maher had got in with the wrong crowd and was repeatedly getting into trouble. He perhaps decided a clean break was needed and in 1974 he moved to the south coast. He had found a job at a sheepskin and leather company in Bournemouth, Dorset, and went on to spend five years there.

Yet again, though, he was quickly back in trouble. On 6 December 1977, at the age of 22, he appeared before the Central Criminal Court, more commonly known as the Old

Bailey, in London. This time the offence was more serious –
and so was the punishment.

During a trip back home to east London, Maher had been
caught snatching money from a milkman and admitted a
charge of robbery. Appearing in court, he narrowly avoided a
jail term. Instead, he was given a 12-month prison sentence,
suspended for 18 months. As well as being fined £100, he was
ordered to pay £35 to the milkman and £34 to his employer.
At a time when the average weekly wage in the UK was
£68.70, it was a stiff penalty. And even more so for a man who
had never been good at managing money.

For Maher, it was another wake-up call. He had been
warned in court that any further offences within the next year-
and-a-half would result in an immediate custodial sentence.
With a wife and young child to support, the punishment would
have hit Maher and his family hard. He knew that he needed
to get his life back on track and continued with his job in
Bournemouth.

But trouble seemed to follow him and the 24-year-old
Maher was arrested again in January 1979. He appeared at
Bournemouth Crown Court charged with punching a man
while holding a spirits glass, causing cuts to the victim's ear. He
pleaded not guilty and the case was withdrawn. Had he been
convicted, he would certainly have ended up in jail with the
suspended sentence from the milkman robbery being activated.

Once again, Maher had another chance to get his life in
order and decided it was time to switch careers again.
Following a path trodden by many ex-servicemen, Maher
pursued a job with the emergency services. His convictions

would have ruled out a career in the police but the rules were not so strict when it came to the fire service. So after quitting his job in Bournemouth, he joined the London Fire Brigade in November 1979.

His days of court appearances for petty crimes were behind him. Working as a firefighter in the capital, Maher had found a solid career that would pay a good living. For most people, it was a job that would provide a comfortable income. But despite working his way through the ranks of the fire service, ultimately to the position of sub officer, Maher would rarely be flush with cash.

Each week the crews would chip in for the officers' mess, with everyone putting in a fixed amount of money that would pay for food and refreshments for the week ahead. Some of the shifts lasted 12 hours and it was important no one went hungry. Once the money was collected, a nominated officer would go out and purchase enough supplies to see them through. Maher was a notorious late payer, despite boasting of fancy holidays, including one to America in 1989.

One of his former colleagues told police, 'He was always known to be short on paying back. He could always afford to go on nice holidays and talked about going to America but couldn't find the mess money.'

This trait did not endear him to his colleagues, but his career was going well. His personal life, though, was looking far less rosy – his marriage to Sandra was in trouble. Cash problems meant the relationship was being placed under an increased strain, with Maher accumulating a series of small debts that made life at home difficult.

Matters came to a head during the Christmas holidays of 1987, resulting in Maher and Sandra splitting up, a process that was far from harmonious. Maher left Sandra, who later remarried, with a string of debts, some of which took years to pay off, one of her family members claimed. It was also a separation that would lead to Maher spending much less time with Terry, although they remained close. In later years, Terry would follow in his father's footsteps by serving in the Army and joining the fire service. He also became an avid West Ham United football fan.

Months before the separation, Maher had met an air hostess called Debbie Brett at an event in a hotel in the Leicestershire town of Castle Donington, close to East Midlands Airport. Then in her early 20s, Debbie was training to work for the British-owned Orion Airways, which was based in the town. Maher was visiting on a business trip with his brother Michael.

After the initial contact, Maher and Debbie kept in touch and, following Maher's marriage split, they soon got together. Having been born in York, Debbie's mother and father divorced while she was young and she grew up with her father in Nottingham. She was one of three children – all girls - and went on to work for the fire service as a call handler, before taking up a similar position with Essex Police.

Maher soon moved in with his new partner and, in the late 1980s, they flitted between Ilford, Romford and Dartford. By this time Maher was in his thirties. But in some ways his relationship with Debbie seemed to be following a pattern similar to that of his marriage, when he was aged just 16. Like Sandra, Debbie became pregnant early in their relationship.

Within two years of getting together with Maher, Debbie gave birth to their son, Lee, in Dagenham. Their home in Dartford was in Humber Road, close to the town's railway station. It was a neat, newly-built estate with a mixture of terraced, semi-detached and detached properties. Maher, Debbie and baby Lee lived there from September 1990 until August 1991. Their home was semi-detached, with a garage built into the house and a narrow grass lawn leading to the front door.

The birth of Lee was just one of a number of major changes in Maher's life around this time – both at home and at work. After 12 years in the fire service, he was forced to leave after injuring his back while on duty. He was pensioned out of the service in 1991, receiving a five-figure pay-off in the process. He left with an unblemished service record and a pension pot worth £129,000. Now it was time for another career change.

Using £10,000 of his fire service pay-off, Maher bought the tenancy of a pub in Kent. Along with his young family, Maher moved into the Gardener's Arms in Higham, near Rochester, in August 1991. It was a small, isolated village on the Hoo peninsula in north Kent, with a population of about 4,000. Its remote location was both its attraction and downside. Higham was less than 30 miles from central London, yet had the feel of being in the middle of nowhere. It was the type of place where everyone knew each other and where outsiders often took a while to be accepted.

When he arrived in Higham, Maher certainly did not give the appearance of being someone short of money. He quickly earned the nicknames 'Flash Eddie' and 'Two Jags Eddie' among locals, in reference to the fact that he owned two Jaguar sports cars. One was a four-year-old Jaguar XJS. Neither was a top-of-the-range new model but they were enough to draw attention. He was the flash new pub landlord in the village.

But the transition from firefighter to pub landlord proved to be a difficult one. Although they made friends with some regulars, there were tensions with others. In particular, Maher had a falling out with a group of travellers. Just a month after taking on the tenancy, the pub was fire-bombed. Extensive damage was caused to the bar area in the attack on 4 September 1991. It was a crime that shocked the village – a place where offences of that type were very rare.

The dream of running his own pub had turned sour within weeks. No one was ever arrested or charged over the incident but police were satisfied that the pub had been deliberately targeted.

The effect on Debbie was immediate. Fearing for the safety of herself and her young baby, she moved out and took Lee with her. They went to live with Maher's mother in Ilford. The pub was refurbished but the damage was permanent as far as Debbie was concerned. She vowed not to return.

With his family living in east London, Maher was left to run the pub alone. By now, he was already desperate to get out and advertised the tenancy for sale in November 1991.

Brian and Terrie Covington stepped in to take over on 24 January 1992. Terrie, who now runs a guest house in Lyme Regis, Dorset, said, 'One of the things that struck me at the time we were buying it was at the time you had to live on the premises as a condition of the tenancy and every time we went there everything was exactly the same as before. The bed was made the same, etc. It was a bit odd. We couldn't work out what it was. We just couldn't put our finger on it.'

It later became clear that Maher was no longer living at the pub in the final weeks of owning the tenancy. Like Debbie, he had moved to back to his childhood home to live with his mother. It was a pattern common among the Maher siblings. Each time anything went wrong, Leyswood Drive would become their temporary home.

Maher did not stay long and, later in 1992, moved to rented accommodation in Brentwood, an Essex town just north of the M25 that would be made famous decades later by the ITV television show *The Only Way Is Essex*. Maher had been keen to get out of the pub as quickly as possible and sold most of his possessions to the Covingtons at 'rock bottom' prices.

The Covingtons had recently moved back to the UK from Portugal and the arrangement suited them perfectly. They were keen to snap up all the bargains on offer. Terrie said, 'We bought bits and pieces from him, like a TV. He sold everything, lock, stock and barrel. He sold it to us at a rock-bottom price. It was just amazing. It was an offer we couldn't refuse.' At a time when Maher was haemorrhaging money from the failed pub venture, it was another example of how he was easily able to squander cash.

The Covingtons saw Maher less than half-a-dozen times. On one occasion, Maher met them at the pub with his mother and Debbie in tow. Terrie said, 'Towards the end, they didn't live on the premises and trade wasn't particularly good. He never used to open the pub during the day but they used to meet up as if they were living there. It was a bit peculiar. Eddie Maher was pretty outgoing, but Deborah was quite quiet.'

Brian added, 'He was pretty ordinary really. They went into the pub trade and realised it didn't suit them.'

The impression they got was that Maher was very happy to leave the business. Terrie said, 'We knew he was going to live back in Essex, but didn't know what he was going to do.'

According to the Covingtons, Maher did not seem to have forged any close friendships with any of his regulars. Terrie, who went on to run the Gardener's Arms for 10 years, remembered the fire that hit the pub during Maher's time in charge as an incident completely out of character for the village. 'Higham's a sleepy little village,' she said. 'Nothing ever happens there.'

Maher's determination to get out of the pub as quickly as possible meant he had no job to go to, and the experience had been bruising both financially and emotionally. For the next six months, like tens of thousands of others in the recession-hit Britain of the early 1990s, Maher was forced to sign on. Jobs were hard to come by and he had to be patient. But for a man with expensive taste, Maher's dole cheque would not have gone far in providing for his wife and child.

By 1992, he had accumulated a series of debts. None were much more than £1,000 but they were amounts Maher was unable to repay. Credit card debts went unpaid and county court judgements were made against him. Rent on previous properties was left in arrears … debtors were starting to chase harder.

The couple had a habit of moving regularly and, later in 1992, found a detached three-bedroom house in Fremantle

Close, South Woodham Ferrers. By now, Debbie was solely a housewife, so income was short.

It was while living in the quiet cul-de-sac that Maher got a break as he found a new opening that could bring a healthy monthly income – it was a job as a security guard at internationally-renowned security firm Securicor.

6

SECURING
A FUTURE

The case of 'Florida Phil' was still all too fresh in the memories of people who worked in the security industry. Phil Wells became one of Britain's most wanted men in 1989 after stealing nearly £1m in foreign currency from London's Heathrow Airport. He travelled the world between the theft in July 1989 and his capture in London in May 1993. He was 48 when he was sentenced to six years in jail in January 1994.

Wells, of Hounslow, west London, was a £2.50-an-hour security guard for Ealing security firm Chalmers when he collected the cash, held in shoe box-sized containers and carried on a Portuguese plane at Heathrow. He fled with the money in his Ford Fiesta. He became known as Florida Phil in the British press after investigators suggested it was likely he would have fled to the American state.

But while the international manhunt was launched, Wells hid in Essex. Two months after the theft, when the trail had gone cold, he went to Malta. He was relying on a regular

67

supply of cash being sent to him from the London accomplices who were involved in the theft but were never apprehended. He only returned to the UK when the £928,000 haul ran dry. On his return, he reportedly attempted to sell his story to a British newspaper but police were tipped off and he was arrested.

Despite the evidence against him, Wells pleaded not guilty, claiming a defence of duress. He said he had been forced into the theft by thugs. He was convicted following a trial at Isleworth Crown Court and jailed.

At the time, the theft was one of the most brazen and high profile to hit the security industry and had proved highly embarrassing. Securicor, although not involved in the Wells case, was keen that it would not fall victim to a similar sting. It had much to lose as, by 1993, the British-based multinational company was the biggest cash carrier in the UK. It had begun life in 1935 as a small group of guards in London's West End and continued in the post-war years, guarding properties in the Mayfair area of London to deter burglars. Night Watch Services, as it was originally known, began to thrive and the name was changed to Night Guards in 1939 when the company was taken over. The company's payroll grew to 150 during the 1950s and, by 1953 it had been renamed again as Securicor. The company established an armoured car service in 1957 and began cash-in-transit services as it sought to expand from its London base.

The speed of the company's growth was rapid and it soon expanded to include document and data delivery services in the 1960s, as well as developing its own two-way radio network.

It tapped into other emerging fields, including the mobile phone business in the early 1980s when it joined forces with British Telecom to create what became the Cellnet mobile telephone network. By the 1990s, it was firmly established as one of Britain's leading companies. And it was determined to maintain its reputation for 'integrity, reliability and security'.

When one of Securicor's engineers had his van stolen from a public car park around January 1992, one news report said the theft was about as 'embarrassing as a weather forecaster being soaked in a rain storm'. It was not a cash-in-transit van and carried no money but it was embarrassing all the same. However, Securicor was proudly able to proclaim that its Datatrak radio tracking system, which by 1992 was fitted to most of its vehicles, had successfully identified where the van had been taken. The engineer was able to report to the police both the theft and the location of the vehicle.

The Datatrak system was, according to Securicor, one of its latest weapons in a growing armoury to foil gangs intent on targeting its business. It worked using terrestrial radio and offshore navigation technology. The intention of the system was that a control centre would immediately be alerted the moment a Securicor van diverted from its appointed route. On that occasion, it had worked perfectly. A year later, it would not be attracting quite so much positive attention.

For a company responsible for carrying £100bn in 1,500 armoured trucks each year by the early 1990s, it was important for it to stay ahead of the game as new technology emerged, despite some apparently encouraging national trends relating to smash-and-grab raids. Figures from the

British Security Industry Association (BSIA) showed attacks on cash-in-transit vans in 1991 had fallen; the statistics suggested there were 7 per cent fewer attacks and about 45 per cent less cash lost in comparison with 1990. That figure was slightly skewed as 1990 had been one of the worst years on record, according to the BSIA.

However, Securicor had bucked the trend, suffering a 33 per cent increase in attacks, its chief executive Roger Wiggs revealed in January 1992. On average, a Securicor van was attacked once every working day in 1991. That compared with just one a month in the mid-1970s, rising to a peak of 376 by 1987.

The cash-in-transit industry was already big business by the early 1990s, worth an estimated £240m a year, of which Securicor had an impressive 56 per cent share. But while there was money to be made, the threat to its loads was an ever-increasing problem. For Mr Wiggs and his team at Securicor, it was an endless quest to 'second guess' what techniques would be used by 'bandits' on their next strike. In short, they had to be one step ahead. And that meant anyone joining the company needed to be thoroughly vetted.

The last thing Securicor wanted to do was to expose itself to any risk that would threaten its reputation as the market leader, so the recruitment process was designed to make sure only the most suitable candidates were employed. Anyone with a criminal conviction would be turned away; people known to have significant debts would also be seen as unsuitable.

Guards would be paid about £800 a month in 1993, which equated to about £5 an hour and a yearly salary of about

£9,600. Shifts would normally start at 6.00am with a five-day week, although overtime was available. And anyone going into the job would be warned of the dangers beforehand, although most would be fully aware that any role involving handling large sums of cash always carried with it a potential threat of being targeted. Two weeks of training would typically be given before starting the job, with rules laid out in terms of handling cash, avoiding risk and advice on what to do in the event of a hold-up.

As technology developed, a major part of the training surrounded getting to grips with the various alarm and locking devices fitted to each armoured vehicle. The intricacy of the systems used ensured maximum protection. Different buttons could be used to release certain locks and there was also constant radio contact with the Securicor branch control room. The hand-held radios would also enable contact between the two guards as they made their deliveries.

For many people, the responsibility of carrying such large sums proved too much and there was a high turnover of staff. With increasing numbers of employees being attacked it was a risk some were simply not prepared to take; for many guards, it began to feel like a game of Russian Roulette, with several million pounds effectively passing through their hands each week.

There were various ground rules that were set down to staff to maximise security: no more than £25,000 could be carried across the street at any one time, which meant that guards often had to complete two journeys to make their deliveries; and anyone found to have carried more than that would face instant dismissal under the conditions laid down by the insurance company. Similarly, it was also a sackable offence if a guard was seen working without wearing his protective helmet. Each job would also be double-staffed, with one guard waiting in the van while the other made the delivery.

As each cash drop was made, the guard would need to collect the signature of the cashier to confirm the delivery had been made. That also applied to any cash the guard would collect along the route. They would have to sign for it, creating a paper trail for every penny in the system.

Time would be of the essence on each job. While it was good to establish a relationship with the cashiers and staff at the various banks, post offices and building societies along the routes, it was important not to delay the departure unnecessarily. Not just for security reasons, but there was also a schedule to keep to.

In a typical week, the vans would clock up thousands of miles as they made drops and collections. In East Anglia, there were Securicor branches in various towns, including Chelmsford, Ipswich, Colchester and Norwich, each being serviced by about 20 vans. Each vehicle looked the same, aside from an individual marking on the roof, meaning it could be identified and tracked from the air if necessary. Experts said the tracking devices were designed to trigger once the van had been reported as either missing or stolen.

Despite the separate Securicor bases, county boundaries would not come into the equation when routes were being formulated. Guards working in Essex would be expected to work in Suffolk, and vice-versa. A day that started in Norfolk could end in Cambridgeshire. On longer routes, it would be common for the two guards to share the driving, with one acting as leg man in the morning before the roles were switched in the afternoon. It was to provide both variety in the job and also help to avoid tiredness from spending too much time behind the wheel.

For the guards, their van would become their second home during work hours. They would only leave it for a matter of minutes throughout an average eight-hour shift. The layout and functions of the vans would also need to be studied in precise detail. Every button had a use and the guards were expected to know what each one did.

Everything possible was done to deter would-be raiders. A warning was printed on the side of the van that stated, 'This van contains a locked safe to which the crew have no access.' Another message, printed in large font, read, 'Should a vehicle be stolen or unlawfully removed, Securicor will track its precise movements and will pass the information to the police immediately.'

Some days could see dozens of pick-ups so the cash would quickly pile up. Similarly, a packed day of drop-offs could see a similar number of stops. But whether the job involved picking up cash or delivering it, the procedure would remain the same. On collection runs, the driver's contact with the cash would be fleeting. Once picked up, the money would be placed straight into a vault which could only be unlocked once they returned to their base. When making deliveries, however, the procedure was slightly different. On these jobs, the cash would be in full view of the guards and would need to be individually packed for each order.

Securicor operated many contracts and most varied in their nature. Some would be very specific, like the regular run made exclusively for Lloyds Bank branches. Others would be more general and include a variety of high-street banks, building societies and post offices. Guards would normally find out what route they were taking a week in advance, although there were no guarantees the plan would not change.

Securicor described the vans as 'impregnable'. Each one was fully armoured with bullet-resistant glass and weighed two tonnes. There were no driver's side and passenger's side doors to get in and out of. If anyone wanted to leave, they would have to enter an air-locked passageway. Once inside, the person in the van could press a button to unlock the outer door, but first the inner door had to be shut. No two doors could be open at the same time – the electronic system would not allow it. The inner door had to be closed before the guard could step out on to the street. The passageway was surrounded by armoured glass so the guard inside the van could identify their colleague before releasing the lock to allow them back inside.

When it came to unloading the money, there was another set of rules to follow. The cash would be bagged-up inside the van, with every penny logged and accounted for. Each of the Securicor-branded white bags would have the branch name printed on it with a unique number code. That was the only thing that would identify the amount of money inside. The only clue for the guards was the weight – they would not be able to see the notes or coins, and they were never told how much money they were carrying.

It was the role of the guard inside the van to check the order sheet and place the bags inside the receptacle. Once that was done, the receptacle would be placed into a chute; the inner door would open with the touch of a button for the money to be placed inside. After that was closed, it would be possible to open the outer door, which would also be released by the guard inside the door.

From the moment the guard collected the receptacle from the back of the van, it would be a case of delivering it as swiftly as possible. Part of the guards' training had focused on the need for speed. This was the time they were at their most vulnerable; if anyone was going to challenge them, it would be now.

It was because of this the vans always pulled up as close to the entrance of their destination as possible. Parking restrictions were ignored, occasionally to the annoyance of traffic wardens. They always had to stop on the same side of the road as the destination venue; there would be no crossing of streets or walking through shopping areas, and the length of the journey from the van to the bank would be kept to an absolute mini-mum. If anyone was going to snatch the carry case – each of which was fitted with a rolling number lock – the insurance companies knew £25,000 was the maximum amount they could get away with. And even if an attacker was able to snatch the cash, they would not be able to travel far. Each guard had a device fitted to a belt that required the receptacle to remain within a certain distance. If it went any further, the box would explode and the cash would be destroyed.

And that was not the only gadget the guards had at their disposal – they would be able to remain in constant contact with the Securicor control team via the radio system inside the van. They would be expected to stay in regular contact, providing an update each time a delivery had been completed and reporting any issues. While the guards inside the van could hear the controller's voice, they would not be able to listen to the conversations of their colleagues over the radio.

Under the system operated by Securicor, the driver was the person in complete control. They would oversee all of the various functions, most of which were operated from the dashboard. They would even be able to override the complex locking systems if necessary. And it was accepted that no technology was faultless, so if there was a problem there was always a back-up plan. The driver could hit a button on the dashboard that would immediately isolate the electrics. Locks would be disabled and security compromised. It was a function to be activated only in extreme circumstances.

Peter Bunn said his typical hours as a guard would be between 6.00am and 5.00pm. He often worked six days a week as he was keen to snap up any overtime on offer. When he retired in 2006, he was on an hourly rate of £8.50. 'I just loved it, being out on the road,' he said. 'I met some fantastic people.'

He was the victim of two hold-ups during a career that started in 1971. 'One was with a gun in Leigh-on-Sea. A bloke pointed a pistol into my stomach … I gave him the box but it was empty. The bank ended up giving him some money and he was happy.

'The other one was out in the sticks somewhere in Essex. I had coins weighing 80lbs. Someone knocked me down from behind and tried to pick up the box but couldn't. I watched them drag it to a car and the box blew up. I found that one funny.'

Like all new applicants, Maher would have been made aware of the risks and responsibilities of the role when he applied for the job at Securicor in March 1992. He had also sent in an application to join rival firm G4 but never made it to the interview stage. It was clear he had set his sights on a job as a cash-in-transit driver and, in August that year, signed a six-month casual contract with Securicor. Two months later, he became a permanent full-time member of staff.

His background in the Army and the fire service would have impressed his new employer. It was common for former servicemen and emergency services workers to go into security roles later in life and Maher seemed to fit the bill. But what his new employers did not know was that he had a criminal past, even though that was something he was required to disclose as part of the application process.

'He wouldn't have got the job if they had known,' Bunn said. 'The security checks must have gone a bit awry with that. We had a police liaison officer, I think they were called. I'm sure they would've done check-ups. They must've missed that one.'

It was a different matter with the thousands of pounds of debts Maher had accumulated, according to Bunn. There would not have been a requirement to pass on the information. Bunn said, 'They couldn't check bank accounts or anything so they wouldn't have known if he had debts or not, unless he told them.'

FAST EDDIE

Maher's failure to disclose his criminal past was not the only way in which he misled his new employers. Applicants were banned from using family members as potential references. On his form, Maher listed his sister, Margaret Francis.

Even before he had joined Securicor, he had already begun to compromise the organisation's security systems.

7

THE MANHUNT
BEGINS

The 22nd of January is a date John Barnett could never forget. Well before 1993, it was already firmly etched into his mind as his second daughter's birthday; that year, she turned 17.

That morning, Barnett, then a detective inspector, was working at Felixstowe Police Station, where he was based. He had been involved in the arrest of a man who was being held in custody ahead of an appearance at the town's magistrates' court. As he was midway through preparing the case for court, he heard a message come over his radio. It mentioned something about a Securicor van going missing in the town. He remembers the time exactly – it was 9.38am.

'This came in and I thought, "Ah yeah, there's been a mistake here … that can't be right,"' he said later. It was a natural reaction and Barnett was not the person tasked with establishing whether the details were correct. The message was not intended for him directly, he was simply overhearing the conversation so he had no reason to think any more of it. As detective inspector, it would be up to lower-ranked officers to find out further details before he would get involved.

His role involved dealing with major crimes. At this stage, it was not even known if a crime had been committed. However, Barnett had been intrigued nonetheless and was listening out for the expected follow-up call confirming there had been an innocent mix up.

But the call never came. Time was ticking by and, with each passing minute, concern was growing that something had happened to the money. Within 10 minutes of receiving the first call from a Securicor controller based in Chelmsford, the first police officer had arrived at the bank. There he found Peter Bunn standing next to an empty cash box in the reception area.

Information was quickly relayed back to the police control room, where other officers had already been drafted in to handle the job. A search was already under way for the missing van. This was rapidly becoming a full-scale incident for the police, who knew they had to act quickly.

At about 10.15am, any remote hope of an innocent explanation disappeared. The Securicor van had been found, minus the £1,172,500 in used banknotes that it had been carrying. The load had been closer to £1.2m when it had set off from Chelmsford but about £25,000 had been delivered to Lloyds Bank. Soon after the discovery, the van was taken away for further investigation. And along with most of its precious cargo, the driver had also disappeared.

Barnett said, 'It was now a proper job. At a fairly early stage, we had a good idea it was big.'

Securicor had told police how much was in the van when they reported it missing. 'The first thing I did was meet the Securicor rep,' Barnett said. 'He came to the police station in Felixstowe, where I was.'

After being briefed by the worker, who had travelled from Chelmsford, Barnett rushed to Martlesham Heath where an incident room was already being set up at the force's head-quarters. The bank job was now his sole focus.

DS David Moss was quickly installed as senior investigating officer, with Barnett and DI Peter Noble working alongside him. Barnett was to be the deputy senior investigating officer behind Moss.

At this stage, the police were attempting to piece together what had happened while trying to trace the van driver. There was the possibility Maher had been kidnapped and his family harmed; the van could have been hijacked ... there were numerous theories that officers could not discount at this stage.

Barnett's meeting with the security firm's representative had provided him with useful information about the van, its driver and details of the load. And further information was gathered after driving Maher's colleague, Peter Bunn, to the van in Micklegate Road, satisfying them that Maher had not been tied up inside and left for dead. An alert was then sent around the force urging officers to look out for the missing guard. Ports and airports had also been made aware in case Maher was attempting to leave the country, voluntarily or not.

The closest port was Felixstowe, offering ferry routes to Europe, but airports were not far away – Stansted was 60 miles to the south, in Essex, and Norwich 62 miles to the north, in Norfolk. Ipswich Airport was also in operation in 1993, although not for commercial routes. The other London airports of Heathrow and Gatwick were both more than 100 miles from Felixstowe. From any of the locations, flights around Europe would have been available.

By the end of Friday, the day of the theft, police were still uncertain as to whether Maher would turn out to be a key witness or a prime suspect. Barnett said, 'We had concerns that his wife might have been kidnapped.'

Details of the theft were released to the media just after 2.00pm and it had an instant impact as police received a succession of calls. Barnett, who was in the Martlesham incident room, said, 'Once it was made public, the telephones were ringing constantly.'

It proved to be a long day for the detective. His eight-hour shift had been due to finish at 4.00pm but he found himself working until 10.30pm. His weekend off was also cancelled and he found himself working more than 12 hours on Saturday and a further eight on Sunday. Officers had to be ready to drop everything at a moment's notice if a big job came in and it was part of the role that Barnett readily accepted. 'That's just what we did. It wasn't a problem,' he said.

The first press release confirmed brief details but did not name Maher, or confirm the amount stolen; that would have to wait until the next day. Then, early on Saturday morning, fax machines in newsrooms around the country buzzed with the latest update. It read: 'Police can now reveal the identity of the Securicor driver missing after the theft of about a million pounds in Felixstowe yesterday (Friday, 22 January). Detectives investigating the theft are anxious to trace Edward Maher, aged 37, of Fremantle Close, South Woodham Ferrers, Chelmsford, Essex. Police also want to find his common law wife, Deborah Brett, aged 27, of the same address and her three-year-old son.'

The release went on to confirm further details of the theft for the first time. 'One guard made a delivery to the bank and returned to find the van and driver missing. The empty Securicor van was later found abandoned in Manwick Road, Felixstowe. Police today confirmed the value of the theft was in the region of a million pounds, made up of £5 to £50 denomination notes – but mainly £10 and £20 notes. The driver has not yet been located and extensive enquiries are being made to trace him and his common-law wife. Securicor are offering a reward of up to £50,000 for information leading to the arrest and conviction of the offender(s) and the recovery of the money.'

The use of the brackets indicating possibly more than one 'offender' was also telling. Police already suspected that more than one person was involved but could not be sure enough to say as much categorically. Moss said at the time, 'We still have an open mind about this incident. Any extra information would prove invaluable. Hopefully the reward being offered by Securicor will persuade people to come forward. It is essential we trace Mr Maher as soon as possible because, until we do, we cannot say with any certainty what happened after the van left the bank.'

A full-scale manhunt - now officially called Operation Ramble - was under way but detectives had many holes in the investigation that needed filling. Tracing Debbie was as crucial a priority as locating Maher – find one and they would probably find the other, detectives believed. And a significant element of the early stages of the inquiry was to trace anyone known or related to Debbie and Maher. Barnett said, 'We had a team looking at their friends and family. We wanted to know where they might have gone. We didn't have any reason to suspect that any family member had anything to do with it.'

The information police garnered from the several hours they spent questioning Maher's fellow security guard Peter Bunn had proved useful to the investigation. His description of how the van operated and his belief that it would not have been possible to remove the money single-handedly was another indicator that Maher had not acted alone.

Another early task in the investigation was to 'prove the money', as police described it. Securicor had told them the exact amount that was inside the vehicle at the time of the theft but officers needed to see documentation to confirm that. It was a laborious process but one police needed to go through to be satisfied that the money had actually been inside the van at the time it was taken.

One by one, each piece of paperwork was made available by Securicor. The company's record-keeping had been meticulous and the paper trail was complete. There was no doubting the figure – this was the biggest cash theft Suffolk Police had ever dealt with.

By Monday, the investigation had progressed with dozens of witnesses interviewed. No one had seen Maher being robbed; his partner and child had also vanished. Maher remained firmly in the frame and the prime suspect. 'It now seems less likely that Mr Maher or his family have been harmed,' said Moss. 'However, until we have spoken to him or have firm evidence to the contrary, we still cannot discount anything.'

All options were open, mainly because there were so many unanswered questions about the case. In the hope of encouraging more witnesses to come forward, detectives decided to release further information to the media on Monday, 25 January. By this time, police had corrected the error made in the first two press releases about the street in which the van had been found. Manwick Road had been replaced with Micklegate Road.

'Suffolk Police today – 25 January 1993 – are revealing more details surrounding the theft of £1 million from a Securicor van in Felixstowe on Friday,' the press release began. 'Detectives were able to issue the details of two vehicles and a picture of missing Securicor guard Edward Maher's common-law wife, Deborah Brett.' It went on to describe how a grey, seven-seater Toyota Previa Space Cruiser, with the registration plate J540 LMD, had been found in a viewing area opposite Landguard Fort in Felixstowe. 'This was stolen from east London in November and is now believed to have been used in the incident,' the press release revealed. 'Detectives are appealing for anyone who may have seen this vehicle in Felixstowe on Friday to contact them. They are also anxious to trace Mr Maher's own car, a reddish-brown Opel Ascona with the registration number BMG 389T.'

A description of Debbie was included, along with details of her recent job as a 'communication aide' at Essex Police. Detectives knew it would be a fact that would grab headlines and ensure the story maintained its position high up the national media agenda.

Essex Police confirmed Ms Brett had answered 999 calls in its force control room in Chelmsford. Debbie was said to be 5ft 6in tall, of slim build, with brown, shoulder-length hair which she often wore tied back. Lee, the couple's son, was also referred to by name for the first time in a police press release, instead of simply as a 'three-year-old child'. And as the request for information gathered momentum, Maher was now being openly identified as the most likely perpetrator of one of the most audacious thefts in British criminal history.

The 20 detectives immediately assigned to the case were playing catch-up – and they had plenty of ground to cover. There were numerous enquiries that needed to be carried out, which were of a scale that the area had seldom seen. Felixstowe was not the type of place where a major crime would take place. Murders were extremely rare and even assaults were infrequent. Million-pound security van thefts were completely unheard of. It was a place already well known to many for its beach and port. Now it was on the map for an entirely different reason. And everyone had been taken by surprise - Maher's colleague, the bank, Suffolk Police and the town as a whole.

In the early stages of the investigation, police had been careful not to point the finger of suspicion at Maher. Four days later, on 26 January, they were being less subtle and went as far as hinting at a possible motive. Police confirmed officers were investigating claims that Maher had gambling debts, and they also revealed that he 'may have had some training as a locksmith'.

Moss said, 'There is some suggestion that he made some enquiries about training in this field but at this stage we have been unable to confirm this. There has been much media speculation about the whereabouts of Mr Maher and Ms Brett. However, I must reiterate there is nothing at this time to indicate where they are. Their details have been circulated to every police force in the country and also Interpol and we are waiting for any information back.' A description of the couple was sent around Interpol, including details of a tattoo Maher had, which included the words, 'Homeward Bound, London Town'.

At this stage, police were still appealing for help in tracing Debbie, and continued to ask for sightings of Maher's Opel Ascona, which had still not been found. And although police believed Maher was primarily responsible for the theft, they remained certain he had been given help. This was yet another line of inquiry that had drawn a blank.

There were no suggestions of an 'inside job' that went any further than Maher. 'We do know a number of people were used to carry out the crime,' Moss said. 'It would need at least two people to do it, so there's no doubt he was assisted by someone.'

Although keen to give the impression of being open and transparent, every detail disclosed to the media was being carefully considered by senior detectives. The statement concluded with a note to editors, 'After a briefing with DS Moss this morning, it appears there is no additional information other than this to be released at this stage.'

Two days later, on 28 January, police confirmed that Maher's car had been found at 8.30am the previous day in Nazeing, Essex. Unfortunately for detectives, it provided few forensic clues as it had been destroyed by fire. There was no cash and nothing of evidential value at the scene.

Police released details of the discovery but would not allow journalists to photograph or film the car. Instead, they released a grainy photograph to the media. It was another sign of how police were trying to control what was being released. There were certain things they did not want the public to know. In the press release, Moss said, 'The car was found on an unmade road near the Lee Valley Leisure area at 8.30am yesterday and had been completely destroyed by fire. This single track road leads down to the River Lea, which separates Essex and Hertfordshire. We would like to speak to anyone who saw the vehicle prior to it being found.'

For police, there were numerous possibilities about where Maher could be; this had become an international manhunt, and they had to accept that he could be anywhere in the world.

All three vehicles involved in the theft had by now been found – the Securicor van, the Toyota Previa and the Opel Ascona. Yet the trail had gone cold. Detectives had no knowledge of where the Opel had been driven between 22 January and 27 January. They were not even sure when it had been abandoned. 'We don't know what happened to it,' Moss said. 'It could have been driven to Scotland, Wales, anywhere before it was dumped.'

A week after the theft, police said they would be staging a reconstruction of the events on 22 January. The Securicor van and the Toyota would be 'relocated where they were found on the day of the theft as part of the reconstruction in the hope it will jog the memories of any potential witnesses,' a press release revealed. Police hoped that people who were in the area at the time would have returned seven days on.

DI Barnett conducted media interviews at the event. It was the first time he had visited the bank in the seven days since the crime. He was quoted in the local media describing the initial response from witnesses in the town centre as 'quite good'. But on the seafront and in the Landguard Fort area, where Maher had dumped the van, it had been 'poor'.

Witnesses later came forward to tell police they had seen people helping a man load a 'space cruiser' type vehicle at Landguard Fort, one of whom could have been a woman. The man they were helping was wearing a uniform similar to that of an ambulance worker, witnesses said. It fitted the description of Maher and supported the theory that he had been given help. And following this line of enquiry, Maher's colleague, Peter Bunn, had been questioned as a witness over 'a number of hours' by detectives, Barnett revealed at the anniversary appeal. Despite obvious initial suspicions, Barnett ruled him out as a suspect, saying, 'He was with us, as any witness would be, for a number of hours on Friday but has now been released.'

Meanwhile, rumours were circulating of a possible flaw in Maher's plan. It was thought much of his haul included £20 notes that would go out of circulation in less than two months' time – on 19 March 1993. If true, it meant a large part of the missing cash would soon be worthless, prompting newspaper stories to that effect. But it proved not to be the case; the bank had stopped taking delivery of the old £20 notes several months earlier. Police quickly dismissed the claim as an 'invention of the media'.

One thing police did have in their favour was one of the

earliest versions of the police national computer, HOLMES – the Home Office Large Major Enquiry System. It meant information could be stored centrally and easily accessed, although many officers were still not confident using it. They were more familiar with piles of paper and scribbled notes. The towering computer represented a steep learning curve that some were quicker to master than others.

In any case, the pace of updates to the investigation had now slowed. For the majority of the first two weeks, DS Moss had seen large chunks of time taken up by media interviews. Although it was drawing him away from the investigation, senior officers knew it was a necessary job in terms of making direct appeals for witnesses and to ensure the case continued to receive coverage on television, radio and in newspapers. However, it was beginning to reach the point where there was little new information that police could pass on to the media, and some details had to be kept confidential for operational reasons.

There was a six-day gap between press releases, with the next one sent out on 3 February. Instead of including fresh revelations, it simply recounted the investigation so far: 'There has been a mass of information to work through and quite a complicated string of events to piece together,' Moss said. 'So far, we have pursued more than 500 lines of enquiry. Officers are painstakingly sifting through every snippet of information gained from witnesses and people who have contacted the investigating team. Even the smallest piece of information can be of value in an investigation such as this.'

The release said 30 uniformed and CID officers were

working on the investigation, 'piecing together Maher's movements and speaking to everyone who knew or dealt with him'. It added that 200 people had called the incident room at Suffolk Police headquarters, with more than 450 people interviewed in 15 countries since the investigation began. New leads had also come out of the anniversary appeal a week on from the theft, police said.

DS Moss added, 'We have had a good response from the public since Mr Maher's photograph appeared in the media but we still need to trace these people and need more information. Anyone with anything to tell us should ring on 0473 610610.'

A key detail about the family was also revised. For the first time since the incident, police mentioned Maher and Debbie and referred to 'their three-year-old son'. Previously, Lee had been identified as 'Ms Brett's son' by police.

Moss was made available to speak to the media at 2.00pm on 3 February. In his comments, published in the next day's newspapers, he was making no promises that he would be able to track down Maher. 'I can't say how close we are to catching him,' Moss told the *Evening Star*. 'We may never fully know what happened. We hear reports of sightings of her [Miss Brett] on her own, both of them separately, them together, with the kiddie, both in this country and in several countries abroad. We are totally reliant on another country's police force doing this investigation for us on these sightings.

'If I get to the stage where it was better than 50/50 that there was something in a report there's a good chance that an officer from here would go and investigate. We have to be careful – the people of Suffolk are largely paying for this investigation.'

From the initial stages of the inquiry, it had been stressed to officers that foreign trips would only be authorised if there was sufficiently strong information to point to the particular country. Budgets had to be kept under control.

One of the many calls to police saw a businessman come forward to tell officers he had seen two men and a woman keeping watch on another Felixstowe bank over a two-week period, four months before the Lloyds bank raid. He said they had been positioned outside National Westminster Bank, further along Hamilton Road. Like many other pieces of information received, it was not enough to move the inquiry forward, and there was nothing to suggest that one of the men was Maher. Little progress was being made.

In the second week of February, the investigation received a potential boost. The reward put up for information leading to the conviction and return of the cash was doubled. The £50,000 offered by Securicor was increased to £100,000 by loss adjuster Cunningham Hart, based in Romford, Essex. A spokesman for the company said it had decided to step in because the initial reward offered by Securicor 'could have been better'.

DS Moss hoped it could lead to a breakthrough. 'If anyone has any information about the theft which leads to a result, they could be entitled to a substantial reward,' he said. 'Hopefully, this may encourage people with vital information who have not previously spoken to us to come forward.'

To the frustration of officers leading the hunt for Maher, the promise of money failed to tempt anyone with knowledge of the crime to come forward. Maher, with piles of cash at his disposal, could already have bought the silence of his key accomplice or accomplices. Or maybe they had paid him to simply disappear. Either option was a possibility.

The continued public appeals and reward had failed to provide police with the information they needed. The force had also refused to comment on how Maher would have been able to open a locked safe that was inside the van. Other theories centred on the suggestion that Maher could have passed keys from the back of the van through a hatch and to an accomplice, possibly disguised in a security guard's clothing.

Securicor was refusing to speculate and a spokesman for the firm was blunt: 'There would be little point in having security arrangements if we told everyone what they were,' he said.

Meanwhile, detectives had another major investigation on their hands. On 11 February 1993, Doris Shelley, an 82-year-old widow who lived in Martlesham, close to the police headquarters building, was found dead in her home. She had been murdered with what police called a 'blunt object' and was discovered lying in a pool of blood. Murders were rare in Suffolk and this obviously required extensive investigation.

With the Securicor inquiry still ongoing, the force was now at full stretch with two major incidents to contend with. It meant some officers, including John Barnett, would have some of their time diverted to the murder investigation.

In an attempt to remain on the front foot in respect of the Securicor theft, police released further new details on 11 February 1993. In an unusual move for most police forces, they had turned their attention to three-year-old Lee, and appealed for help in tracking down the child as part of the criminal investigation.

Normally, unless the child was officially reported missing, everything possible would be done to shield their identity. But these circumstances were different; this child's whereabouts formed a key part of a major theft inquiry.

Detectives had held back initially but were now prepared to authorise the release of an image. The press release said: 'Suffolk Police this afternoon issued a photograph of the young son of missing Securicor guard Edward Maher. It is believed the photograph was taken just before Christmas.'

A side-view image was made available. The poor quality of the photograph had little impact on its usage as it was promptly published across various media outlets. DS Moss, quoted in the press release, said, 'We still cannot discount anything. All we can say for certain is that this three-year-old boy is missing with his parents. Is he all right? Is he in danger? This is one cause for concern. When Mr Maher and his family are traced, we would obviously like to speak to them. Only then will we know the full circumstances of this incident.'

He again confirmed it was an international inquiry. 'The incident room has received several unconfirmed sightings of Maher, alone and with his family, both in this country and in several countries abroad,' he said. 'We have been liaising very closely with forces abroad through Interpol. It is impossible to say how close we are to tracing Mr Maher or his family. As with any major investigation, the next inquiry could lead us to them. Several positive lines of inquiry are still being pursued.'

Included in the statement was another terse warning to the media that police 'would not be prepared to discuss specific lines of enquiry or countries where enquiries had been made'. Moss said, 'Furthermore, we have received numerous requests to disclose personal details about Mr Maher, Deborah Brett and their families. From the outset of this investigation, I made it clear that I had no intention of releasing personal details and this has not changed.'

It was a delicate balance for the police; they needed to keep the case in the media to ensure witness appeals were publicised. But the senior officers in charge of the inquiry were determined to remain guarded over what they released.

At 9.30pm on 18 February 1993, nearly a month on from the theft, the case was featured on the BBC *Crimewatch* programme. Photographs of Maher, Debbie Brett and Lee were shown, along with images of the Securicor van and Toyota Previa Space Cruiser. Quoted in the press release, Barnett said, '*Crimewatch* has proved an effective tool in the past. We hope the family's photo appearing on national television might jog some memories.'

Like the other tactics employed, the television appeal failed to provide the crucial breakthrough. Despite their best efforts, the initial police inquiry was rapidly grinding to a halt.

8

A STREET
IN SHOCK

Fremantle Close had never seen anything like it. Most people in Suffolk and across the county border in Essex were just hearing about the audacious £1m theft in Felixstowe when the residents of the normally quiet South Woodham Ferrers cul-de-sac were seeing the drama unfold before them.

First came the police. Officers arrived in large numbers and their attention was focused on No 27. Most of the residents in the Essex street knew little about the couple with a young child who lived there. They hadn't been there long and had made little or no attempt to get to know their neighbours. But soon the locals would know more about them than they could ever have imagined.

Police cars were parked all around the three-bedroom house Maher rented with Debbie, then 27, and three-year-old Lee, within hours of their disappearance. They had moved in five months earlier but had – until now – not made much of an impact. That day though, they were the topic of conversation on everyone's lips.

Even 20 years on, some residents remember it as their five minutes of fame. Others describe those days as 'chaos', a time when they found themselves at the centre of England's hungry press pack as it feverishly chased a story that would only become more enthralling as each new detail emerged.

The police gave some neighbours a warning of what was to come. Simon Butterworth, who at the time was among Fast Eddie's closest neighbours, answered a knock at the door and found police officers on his doorstep. 'They said, "You should have noticed a bit of activity out the front,"' he recalls. And knowing the scale of the robbery and the size of the story it would become, the officers warned him, 'He's been involved in a theft … you might hear about it on the news soon.'

But soon the news came to them. It wasn't long before the reporters arrived, along with TV cameramen and photographers. TV reporters from the BBC and others, radio reporters and journalists from the local newspapers – the *East Anglian Daily Times* and Ipswich's *Evening Star* – as well as the national papers all converged on the area. They set up camp in the street and began asking the neighbours for any tit-bits of information they could remember about the couple at No 27. That night, the street was on every channel as news of the robbery gripped the country.

When the police sent to Fremantle Close to check on Debbie and Lee had entered the house, they found it empty. There was no sign of a struggle and nothing to suggest they had been harmed. Searches of the house revealed that their passports had gone. There was also no trace of Maher's Securicor uniform, or his 'reddish-brown' Opel Ascona. Everything else appeared perfectly normal.

Reports from the time suggest two cars belonging to Maher were parked outside – a light blue, A-registration Austin Ambassador and a battered yellow, T-reg Austin Allegro, which had a child's teddy bear on the back shelf. The ownership of the cars would be queried years later, with lawyers suggesting Maher had only owned the Opel at the time of the theft.

In the garden of the house were three children's toy tricycles – one of which was a miniature police motorcycle. Pegs were still on the rotating washing line in the middle of the lush grass lawn in the back garden.

It was obvious the family had left in a rush. There was not even time to cancel the milk delivery. Three pints had been left untouched on the doorstep. An outside light next to the front door had also been left on, perhaps with the intention of suggesting someone was at home.

Little was known about Maher and what had happened to him and the speculation generated headlines for weeks. The tabloids took hold of the story and Fast Eddie became one of their favourite criminal characters. The reporters appealed to Maher's neighbours for any detail that might lead to another headline. For their part, the residents of Fremantle Close were left shell-shocked and wondering where their peaceful street had gone. One resident later recalled, 'They descended on us … there was just chaos around here. We didn't want all that. For a number of days it was like that.'

Number 27 sits squeezed into the end of the T-shaped close,

overlooked to the rear by the house then occupied by Simon Butterworth and his wife Jill and their children. The front is open to the close and looks over the parking areas for a number of other houses. It is only a few hundred metres from the open fields which surround the town but, once within the close itself, the fields are blocked from view. Beyond the fields to the north is a rise known as Bushy Hill, which overlooks the town and has been used as a radar testing site for many years, first by the British telecommunications firm Marconi and later by defence firm BAe Systems.

Maher would have known the roads in the area like the back of his hand, not only because he drove them for work but because he grew up only about 30 miles away; even the pub in Higham was only 40 miles from where he had now settled. He had spent his life in this part of England, without ever finding a place to put down solid roots.

Number 27 Fremantle Close is an unremarkable house that would rarely warrant a second glance from a visitor to the street. On 22 January 1993, however, all eyes were focused on it and the police activity within.

Jill Butterworth remembers returning home to find police looking for clues right on her doorstep. 'I'd collected the children from school and, as I drove up the road, there was all police outside our front door. They were all over our driveway,' she said. 'I pulled up in front of the garage. I said, "Right kids, straight out and in." Then the police came and knocked.'

The officers were looking for any possible detail that might help them to get their heads around what had gone on. It was still not certain whether Maher had run off with the cash himself or been the victim of a kidnapping. He had the jump on the police and, unfortunately for the investigation, Maher and Debbie had been far from outgoing when it came to building relationships with their neighbours. Despite living just metres from them, the Butterworths had not had a single conversation with either of them. The best they could offer the officers was a few sightings now and then. Jill Butterworth said the only time they had cause to pay attention to Maher was when they found his car blocking their driveway, which ran along the side of his house. 'You'd see them backwards or forwards to work,' her husband added. 'I knew he was security of some sort because he used to wear a uniform.'

As is the case in many of England's tightly-packed housing developments, neighbours remember each other for their cars and where they park them. A badly or inconsiderately parked car will make you no friends with your neighbours. Maher often parked his car by the wall of the house of one particular neighbour. That neighbour recalls, 'He regularly put his car there. It made it difficult [for me]. It was difficult to gain access and go off.' He remembers the car being moved 'fairly early' each morning, most likely as Maher left for Chelmsford.

The drive each day would have given him time to run through his plan for the theft in his head – calculating the risks, escape routes and how that very car would play its own role. But while his car was well known and Maher's face and security uniform recognised in the street, who he worked for and what his role was had been, until then, a mystery. Other neighbours would later say that Maher rarely even met their gaze, let alone stop for a friendly chat.

'They never seemed like horrible people, they just kept so much to themselves,' Simon Butterworth said. 'He was just an average sort of guy. We didn't really have a lot of contact with them,' he added. Another neighbour, now wary of having his name associated with the case, said, 'It's a small close so people know pretty much what's going on around them. In a small close like this it's difficult not to come into contact. They made a point from my memory of keeping their eyes in front.'

Of Debbie, Jill Butterworth remembers, 'She had long brown hair and it was always pulled back in a tight ponytail and I used to think it made it look like she was very harsh.'

Another neighbour, Brenda Draper, who was managing a baker's shop in nearby Maldon at the time, said, 'They hadn't lived here that long. I remember coming home from work and seeing the TV crews at the end of the road. My son was in when the police knocked on the door. He was interviewed by the police but we didn't know anything about it. I think they just asked if we knew the family. We were all out at work all day. We didn't really see our neighbours. Now we're retired we know everybody.' Like many in the street, she found out about Maher's crime through the reporters. 'They said there had been an incident. I remember it being a Saturday and all the media were there.'

While the tenants in No 27 went out of their way to avoid contact with their neighbours, their movements couldn't go totally unnoticed in such a small street. The Butterworths' dining room overlooked Maher's house and from there they could see the comings and goings of the street. Although they couldn't tell police much about the day of the robbery, when the officers turned their questioning to the previous day, they stumbled on a piece of information which focused their suspicion directly on Maher. It was then that Simon Butterworth, a printing industry worker-turned-driving instructor who still lives in Essex, remembered what he had seen while doing housework. He said, 'I was in the dining room hoovering and I noticed her walking down the road with a suitcase and the little one. I thought, "OK, they've had a row." She looked like she was leaving.' Of the suitcase, he told the police it was much more than an overnight bag.

It was the kind of lead the police had been hoping for. They now had a neighbour who had seen Debbie walking away from No 27 with Lee at about 10.00am on 21 January. She was dragging a suitcase on wheels and pushing Lee in a pushchair. Further door-to-door enquiries revealed that another resident had seen her leave, too. But, crucially, neither saw her return.

At the time, police said the sightings were 'potentially significant'. Debbie had been seen walking out of the street with her child and a packed suitcase less than 24 hours before her partner disappeared with almost £1.2m. It quickly pointed the police in the direction of the theft being the work of Maher, not someone who had done him harm and taken the money from him.

Simon Butterworth's early suspicions of Debbie leaving due to a row with Maher weren't correct. But the tightly-packed Fremantle Close had meant even someone who deliberately avoided attention could not go unnoticed. And the residents could hardly believe what had gone on under their noses. 'Until that happened you just thought they were people who lived in that house who kept to themselves,' Jill Butterworth said. 'The majority of people felt, "Well, he's not hurt anyone, good luck to him!" but I thought it was wrong.'

By now the media was conducting its own enquiries, hungry for more information. Reporters were knocking on the doors of each of Maher's neighbours. One resident, speaking on 25 January, summed up what many people in the area were thinking. 'He seemed fairly miserable most of the time – but I bet he has got a big smile on his face now!'

Fast-forward a year, and the BBC's regional evening news programme *Look East* returned to Fremantle Close. By then, Maher's status as a 'hero' was cemented in the eyes of some. One resident said, 'Good luck to him. It's a bit unfair and very unlawful obviously, but he has got away with it so he has obviously planned it.'

After Maher and Debbie disappeared, police closed up their house and it remained empty for some time. Several weeks later, there was more activity when a group of people, who neighbours presumed to be related to Maher or Debbie, were seen emptying the house of its contents.

9

THE INQUIRY WIDENS

Days after Maher drove away with £1.17m in the back of his Securicor van, detectives on his trail received information that could have potentially led to a major breakthrough in the case. At that stage, police were pursuing dozens of lines of inquiry and reacting to reported sightings all over the UK and abroad. Then, in a call to the incident room set up following the crime, they were given their first major clue as to where Maher might be hiding.

They knew Debbie and Lee had been seen leaving the family home in Fremantle Close, South Woodham Ferrers, the day before the theft, with Debbie dragging a suitcase. They had also discovered that her passport had been used to leave the UK on a flight to Boston, Massachusetts. Beyond that, they had no idea where she was heading. That was all about to change.

Irene Bailey, who lived in Humber Road, Dartford, Kent, knew all about Maher and Debbie long before 22 January 1993. They were the couple who had lived in the house before her. They had moved out three years earlier but 'red letters' containing demands for cash were still turning up. On one occasion, she reported a burglary at her house after returning home to see someone attempting to force entry. It turned out to be bailiffs in pursuit of Maher and Debbie. They had been granted a seizure order by a county court and believed the couple still lived at the Humber Road house.

Maher and Debbie had taken over the tenancy of the Kent pub by that stage but were still giving out their old address on credit applications. Bailey had become used to seeing mail addressed to Ms D Brett and Mr E Maher drop through her letterbox. It had become a regular occurrence and one that was increasingly irritating her. So it was no surprise when a letter landed on her doormat towards the end of January 1993 bearing Debbie's name. The only unusual thing about it was the fact it had been stamped with an American postmark. By that stage, she knew Maher and Debbie were wanted by the police. It had been almost impossible to escape the fact as it was blasted across newspaper front pages and on television reports. She had followed the story with interest and, intrigued by the letter, decided to open it.

Inside was a short and polite note addressed to Debbie from the Buckminster Hotel in Boston, Massachusetts. It explained that a refund was enclosed for the remaining five nights she had been due to stay at the hotel. She had checked out after just two nights. The refund came in the form of a cheque, made out to Debbie.

Realising the potential significance of her mail that day, Bailey came forward to make a statement to the police. For them, it was the first clue, albeit indirectly, about Maher's potential whereabouts. They knew that it was likely he and Debbie would be reunited at some point; this was the first indication of where that could happen.

After receiving the letter, police were able to correlate the hotel reservation with Debbie's flight booking, made on 20 January in her name, departing from Gatwick Airport, south of London, bound for Boston.

It is not known why Debbie chose to give the Humber Road address to the hotel when checking in. Without a false passport, she had to travel in her own name and perhaps felt she could explain it as a misunderstanding if anyone confronted her about it. However, it did seem an odd decision if she was trying to cover her tracks. Although it was a false address, it was one that could be easily linked to her, along with any of the four other addresses she and Maher had used as residences since 1991. By accepting the refund of a few hundred pounds, she had taken a gamble that would give the UK authorities a crucial clue in their attempts to trace her and, ultimately, Maher.

It is possible that the issue of the refund would never have been discussed with Debbie when she checked out. There are no records of the conversation she would have had with hotel staff but agreeing to have the money returned to a false address would have been of no advantage to her. The cheque would not have been forwarded on to her last known address in South Woodham Ferrers – and even if it had been, she had no plans to return there any time soon, and there were certainly no plans to leave a forwarding address. It was money neither she nor Maher would ever be likely to see again. Secretly, she might have thought she would never need it.

Regardless of the figure involved, the fact remains that there was no benefit to her in asking for the money to be sent back. One theory of the investigation team is that the refund was processed automatically following her departure, without her knowledge. But whatever the circumstances, it represented the first slip-up in the days since Maher had vanished. For detectives back in Suffolk, it was a stroke of luck and a massive boost to the investigation.

As the days rolled on after the theft, various media reports had quoted former associates of Maher on how he had had an 'American dream'. Police had done their own background checks and knew the couple had holidayed in the States in 1989, as well as enjoying a trip to Canada.

Sightings of Maher were coming in from around the UK and across the globe, some of which described a man and a woman together. But now that police knew Debbie had been alone when she left the hotel, it meant a lot of the reports could be eliminated from the investigation.

In the initial fortnight after the theft, the inquiry picked up pace. Speaking in 2013, DI John Barnett said it had quickly been established in the minds of officers that Maher was definitely responsible for the theft, having discarded initial theories that he might have been kidnapped or harmed. 'We knew who had done it,' he said. 'The actual amount of detective work to find that out was pretty minimal. We then found out fairly early on that she had gone to the Buckminster Hotel in

Boston, at which point we then started to think he had gone to the States.'

Police suspected Maher might have left the UK within days of the theft. They knew he had not used his own passport but realised he might not have travelled using his own identity. The fact that Debbie could now be placed in America was crucial but, on its own, not enough to go on.

The initial buzz of excitement died down when further enquiries linked to Boston drew a blank. From the moment she stepped out of the Buckminster Hotel, Debbie had vanished. It would be the last time the police had any knowledge of her whereabouts for the best part of two decades.

Despite the American link, calls continued to flood in with claimed sightings in various locations. 'We had phone calls from people who had seen him all over the place – South Tyneside ... Scotland ...' Barnett said. Reports were received that Maher and Debbie had been seen at a hotel in Leeds; another sighting was made in the West Country. Both were proven to be incorrect.

While Debbie was known to have entered America, detectives could not be sure she had stayed there. So when a link to Cyprus cropped up three months into the inquiry, it was treated very seriously. The country triggered an alarm bell in the heads of officers: background checks had revealed Maher's military history and the fact he had completed a tour of duty there. The island would not have been unfamiliar to Maher, even though it had been more than 15 years since he had left the forces.

The intelligence being fed back to Suffolk Police about apparently 'secretive behaviour' and the family profile of the person under suspicion also added credence to the tip-off. It was enough for Moss, still leading the investigation at the time, to authorise a four-day trip, and the team had high hopes of a positive result.

Barnett, one of the officers who went on the trip in May 1993, was matter-of-fact in his memory of it. 'We went to Cyprus … we thought we had him … it wasn't him … and we came back,' he said.

Reported sightings around the world were being treated with caution by Suffolk Police, aware of the potential for the cost of the investigation to spiral. Wherever possible, the force found itself relying on other countries to carry out initial enquiries for them, something that often proved frustrating. Barnett said, 'We've always had people phoning up. We had one from the West Indies … all we could do was to rely on other agencies to do what they said they would do. Unless your force says you can go, you have no choice. David Moss said earlier on that if there wasn't a big chance of success, he wasn't going to say yes. It was a real struggle to get other forces to do the enquiries we wanted them to do. It was a big deal for us. But Maher was our villain and it was our inquiry. I learned quite quickly that it wasn't a big deal for them.'

The Cyprus trip had been given the go-ahead but an earlier request Barnett made for another foreign trip had been unsuccessful. On the back of the information that came in from America, he asked if he could fly to the States. It would have been a speculative trip but he was confident he would be able to find information once he was out there. However, with little other than the Boston hotel sighting to base his case on, his request was refused by DS Moss. 'I think a decision was made at the time that I had no argument with. There was insufficient evidence. If you look back with hindsight, yes, we probably should have gone. I asked if I could go somewhere and they said no. Had I went out there, I would have probably found out stuff. In fairness to him, as soon as we got that Cyprus lead he said, "You had better get out there." It turned out to be a villain … but not our villain.'

Much of the early part of the investigation involved speaking to members of Maher's large family, as well as other associates. The majority were based around the south Essex and east London areas, including Maher's mother, Elsie, in Ilford. Within two weeks of the theft, each one had been tracked down and spoken to.

The same applied to Debbie's family. Barnett said, 'We were looking at Maher's family and Debbie's family. Not because we thought there was anything they had done wrong … It wasn't anything other than the fact we wanted to know if they knew anything about where he might have gone.'

One source close to the investigation said Maher's family had proved difficult to gather information from in police interviews. 'They were consistent in that they said as little as possible when officers visited them,' the source said.

Background checks on Maher revealed details of debts and his previous convictions. He mixed with known 'faces' in the south Essex and east London areas but had not been heavily involved in any criminal underworld activities. 'I really don't think he went out of his way to mix with villains,' Barnett said.

'I think he was one of these people who got themselves into debt. It was a way to solve his problems.'

The problems detectives faced in looking for him were far from being resolved. Their main struggle was in moving the investigation on after the first two weeks. Phone records were an area of particular interest that helped build up a pattern of activities in the weeks running up to the theft. As well as telephone records, travel patterns were also being scrutinised.

Several known associates of Maher all lived within a very short radius in south Essex and east London. One source said, 'They were all in the same locale. If you plotted a map and started to put all the relevant sites on the map, you get a telling picture. It's this East End sort of thing. It was the way the criminal fraternity operated. Smaller gangs had allegiances with bigger gangs.'

A key location in the inquiry turned out to be The Retreat pub in Chigwell, then owned by different landlords. Telephone analysis showed links between the establishment and people known to Maher. 'It was one of those places known for its clientele,' said one source close to the investigation. 'The boys all went there, the East End faces. It would have been all Jags and Rollers. The criminal fraternity of east London used that pub on a regular basis, it would be fair to say. It was full of old lags and faces. It just shows another link between Maher and the criminal fraternity.'

In their attempts to investigate Maher's extended network, the police were building up a significant amount of circumstantial evidence. But it was felt there would never be any realistic chance of prosecution without the main culprit being captured first. 'It was decided that, without Maher, the chance of any prosecution succeeding was minimal,' said the source.

Meanwhile, Peter Bunn found himself on the receiving end of further police attention in the weeks that followed the theft. He said, 'On two or three occasions, they visited my home in the evening. They just happened to be passing and they would pop in to see if I had remembered anything. It maybe happened two or three times over a couple of months. It was fairly obvious what they were doing. I wouldn't be surprised if they investigated my finances. I have got to be a suspect.

'There was always somebody wanting to go to the loo upstairs. They were probably looking to see if I had bought a new £1,000 bedroom suite or something like that. For all I knew, they could've tapped my phone.'

Bunn was also facing scrutiny at work, although it was light-hearted banter directed at him by his colleagues. He said, 'I became the butt of some humour. People asked if they could borrow a few quid, stuff like that. The most iconic joke was when a mystery parcel was sent to the branch, addressed to me. It was a couple of weeks after what had happened. Because it was addressed to me, the police were called. It turned out to be a clay pipe, to replace the one that was left on the van. The police didn't find it very funny, in the middle of a major investigation.'

Plenty of people had come forward and the police had managed to rake over Maher and Debbie's past. Beyond that, the investigation was slowly petering out. Many questions were left unanswered. At this stage, the prospect of finding Maher seemed remote. He had disappeared without a trace from the moment he drove out of Hamilton Road. No one saw him unload the cash in Micklegate Road and no one saw him after he drove out of Felixstowe minutes later. Barnett said, 'The nearer to the time of the offence you are, the easier it is to get him. Once you have got a month or two down the line, it becomes a lot harder.'

Various rumours were flying around the investigation, with speculation that Maher could have been linked to other crimes. Newspaper reports suggested that Maher could have been involved in a raid three years earlier that saw £2m handed over to robbers in December 1990. It was claimed Maher gave the cash to an armed gang, who had taken a man hostage. The report went on to say that Maher had been treated as an innocent victim at the time but had now emerged as a key gang member. It was a theory dismissed by the investigating officers.

His family were also being questioned about whether he had ever been linked to any thefts. In one quote, published in the *Daily Mail* on 26 January 1993, Maher's sister, Margaret, made light of the false links to other spectacular crimes. 'He did not have anything to do with the Great Train Robbery, he does not know where Lord Lucan is and he had nothing to do with Brink's-Mat,' she said.

Brink's-Mat had been one of Britain's biggest unsolved crimes. Gold worth around £26m was stolen from the company's warehouse close to Heathrow Airport by six armed robbers in 1983. It was reported that the raiders had been expecting £3m in cash to be stored at the warehouse but instead stumbled across three tonnes of gold bullion worth nearly 10 times as much. It was soon melted down and made those responsible instant millionaires. The majority of the gang were never captured. And the similarly audacious £2.6m Great Train Robbery of 1963 is now estimated to be worth about £41m in today's money.

Despite the almost light-hearted references to other crimes, police were confident that Maher had not struck before. He was certainly not living the lifestyle of anyone with significant money, moving between rented houses and even living with his mother for a short time. 'We didn't link him to anything else,' Barnett said.

There were also claims within media circles that he could have been harmed, including one that Maher had been 'buried under a motorway'. Freelance reporter Andrew Young said, 'There were all sorts of rumours that he had been done in. As time progressed, we thought that it was a likely scenario – that he had got in with some dodgy characters and been bumped off. It was thought that it was impossible for anyone to just disappear.' But Barnett said the police never received any information that Maher had been harmed.

By 28 February, 450 people had been questioned in 15 countries, 650 lines of inquiry followed and 250 witnesses interviewed. The number of detectives working on the case had swelled to 30, and numerous reports were being followed up.

There were 20 reported sightings of Maher around the world in the years that followed; none were confirmed. Officers were certain he had flown to America after the theft but, as the years passed without any trace of him, they refused to rule out the possibility that he had returned to Britain.

While the police had numerous unanswered questions, the families of Maher and Debbie were in the same position. And further questions surrounded the security precautions of Securicor. Some were puzzled about why the alarm had not been raised when the van took a detour from its regular route to be dumped on Felixstowe seafront. Experts countered this by saying that the tracking devices only came into play once the van had been reported as either missing or stolen. Other theories centred on the suggestion that Maher could have passed keys from the back of the van through a hatch and to an accomplice, possibly disguised in a security guard's clothing – a theory Securicor refused to speculate on.

It was anyone's guess where Maher and his family were hiding, although there were plenty of people willing to put forward their ideas. As the two-month anniversary of the heist approached, the case was already being scaled down. A Suffolk Police press release, dated 19 March 1993, confirmed that the 30-strong team working on the inquiry had been cut. 'Although the team has been scaled down, this does not mean this investigation is at a close,' said DS Moss. 'A small, specialist team of detectives is still pursuing a number of lines of inquiry. We are still confident that we will find those responsible.'

Police refused to reveal how many detectives had been left working on the inquiry but said information was still coming in to the incident room. Moss said, 'Members of the public are still contacting us with information and we are still following up every lead. However, to date we still have no confirmed sightings. Although concerned about the welfare of the family, especially the young boy, we have no reason to believe they have come to any harm.'

Police were now saying publicly that it was likely that Maher and his family had left the country within hours of the theft. Although police believed Maher was behind it, it was clear that he had been given help. 'We do know a number of people was used to carry out the crime,' said Moss. 'It would need at least two people to do it so there's no doubt he was assisted by someone.'

John Barnett, speaking in 2013, added, 'My own personal opinion at the time was that he was not the main beneficiary of the theft.' But this was another line of inquiry that drew a blank. No one was ever publicly linked to the theft in 1993, even though detectives had their suspicions.

Barnett had continued working on the inquiry but, by July 1993, the majority of his time was being spent on other jobs. He still had his policing work in relation to Felixstowe to complete and was involved in a murder investigation. Single mother-of-two Mandy Duncan, 26, was murdered while working as a sex worker in Ipswich on 2 July 1993. Police believe she turned to prostitution to pay off mounting debts. Her body was never found but it was a high-profile investigation for Suffolk and one that dominated Barnett's time for several weeks. Fast Eddie was no longer the number one focus of his attention as police pursued a murderer.

An anonymous letter had been found at Miss Duncan's flat, in the town of Woodbridge, on the edge of Ipswich, threatening her life if she failed to pay her debts. Barnett's priority was to find the person who sent that note.

Operation Ramble to find Fast Eddie was slowly coming to a standstill. The trip to Cyprus in 1993 remained the only foreign excursion that officers had undertaken as part of the inquiry and, as one police source put it, the investigation had not rambled very far.

Ironically, that was in stark contrast to the distance Maher and Debbie had put between themselves and their pursuers.

10

SPEED OF
FLIGHT

While Suffolk Constabulary were devoting hundreds of hours to interviewing witnesses and doing everything they could think of to track down Maher, he was honing a skill that he would need for years to come – the art of lying low.

Police and prosecutors have never been able to establish fully Maher's next move after his Opel Ascona was found dumped and burnt out in the lane in Nazeing, Essex. In short, he had simply vanished.

Up to this point, his plan had been executed perfectly. The money was in his possession, the car used to get him – and possibly an accomplice or two – out of Felixstowe was now a pile of charred metal and ash and seemingly no one had spotted him making his getaway after leaving Landguard Fort. Every avenue the police tried revealed nothing.

With Debbie and Lee nowhere to be found and no evidence of any accomplices at this stage, the officers had little to go on. As he had been from the start, Maher was a step ahead. After all, he had been planning this for weeks, if not months.

It was now well known to Suffolk Police that Debbie and Lee had been booked on a flight to Boston from Gatwick on 21 January. Records showed she was at the airport and had her passport stamped at border control. Earlier that month, she had contacted the authorities to arrange for Lee to be put on her passport so he could travel overseas with her. And on 20 January, a woman giving her name as Debbie Brett called the passport office in Peterborough asking when the passport would be ready. A check of phone records showed a call had been made from the South Woodham Ferrers house the day before for last-minute flight bookings for 21 January. So when neighbours in Fremantle Close saw Debbie walking away with Lee, pulling a suitcase behind her, she had been on her way to Gatwick. They would be her last hours in the UK for 20 years.

Just as Debbie had walked out of sight, never to be seen in South Woodham Ferrers again, Maher too had dropped off the radar. And now the police have their theory about where he went next. Maher's Opel car was found in Mead Gate Road in Nazeing, a village near Harlow with a population of about 4,000. It lies about 70 miles south-west of Felixstowe in the Epping Forest district. It is a village with a great of history and was mentioned in the Domesday Book in 1066 as having seven villagers, 12 smallholders, seven cattle and 30 pigs. In the years that followed, it grew into what is claimed to be one of the largest villages in the UK, with pubs, churches and a golf course. The nearest train station was two miles away in Broxbourne, making it prime commuter belt territory for central London.

The car is thought to have been left there sometime between 25 and 27 January, but it is not clear if Maher dumped it himself or if someone torched it for him. What is clear, though, is that Nazeing is much closer to Maher's home turf. By this time, his mother had moved from Ilford and was living in nearby Barkingside, an area of Redbridge he would have known well from his youth. Barkingside is just 20 miles from where the Opel was torched. Police now know that, at the time, Maher's brother Michael was living with his mother. Even closer was his sister, Margaret Francis. She was living just nine miles away with her husband Alan in Abridge in Essex, a tiny village near Romford built around the River Roding.

The fact that Maher's own car was used in the getaway perhaps showed how brazen the theft was. Whether it was driven by Maher or an accomplice, it showed that little was being done to distance the guard from the crime.

While Maher was keeping his head down, Debbie had arrived in Boston. Her flight touched down late on 21 January and she checked into the Buckminster Hotel in the city's Kenmore Square under a booking she had made before she left England.

The Buckminster was an interesting choice. The hotel had been connected to one of the most infamous crimes in American history – the fixing of the 1919 World Series, baseball's Black Sox Scandal. It was after the Chicago White Sox lost to the Boston Red Sox in September 1919 that bookie and gambler Joseph 'Sport' Sullivan met White Sox first baseman Arnold Gandil to hatch a match-fixing scam that would lead to life bans for eight players and the creation of a commissioner of Major League Baseball to crack down on match-fixing and acts that tarnished the image of the game. The hotel's role in the scandal has become a key part of its history.

Having just endured a flight from the UK with a three-year-old, it's unlikely Debbie took much time to discover its past. After her two days at the hotel, she checked out and wasn't seen in the city again. By the time police had traced the booking, she was long gone.

Maher, though, was still closer to home than police imagined. He would later tell the FBI he flew to the USA on 22 February – a full month after disappearing from the bank.

Police have spent years piecing together the events of that month. What is now known, according to the Crown Prosecution Service, is that on 26 January a man connected to Maher booked a flight to New York through a firm called Felton Travel. Prior to leaving for New York, he was in contact with another associate of Maher on two occasions. Police would later say the second man had been 'in contact' with the Toyota Previa used to take the money from the Securicor van to Landguard Fort about the time it was stolen in November 1992.

After flying to New York, the first man caught a return flight from Boston on 29 January. The purpose of the trip has never been fully established, and neither have Maher's movements up until 22 February. It was then that a man using the name Michael Maher flew to Orlando, Florida, with another man.

Michael Maher had a single ticket while his travelling partner had a return, and Maher's had been purchased on a credit card.

Years later, prosecutors would tell Southwark Crown Court that it had been purchased on a card in the name of AW Francis of Abridge. Alan Francis, the husband of Maher's sister Margaret Francis, who has since died, had the initials AW.

Prosecutor Richard Southern said records show the woman making the booking confirmed to the travel agent that the person who was travelling on the flight had a Green Card. And like Debbie's flight in January, the 22 February flight had been booked just two days in advance, and it had also been made with Ilford travel agent Felton Travel.

Police also discovered that a phone linked to a man believed to be connected to Maher was used for a 'lengthy conversation', according to Southern, with the passport office at about the time of the theft.

Police believe while Michael Maher stayed in the UK, his brother Eddie made the most of their similar appearance to use his passport to exit the country, although that was disputed by Maher's lawyers. 'There was a physical resemblance between the defendant and Michael Maher and we say he would have been able to use his brother's passport,' Southern told Southwark Crown Court. This would have been possible, according to Paul Scothern from the CPS, because of the 'uncanny' physical similarities between Eddie and Michael Maher. 'There are a series of photographs from passport applications for Maher and Michael. They show an amazing likeness between them throughout their lives. You couldn't tell the difference,' he said.

Another theory considered by police was that it had actually been Michael Maher on the 22 February flight and that his brother, already in the USA somehow, had collected his Green Card there. But, Southern said, no evidence could be found of Michael Maher ever returning to the UK. 'He had a one-way ticket and investigations have not revealed he had returned to this country. But he certainly was, according to records, back in this country in the middle of 1993,' he said.

One thing that is for sure, police say – Maher could not have left the country on his own passport. Police think he would have been able to enter the USA with a single ticket because years before, in 1984, Michael had married an American woman in the Californian city of San Diego and had obtained a Green Card which would have allowed him to stay in the country. The pair had one child but later divorced and Michael returned to the UK.

So, under the name Michael Richard Maher, Fast Eddie was on the verge of realising his dream of a new life in the States. The plan, though, involved a huge amount of risk. In the four weeks since Maher's disappearance with the cash, his picture had been plastered all over the country's newspapers. From tabloids like the *Sun* and *Mirror* to the broadsheets and regionals, every part of the media had lapped up the Fast Eddie story.

Police had released his picture and urged witnesses to come forward; officers had made appeals on TV and radio. The name Fast Eddie had become recognised up and down the country. Even media overseas – as far away as Australia – had run the story. For a time, Maher's face should have been among the most recognisable in the UK. Add to that the fact that, from the first days of the investigation, Suffolk Police had been aware that a criminal of this kind was likely to try to abscond overseas. Border agencies had been warned to be on the lookout and had been issued with pictures of Maher.

Yet, police believe, here he was, fronting up to border control using his own surname. If he was recognised or the surname Maher flagged an alert for the border control officer, the game would have been up there and then. All the planning and weeks of patient waiting since the theft would have been for nothing. If Suffolk police's theory is correct, Maher, showing nerves of steel, was risking it all to join Debbie and Lee in the USA.

Remarkably, it paid off. He collected his ticket and made his way through border control. The officer who checked his brother's passport did not spot that the man standing in front of him wasn't the man in the picture; neither did the name Maher raise any suspicion. Incredibly, but not for the last time, Maher had stood in full view of the authorities and got away with it. While the previous month had been spent lying low, he had been forced, for a time at least, to hide in plain sight. It was a risk that would later be described as a clever double-bluff.

On 22 February 1993, Maher was on his way to his new life in the States. He was leaving behind a life in which he was burdened by debts, had no real assets and couldn't even muster the enthusiasm to speak to his neighbours. Soon, his life would be very different. For the first time since his pay-off from the fire service, he was flush with cash. And this time he would spend it very differently. But, if his new life was to be a success, one final thing needed to be sorted out – new identities.

Unsure if Suffolk Police would wake up to the Michael Maher bluff, Maher needed a new name and so did Debbie.

During their investigations, Suffolk Police found that the man known to have had the lengthy conversation with the passport office in January travelled to the USA at the end of March 1993 and returned again in May. Prosecutors would later allege that he had been a key player in Maher's plan.

On 28 April 1993, the United Kingdom Passport Agency issued a passport in the name of Stephen Michael King. Stephen King was indeed a real person but, alongside the name on the passport, was a picture of Eddie Maher. In the picture, Maher had a short, scraggy beard that made him look like he had been sleeping rough for a month and he was wearing large spectacles.

Few people would be able to look at the photo and see past the outlandish glasses and grubby-looking beard. At least, that's what Maher must have been hoping. The passport was valid for 10 years and was signed 'S King'.

The following month, on 5 May, the office issued another passport, this time in the name of Barbara Anthony. Again, Barbara Anthony did exist but this passport bore Debbie Brett's picture. Investigations later revealed that the real Stephen King and Barbara Anthony had been living in north London and had, according to Southern, been 'persuaded to allow their names to be used for passports'. The applications for the fake passports had been submitted on 2 and 13 February; they were sent in by post and had a London postmark.

Police now know the real Stephen King, an odd-job man,

signed the application in his name on 2 February. He was paid £50 but officers found no record that the real Barbara Anthony was paid for allowing her name to be used. The passport forms were returned to a townhouse flat in Cross Street, Islington, a trendy north London road.

Police say that, given the date the passports were issued, it would have been impossible for Maher and Debbie to take possession of them in the UK. They assert that associates of Maher made trips to the USA, which coincided with the issuing of his false documents. 'Somebody had to supply the photographs. Somebody had to make the application,' Southern said. 'It shows that there was assistance in this country even after the theft had taken place. We believe the defendant received assistance from people in this country in the months after the offence.'

While Maher's associates apparently knew where to find him in the States, the huge police team searching for him still did not have a clue.

11

THE AMERICAN DREAM

The act of stepping on to US soil represented a series of victories for Eddie Maher. He had outwitted his Securicor employers, one of the largest security firms on the planet, by circumventing their supposedly state-of-the-art, crime-prevention measures and driving away with a truckload of their cash; he had outsmarted the police by leaving them scrabbling in the dark in their search for clues as to his whereabouts; he had escaped his creditors in the UK, leaving them with a string of outstanding debts that would never be paid; and he had fooled the immigration services by pretending to be his brother, even though they were on high alert looking for him. And perhaps one of the greatest victories of all for Maher - one that remains shrouded in mystery to this day - was managing to reap the rewards of his crime by somehow gaining access to some or all of the money he'd grabbed after he'd fled to the States. However he'd achieved it, one thing was crystal clear

- for first time in a long time, money was of no concern to him now.

Suffolk Police have always admitted that they are largely in the dark when it comes to Maher's early movements around the USA. The case they presented against Maher had more questions than answers when it came to his time on the run. The only person to shed any light on it so far is Debbie, who described their journey across the USA when speaking out in support of her husband after his arrest. Debbie said she was still in Boston when Maher arrived – saying it was just 'a few days' after she and Lee had landed.

In an interview with investigative journalist Bob Graham, who covered the story for the *Sun* newspaper, she said she had known nothing of Maher's plan to steal the cash and only learned of what he had done when he revealed all at the hotel in Boston. The trip to Massachusetts in January 1993, she said, had been for a holiday for all three of them but Maher had told her at the last-minute that he wouldn't be able to go because of work. 'Eddie had said the day before or so he had something that had come up at work and he would not be able to travel with us, he would join us later,' she told Graham. 'We'd already bought the tickets, it wasn't our summer holiday, it was January but we'd been saving to come back over. I was furious, absolutely livid. I was so angry I decided to go out of spite.'

Debbie told Graham she should have refused to go but added, 'We'd paid all that money for the tickets, we'd booked into hotels. So me and Lee went and Eddie said he'd be out in a few days. Then when he came over, he sat me down and

The Lloyds bank in Hamilton Road, Felixstowe (*pictured in 2013*).

Photo: ©Mark Bulstrode

 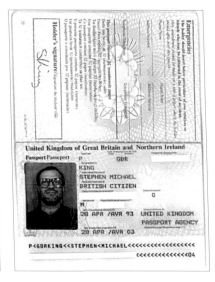

Above left: An *East Anglian Daily Times* billboard in Ipswich following the news of Maher's arrest.   *Photo: ©Mark Bulstrode*

Above right: Eddie Maher's police mugshot after his arrest.

Photo: ©REX/Albanpix Ltd

Below left: Maher in his Securicor uniform in 1992.   *Photo: ©REX/Albanpix Ltd*

Below right: Eddie Maher's false passport in the name of Stephen King.

Photo: ©REX/Albanpix Ltd

Above: Maher's ranch-style home in Colorado, USA.   *Photo courtesy Suffolk Police*

Below: A distant view of Maher's isolated ranch-style home in Colorado, USA.

Photo courtesy Crown Prosecution Service

Above: Eddie Maher with wife Deborah and son Lee, at Lee's graduation while living in the USA.
Photo: ©Kayla Jacoby

Below: The Green Card in the name of Eddie Maher's brother Michael which Eddie is believed to have used to establish residency in the US.
Photo courtesy Crown Prosecution Service

Above: The Securicor van used in the theft, abandoned in Micklegate Road, Felixstowe.

Photo courtesy Suffolk Police

Below: The Toyota Previa used as an escape vehicle, abandoned near Landguard Fort, Felixstowe.

Photo courtesy Suffolk Police

Maher's fellow Securicor guard Peter Bunn displays the police letter thanking him for his assistance (*see opposite*).

Photo: ©Mark Bulstrode

SUFFOLK
CONSTABULARY

Police Headquarters, Martlesham Heath, Ipswich IP5 3QS
Tel: Ipswich 01473 613500 Fax: 01473 613737 (24 hrs)
Calls may be monitored for quality control, security and training purposes. www.suffolk.police.uk

Reference - R v Edward MAHER

6th March 2013
Dear Peter,

This is just to update you concerning the above investigation, which you kindly assisted us with.
The investigation commenced after the theft of £1,172,500 from Securicor on Friday 22nd January 1993 in Felixstowe, Suffolk.
At the time, a team of Officers were tasked with apprehending the offender/s and recovering the money.
Enquiries quickly established that the principal offender responsible for taking the money was Edward Maher, a Securicor employee and former Firefighter.
Despite extensive efforts, Maher and his family could not be located, however he was strongly suspected of living somewhere within the United States.
In February 2012, Suffolk CID was contacted by the FBI, stating that they had arrested Maher in Ozark, Missouri, USA, for firearms and immigration offences. Maher had, up to this point, evaded detection within the US by using various forms of false documentation and moving between various addresses and jobs at regular intervals.
Maher agreed to a voluntary deportation to the UK after learning that officers had commenced extradition proceedings. Maher was arrested at Heathrow Airport at 10th July 2012 and was immediately taken to Ipswich Magistrates Court in Suffolk, where he was remanded in custody.
At a subsequent court appearance Maher pleaded not guilty, indicating that he had been forced to commit the offence by unknown persons.
The not guilty plea initiated a large amount of additional enquiries and as such a team of Detectives were put together to establish Maher's movements and finances over the past 20 years in the USA and to locate the witnesses who had provided evidence back in 1993.
Officers established Maher's cash purchases of property and land within the U.S and officers were able to secure vital evidence linking Maher to the purchases. Maher subsequently sold these houses.
What happened to the money? We are confident that other persons were involved in committing the offence and were likely to have obtained a share of the stolen money. Maher was financially inept and at the time of his arrest; he had no significant funds to his name, and, whilst none of the money has been recovered, we have applied for a restraint order for any funds that he should come into possession of post conviction - We look forward to the money being used in the future for crime fighting purposes.
It is because of people like you that we have been able to build a strong case, which has resulted in Maher entering a **guilty plea** to the offence of theft.
He has been sentenced to serve 5 years in prison.

On behalf of Suffolk Constabulary, we thank you most sincerely for your assistance with this significant investigation.

Kind Regards

Detective Inspector David GILES
Senior Investigating Officer

Detective Sergeant Stephen BUNN
Deputy Senior Investigating Officer

Taking pride
in keeping
Suffolk safe

A copy of the police letter sent to Maher's fellow security guard Peter Bunn.

Photo: ©Mark Bulstrode

Above: A recent photo of Eddie Maher's home in New Hampshire, USA.

Photo: ©REX/ Albanpix Ltd

Below: The house in Fremantle Close, South Woodham Ferrers, in which Maher and his family lived before fleeing to the USA (*pictured in 2012*).

Photo: © Grant Sherlock

said what had happened. He just said, "I've got to tell you something and it's serious."

'He then told me what had happened. I felt total dread ... I was angry with him. He then went on to tell me I would not be able to speak to Louise, my baby sister; I would not be able to go home again. It was hard, very, very hard. I couldn't believe it ... I just couldn't believe what he was telling me. It was, like, surreal, that's the only way I could describe it. I didn't want to know anything, I didn't want to see anybody, I just wanted to go home.

'When he told me what had happened, I could not think. I said, "What about everything at home? What about everything in the house ... what about the pictures? What about everything?" I just left the house like I was going on holiday – because I was. I had washing that was waiting for us to come home to, and I'm sure the bins needed emptying. He just said. "We don't have anything any more." I was angry, just angry, like something was in the pit of my stomach and I could not get it out. I couldn't phone family, anything.'

Police and prosecutors would later contest Debbie's assertion that Maher arrived in the USA just a few days after her, presenting instead a case that suggested Maher had taken the flight under his brother's name a full month after Debbie's arrival. Under their version of events, Maher would have arrived in Orlando on 22 February and travelled from there to meet Debbie.

Either way, by then Maher knew what a life on the run would involve. No contact with home, no hanging on to the past. Life would certainly have its drawbacks but he had had long enough to weigh up the pros and cons while he had planned the theft. In doing so, he had made that choice for Debbie and Lee, too. They would have to live by the same strict set of rules, or the police would come knocking in no time. They were fugitives and they had to live as such. No matter how much they craved it, normality was now unachievable. While Eddie had made that choice and would live with it, Debbie says it was made for her without her knowledge. And Lee would only learn when he was old enough that he, too, was living a life on the run.

Although Debbie's fake passport carried the name Barbara Anthony, Eddie told her that her new name would be Barbara King. Under their assumed identities at least, they were to be a married couple. Debbie decided there was 'no way' she was going to be called Barbara and could not stomach the Americans shortening it to Barbie, so she chose the name Sarah for herself. From then on, she was known as Sarah King.

Debbie told Graham, 'When he first arrived in Boston, he told me he'd have to call me something else. I didn't want to be called something else … I wasn't stupid but I knew we had to, so I just said, "Sarah". I have no idea why, I don't even like the name.

'The name King was the name he gave me when he came over – Barbara King – and there was no way I was going to be called Barbara. I'm not a Barbie, that's what they shorten it to, and there's no way I could do that. So I said, "Call me Sarah." He just gave me the identity and said, "This is you now."'

In Maher's mind, there was no going back. He spent his time now focused on looking forward and planning their next move.

Most of those first weeks were spent indoors, hiding away in case the police caught on about Michael Maher's trip and began to follow the trail from Orlando. Soon the fugitives found themselves in New Hampshire but, before long, they were back on the road. They travelled nearly 2,000 miles to Houston, Texas, where they stayed in a hotel which accepted long-term tenants. They were there for two or three months and, according to Debbie, 'stayed in the room the whole time'.

By now they were getting a feel for life on the run and there was plenty not to like - the ever-present fear that a knock on the door would signal the arrival of the police, the uncertainty of where to go next and what the police in England had uncovered about their plan. Every time someone asked about their accent and enquired if they were on holiday, they would have to think up a lie. It was to become second nature to them but, for now, they were just beginners at it.

Debbie told Graham, 'It was not a fun time ... we knew we were on the run. We never picked up any newspapers or bothered with the news; we tried to stay away from it all. We lived off whatever money he had. I can't tell you about money or how he got it out of the country ... he's never told me,' she added.

After holing up in the hotel in Houston for several weeks, Maher made his next move. This time he wasn't going to hide away inside a city hotel room, he was going to use America's vast open spaces to his advantage. And he made his first big purchase with his new-found wealth. In July 1993, six months after he disappeared with the cash, Maher bought a house in the mountain community of Woodland Park in Colorado's Teller County.

The town lies below Pikes Peak – one of Colorado's 54 'fourteeners' at 14,115ft - and the Rampart Range in the Rocky Mountains. It is known for its spruce, pine and aspen and its deep blue skies and clean air. It began as a saw milling town but has grown to comprise more than 7,000 residents. It prides itself on its tourism industry, which is a big driver for the local economy, and boasts that first-time visitors often become lifelong residents.

While Maher didn't stay for life, he did his best to make a home there. The town is surrounded by one million acres of national forest and lies 18 miles west of Colorado Springs. Plenty of space, then, for someone to hide away in if they wanted to.

Using the name Stephen King, Maher signed the contract on 23 July to purchase his first American house for $119,000, which, based on exchange rates at the time, equated to about £80,000. Maher's first public act under his assumed identity, he bought the house from a couple called Kevin and Beth Ellis and paid the £119,000 in full a week later without having to trouble himself with a mortgage. The two-storey, shingle-roof house at 1345 Leslie Circle had been built in 1986, and had wooden cladding which helped it blend in with its surroundings, along with a wood fire needed for Colorado's cold winters – the average January temperature in nearby Colorado Springs is -2°C. It had five bedrooms, a basement and an attached double garage, and was slightly set back from the road, shielded from the neighbours on either side by trees. The dirt drive led to a set of wooden steps and a small covered porch. Inside, the house had a large, open living area with vaulted ceilings and floor-to-ceiling windows, with built-in wardrobes in all the bedrooms.

Kevin Ellis still remembers selling the property to Maher, helped largely by his fake passport giving him the name of one of America's most famous authors. Horror novelist Stephen King had even set one of his best-selling books, *The Shining*, in Colorado, making him a well-known figure in the state. Years later, one of Debbie's fingerprints would be found on an energy assessment form for the house. They were among only a few forensic clues police found regarding Maher's movements across 10 US states.

Paul Scothern, an investigator for the CPS involved in the case against Maher, said, 'It was not a cheap property. It was in an upmarket area of Colorado. If you want to be out of the public eye, that particular area of Colorado would be a wonderful place to go. It was really isolated.'

Seemingly, Maher and Debbie took a liking to Colorado and its remoteness. They spent eight months in the 1,290sq-ft house, and Detective Inspector David Giles, from Suffolk police, who travelled to the area in 2013 while gathering evidence against Maher, got the impression he had been far from slumming it. 'We can only surmise that he lived a quite nice lifestyle,' Giles said. Much later, one of Lee's ex-partners would later recall him telling her about their 'awesome' time in Colorado when they had couches worth $20,000. She claimed he told her he could jump on them and 'his parents didn't care'.

Eddie must have felt a million miles from the cramped streets of east London. The summers were warm and, at times, hot, the land semi-arid and, on average, winters brought 37 inches of snowfall. He was also living in one of the most active lightning strike areas of the country. This was a place where nature ruled, and Maher seemingly took a liking to it. In fact, his next move took him even further into the wilderness.

In March 1995, he sold the Woodland Park house to a man named Gary Raffensperger for a $17,000 profit. And, once again, his alias led to him being remembered. Giles tracked down Raffensperger and discovered he also remembered Maher's unique name. 'That's one of the things people in America remembered. The man who bought his house told people he was buying it from Stephen King,' he said. 'Whilst it was probably a completely random name to adopt, perhaps it wasn't a wise choice.' But while his name stuck in people's memories, there was no real reason for them to be suspicious of the Englishman with enough cash to buy houses outright, even though that in itself might have raised an eyebrow or two.

It was at about this time that Maher and Debbie married. For some time, their assumed identities had them as a married couple – the Kings - but in reality Debbie had been Maher's common-law wife until this point. All police were able to uncover about the wedding was that it took place in Las Vegas in 1994. Seven years after they met in the hotel in Castle Donnington and five years after they had had Lee, they became husband and wife. It was Maher's second marriage. This time around there was no chance to have family and old friends to celebrate with. Debbie had not spoken to her sisters in more than a year and her whereabouts remained a secret.

They chose America's marriage capital; each year, 90,000 people head to the city in the Nevada desert to get hitched in one of the many chapels located around the famous Las Vegas strip and all its casinos and bars. This wedding, though, was just for them. Since they were already living under assumed names, it provided no benefit in terms of their false existence and didn't aid their life on the run. And, depending on what information they put on the official documents, it's likely that in the eyes of the law it wasn't legally binding.

'Whether that counts as an official marriage, we don't know. We haven't been able to trace his marriage certificate,' Giles said. 'We don't know what name he married under.'

In January 1995, two months before selling the Leslie Circle house, Maher had purchased 40 acres of land about 50 miles away in El Paso. The closest town, Calhan, was a 30-minute drive from the new property and, even 18 years on, the closest neighbour is half a kilometre away. The plot at 7550 Mulberry Road cost him $12,000. After selling Woodland Park, he bought another 40 acres which adjoined the first 40, again for $12,000. He spent $58,000 having a prefabricated, ranch-style house built on the land and the family moved in. They weren't living rough but it also wasn't extravagant. Maher had the house built back from the road and access was via a dirt driveway. The single-storey house had six rooms, including three bedrooms, a detached garage, stucco walls and a shingle roof. If the Woodland Park house bordered on luxurious, this was basic by comparison.

DI Giles remembered the location from his evidence-gathering trip. 'To use the term "middle of nowhere" is a bit of an understatement, in my opinion,' he said. 'We know that when it was put there no other houses were around.'

So Maher had found a place where he didn't have to come into contact with anyone other than Debbie and Lee if it suited him. He had an 80-acre hideaway that made the search for him even more like looking for a needle in a haystack. Anyone wanting to find him would have had to have known exactly where to look. Giles said it was clear the choice of location for Maher's latest hiding place was not random. 'If he wanted it because it was isolated, he couldn't have done much better than that,' he said.

The new arrivals soon made a home in their remote surroundings. The house Maher had built was far enough away from the boundaries of his property to mean he was far from view from any inquisitive eyes keen to find out more about the new arrivals. Prying eyes would have faced a more difficult task than at the Woodland Park house, which was only set back from the street about 20 metres and had houses surrounding it. That was a residential street; now Maher was carving out a place to live from the bare open land. He spent $10,000 adding extras to the home, including having a well dug on the land.

And he had plenty of time to enjoy it. Maher's new life meant he wasn't employed full-time, so he had plenty of time to spend with Debbie and Lee. He did, however, find himself a position at the local airport which allowed him to pursue his dream of learning to fly. After his disappearance, the Covingtons had told of Maher's aim of one day running a flying school in the USA. Indeed, the British papers had speculated whether he had fled to America to do just that. But while he wasn't running his own flying school, he was definitely taking lessons at one. Scothern said, 'He certainly started flying lessons. There are records that he was working there fuelling aircraft and doing bits and bobs and taking private pilot lessons. He was living the dream.' Maher didn't qualify as a pilot, but investigators discovered he had 'done a lot of lessons', Scothern said.

The property was to be Maher's haven until 1996, when he became convinced of the need to move on again. He sold all 80 acres to a man called James Lee Rose for $108,000. Maher sold up to return to New Hampshire, where they had been on holiday in 1989. The fugitives had fallen in love with the vast open spaces and remembered fondly the sight of the White Mountains in winter.

For Suffolk Police, chasing the now stone-cold trail some 20 years later was where they lost track of Maher's life on the run. Yet it was only a small part of the escape route that took Maher and his family across 10 states in a journey which seemed to have no direction or overall plan. In her interview with journalist Bob Graham, Debbie told how they returned to New Hampshire to live in Laconia in Belknap County. It was to be the last house Maher bought in the USA. Police still don't know how much he paid for it.

If Colorado was picturesque in its ruggedness, Laconia had a different kind of beauty. It is situated on four lakes – Lake Winnipesaukee, Lake Opechee, Paugus Bay and Lake Winnisquam – and it was destined to be the family's home for some time. Jim Coffey, a landscape contractor who lived across the street from the Kings in Morrill Street, remembers them as 'very friendly' and a 'pleasant family' who made no attempt to hide the fact they were from England. He recalls Debbie being pregnant and his son playing with Lee. 'My wife used to sit on the patio with his wife and their son and she was expecting then,' he said. Maher's neighbours also came to the conclusion he wasn't working at the time. 'He always seemed to be around the place,' Coffey said, remembering that the man he knew as Stephen King would often be seen working in the yard.

He remembers discussing with his wife where Maher had made his money. 'I thought it was odd,' he said, 'he never really worked … he was always around. It just seemed a little odd. He always seemed to be buying things.' But exactly where Maher got his cash never made for conversation when Debbie came to sit on the Coffeys' patio. 'We don't really pry into anybody's world,' Coffey said.

The ranch-style house with a basement and garage below that Maher and Debbie moved into is across the street and one door down from Coffey's. He remembers being pleased when the new family moved in. 'We were just happy to see new neighbours and they seemed like a good family with kids,' he said.

While Coffey was out most of the day, his schoolteacher wife got to know Debbie and Lee quite well. From across the street, he noticed they put in an above-ground pool and erected a deck around it and his wife and son occasionally visited for a swim.

Maher, whom Coffey remembers having a pot belly, also made the most of his surroundings by buying a boat. 'It wasn't a large one, just a nice little one for the lakes in the area,' Coffey said. Maher clearly felt comfortable enough with his finances to splash out on a new pool and buy a boat. But Coffey said his cars were 'nothing flashy'.

Unlike their remote hideaway in El Paso, their actions were

noticed by the neighbours who were keen to learn more about this new family who had arrived suddenly on their doorstep. But despite the curious nature of the Kings' arrival and lifestyle, the Coffeys only have positive things to say about their former neighbours. Their son bonded well with Lee, who they say attended Laconia's Holy Trinity private Catholic school in Church Street.

But while in Laconia, Maher's life changed in three very significant ways. The first was the birth of his third son – Mark Conner King – on 5 March 1997. Maher was now living life on the run with an eight-year-old and a newborn.

The second came in the same year – five years after Maher had driven away with more than £1m, he had reached the point of having to go back to full-time work. It's not clear if he became bored at home of if the last of the money had run out but, whatever it was, it was enough to prompt him to take the test to acquire a heavy goods vehicle licence. Having gained it, he soon found work driving poultry products around.

Along with the new job came the third key development in Maher's life that year – in order to get work, he needed the correct documentation. He didn't have a Green Card to match the fake passport in the name of Stephen King. The passport might have worked for identification purposes but employers would need a valid social security number to prove he could legally work in the USA. Police have said that during the early years in the States, Maher had occasionally used his older brother Michael's name – the same name they believe got him into the USA in the first place. And Michael, significantly, had a Green Card from his 1984 marriage. By switching to his brother's name, Maher was able to get a social security number and driver's licence.

Issued by the US Department of Justice Immigration and Naturalization Service, the Green Card labelled the holder a 'Resident Alien'. It carried the name Michael Richard Maher and a picture of the real Michael Maher. Alongside the picture was one of Michael Maher's fingerprints, listing his date of birth as 17 April 1951 and gave him a unique 'alien number' – A26773349. At the bottom, it was signed 'M Maher'. From that point on, Edward John Maher became Michael Richard Maher. To most people, he was just Michael or Mike.

Just five years since carrying out one of Britain's most high-profile thefts in decades, Fast Eddie was back to using his own surname. He was back to hiding in plain sight.

Debbie later recalled to Graham the moment Maher announced his decision. 'There came a time when he needed to get a job and he just said, "You need to start calling me Mike,"' she said. 'And I'm like, "What are you on about? You mean your brother?" and he said, "Yep, I'm now Michael Maher and you'll have to call me Mike."'

Police have asked themselves the motivation for that brazen move, with desperation borne out of a lack of money one possible answer. Suffolk Police's enquiries suggest that, by the late 1990s, Maher and Debbie were no longer living the high life that Giles witnessed in Colorado and that led to Coffey describing them as appearing 'affluent'. So Maher had gone from driving millions of pounds of cash around the east of England in 1993 to driving dead poultry around New Hampshire in 1998.

Debbie's memory of it was that Maher 'had to get a job'. This wasn't a case of Maher getting bored having spent five years sitting at home spending his ill-gotten gains. The reality of work had been thrust back at him, brought about by five years of costly outgoings with little coming in. Those back home who occasionally wondered whatever happened to Fast Eddie and his £1m could be forgiven for not expecting him to be driving trucks for a living. It was something that would later be used by his lawyers in an attempt to convince a British judge that Maher's life on the run was far from one of Bentleys and cigars.

As the judge prepared to decide his fate following his capture, Maher's barrister David Nathan QC told Southwark Crown Court, 'Mr Maher, Deborah and the children were not living high on the hog. Mr Maher went to work!'

12

THE BOSTON
CONNECTION

As Maher and his family were settling into their latest American home in New Hampshire, the story of the theft was back on the front pages of newspapers in Suffolk. A press release was faxed to newsrooms out of the blue one morning in January 1998 to mark the fifth anniversary of the crime. It contained major new information as far as journalists covering the case were concerned.

For the first time, the media had confirmation that Debbie had travelled to Boston the day before the theft. It was known she had been seen leaving her home in South Woodham Ferrers with a suitcase and her three-year-old son, Lee. But her movements beyond that time were a mystery. Finally, after refusing for 'operational reasons' over many years to comment on speculation that Maher had fled to America, this was confirmation that media reports around the time of the theft were close to the mark. And drinkers in Maher's former pub, The Gardener's Arms, had been correct in their assumption that he had probably gone to the United States.

By now, the media appetite for the story nationally had died down. If Maher was ever caught, it would once again be a massive story but, for many national newspapers and media organisations, this was simply confirmation of what they had been reporting years ago. It was the finer·detail that was more interesting to the local media – the name of the hotel Debbie and Lee had stayed in, and the fact that they were there on the day of the theft.

For the media in Suffolk, it represented big news in what had become the county's most intriguing and high-profile 'cold' case, especially at the county's two daily newspapers. The Ipswich-based *Evening Star*, under the editorship of Nigel Pickover, immediately formulated a plan.

After reporting the news, it was decided that a reporter from the paper should go to Boston. Crime correspondent Brad Jones, then 24, was chosen for the trip. His brief would be to write a 'colour piece' and speak to people in the vast city about the crime. It was always unlikely that anything would come from it in terms of positive information about Maher but, unlike the police, the newspaper decided it was worth a trip.

Jones, now news editor at the *East Anglian Daily Times*, said, 'Suffolk Police put out an anniversary press release saying that Debbie had checked into the Buckminster Hotel in Boston the day before the theft. She was with Lee. It was the first significant new bit of information there had been on that case for a while. It made everyone sit up and take notice and take some interest again.'

The release of the new details had come as a surprise to the local media, especially the timing of it so long after the theft. Richard Cornwell, who had been following the case since breaking the story five years earlier, said, 'It was one of those things that came out and it was new and different. Why they hadn't told us before I don't know. You would think surely they would want people to know that as it could lead to witnesses coming forward. It was so surprising that you could go to America and nobody would take any notice; that they would not be actively looking for you. It was big news for us and we dispatched Brad to America.'

Jones was also surprised by the timing of the press release. 'I can only think they wanted to hold something back from the original inquiry to release,' he said.

But in deciding not to release the information sooner, police had lost any remote chance they might have had of tracing potential witnesses among the 625,000 population of Boston. The city, one of the oldest in the country, is just outside the Top 20 biggest in the United States. It was also the scene of many key events in the American Revolution, which led to some tagging it the 'birthplace of freedom'. A Freedom Trail, marked by a line of red bricks, runs through the city centre, past some of the places that led to the city's prominent role in the revolution. It would have been ironic had the city of freedom been the first stop on Maher's journey out of the UK. But it does not appear that that was ever the case, with evidence suggesting he arrived in the country via Orlando, Florida.

Police files reveal detectives in the case had considered

releasing information about the American link three years earlier but ultimately decided not to. A press release was drafted in 1995 but never issued; much of the information it contained was never given to the media. The document was kept among the thousands of other pieces of paper relating to the case. It stated, 'Suffolk Police believe Securicor van driver Eddie Maher and his family may be in the United States. Detective Inspector John Barnett, who is now overseeing the £1m theft inquiry, revealed that information obtained indicated Mr Maher was living in the south-west of America prior to April 1995.'

It recounted details surrounding the 1993 theft and continued, 'DI Barnett confirmed that Maher's common-law wife, Debbie Brett, 27, and young son, Lee, three, checked into a hotel in Boston a day before the theft. They were at the hotel when the Securicor van was stolen.'

Barnett, quoted in the press release, said, 'We now believe they have been living in the States but, so far, have been unable to trace them. Two people fitting their description were seen in the south-west of America in April 1995. We contacted police in the States but their subsequent enquiries failed to confirm the identification or trace the two people concerned. It is believed they had already moved on. If the two people described were Mr Maher and Ms Brett, they had been living in the area for some considerable time.'

The press release went on to quote several other supposed sightings of the missing Securicor guard, including in France, Germany, Spain and Jamaica. Another was in Cyprus in May 1993.

In September 1994, there had been a further sighting at a 'caravan site in Haltwhistle, Northumberland, England, of two people matching Mr Maher and Ms Brett's description ... The man in question was in possession of two cars, a Jaguar and a Granada Scorpio. It is known that Mr Maher previously owned a Jaguar car,' the press release stated. 'Subsequent enquiries were made by officers in the area but they failed to find anyone matching their description. However, young Lee, who is now six, has not been seen since leaving his home the day before the theft.'

It seems unlikely that the sighting was that of Maher and Debbie; however, at the time, the claim was taken seriously by Suffolk police. Barnett, quoted in the press release, said, 'The new sighting in England has fuelled speculation that perhaps the money has run out and they have returned to this country. I cannot explain at this stage why the young boy has not been seen on either of these occasions. I do not think he has come to any harm, but he may have been left with someone or is being cared for by a relative. At the present moment, I am keeping an open mind on their whereabouts. They could be back in this country or still somewhere in America. It must be stressed that the inquiry is still ongoing and there is still a reward on offer. We would urge anyone who knows anything to contact us.'

The level of information contained in the press release showed that the case remained relatively active in the two to three years that followed the crime, even though the police incident room was shut down after six months.

It seemed the public were responding to appeals from police

and officers had been correct in their belief that Maher had been in the south-west of America, although there were never any firm details or exact addresses at that stage.

What the media, the general public or even the police could not have imagined only a few years after the crime was the sorry situation Maher had found himself in by the late 1990s. In January 1997, on the fourth anniversary of the theft, Suffolk Police spokesman Paul Gainey speculated that Maher's funds might have already run out, in a plight similar to the one that befell fellow fugitive security guard 'Florida Phil' Wells three years earlier. Despite 'a number' of reports in 1996 that Maher was back in the UK, Gainey told reporters, 'We suspect he is probably still overseas, but he could be running out of money now, just like Florida Phil did. It is easy to get through an enormous amount of cash when you're on the run, paying for accommodation, cars, living expenses and new identities. Debbie's son is now seven years old and of school age so there is also his education to think about.'

Mr Gainey's speculative statement proved spot on.

When Brad Jones touched down in Boston late in February 1998, Maher was perhaps not as far away as he might have expected – the fugitive was actually in the next state.

The quickest road route between Boston and Laconia, New Hampshire, where Maher and his family were living, was just under 100 miles. Given the size of America, Jones was remarkably close. But even if Maher had still been in Boston, the chances of Jones finding him would have been extremely remote given the size and population of the city.

Jones' first task was to travel to the Buckminster Hotel, where Debbie and Lee had stayed all those years before. It was a 30-minute walk from the city centre and a 15-minute taxi ride from the airport. Perhaps unsurprisingly, he was met with blank faces when he introduced himself to staff at the hotel's reception. He explained why he was there and started to ask questions about Maher, Debbie and Lee. 'The hotel itself had no idea,' said Jones. 'That was a dead end.'

After checking into his hotel room, the reporter set about trying to find some people to talk to about the case of the 'super thief'. He knew there would have been little point walking down the nearest street to ask people about it, so when he checked into his hotel room, he picked up a copy of the local telephone directory and found a number for a private investigator.

Bob Fitzpatrick, a former FBI agent who had worked on high-profile crimes in America, was happy to help. 'I gave him a call, explained that I couldn't offer him any money but asked if he would be able to help and do a piece with me,' said Jones. 'He spoke about how difficult it should have been for him to disappear. He was very helpful.'

In the front-page story published in the *Evening Star* on 27 February 1998, Fitzpatrick spoke of the problems Maher would have faced during his time on the run. Five years was normally a 'tipping point' in the life of a fugitive, he said. It was a time when things started 'getting difficult'. Fitzpatrick told Jones, 'There are very few that never get caught. There would have been an excitement at first but then all of a sudden it will go. There will be problems of looking over his shoulder every day. He has to take care of the woman, he has to take care of the kid and he could screw up.'

A cursory directory check on the name Edward Maher outlined the scale of the task facing anyone considering looking for the fugitive. At that time, there were 1,653 legal US residents of that name, with 183 in Massachusetts alone.

Another task for Jones on his three-day trip was to make contact with the *Boston Globe*. His editor had hoped to run simultaneous appeals in both titles, on either side of the Atlantic, in the hope it could throw up some new leads for police investigating the case. For the *Globe*, though, it was a story of minimal interest. The Boston link had emerged five years after the crime had been committed and was, in their opinion, a slightly tenuous link to the city. It was clear that Debbie had probably only been there for a matter of about 48 hours. However, they agreed to look into the case, which made for another front-page story for the *Evening Star* back in England as it spoke of the newspapers linking up.

For Jones, relatively early in his career as a newspaper man, it had been a fascinating but ultimately frustrating trip. There were few clues pointing to Maher in Boston and little he could do to generate new lines in the five-year-old story. 'The problem was at the time that people got the wrong end of the stick,' recalled Jones. 'They thought we were sending someone out there to find him. Bearing in mind five years had passed, there was never going to be any chance of him being there. My brief was to do a piece about how a criminal could disappear in America in this type of situation, the steps you have to take and what you would have to do. The idea was to get a bit of colour, describing it all and speaking to a few people about the crime.'

Jones had stuck to the brief and gave readers back home an insight into the scale of the challenge facing Suffolk Police officers having to search for a fugitive in America. It really was a needle in a haystack. With little information to go on, Jones was not even sure Maher was still in the United States when he made the trip.

Like many of his colleagues, Jones was invariably relying on tip-offs for much of the time to move the story forward, or to find new angles. Felixstowe reporter Cornwell had always harboured the hope that Maher himself would offer the ultimate tip-off – by calling him one day to explain how he'd carried out the theft. That never happened but, in July 1997, Cornwell did receive information from someone claiming to be 'close' to Maher. The unnamed source provided information that would be enough for another front-page splash on the crime.

The *Evening Star* edition on Monday, 4 August 1997 carried the headline: 'PLANTED BY EAST END MOB'. It told how the '£1m robbery man' was part of a gang. The exclusive article, under Cornwell's byline, said, 'Security guard Eddie Maher may have been planted by East End gangsters to carry out his daring £1m Felixstowe raid, we can reveal today. New information given to the *Evening Star* says Maher – known as Fast Eddie – was "set up" in his role as a security guard specifically to carry out what may yet be the perfect crime. Villains from London's gangland told Maher to apply for jobs with security firms while they formulated the plan to steal the contents of an armoured van.'

The piece quoted a Suffolk Police press officer who said there was no evidence that Maher was a plant, although the spokesman added it would not surprise them if it turned out to be the case. The source of the article, a former 'close work colleague', told the *Star* that Fast Eddie had been ordered by 'gangland bosses' to find work with Securicor and then report back on their security methods. 'It was not a random theft – it was planned from day one,' said the source, who could not be named, but the information provided would turn out to be close to the truth years later. There was certainly evidence it was a well-planned theft and Maher had actively been trying to get a job as a cash-in-transit driver, applying to two separate companies.

Cornwell has since lost contact details for the source and now has no recollection of who he spoke to in writing the article - understandable considering the number of years that passed. It was not known if the source ever went to the police.

The reason the Suffolk media had been so keen to latch on to the Boston link in 1998 was because new information had become hard to come by at that stage. However, there were still anniversary pieces to be written and most years saw a piece appear in the *Evening Star* newspaper around 22 January. And despite the lack of new information, it was a story that maintained an interest among readers. Cornwell said, 'It's just one of those pipe dreams that you love to read about. There also has been a view that it was a romantic crime in a way. Nobody got hurt. Every year it would raise itself. I can't imagine that he would have ever wanted to come back. He probably thought he was safe. To have come back would've been too risky.'

With each year that passed, there was the chance that Lee, who had left the UK as a three-year-old, would start asking questions about his past. Then Maher and Debbie would have a decision to make over what to tell him, and at what age should he know. It was a factor that led to speculation in the annual stories that Lee could ultimately hold the key to whether his father's past remained a secret.

In a 2003 interview with the BBC News website, John Barnett told reporter Nic Rigby that Lee could ultimately lead to his father's arrest and conviction. 'They do tend to get caught,' said Barnett. 'For instance, if he gets in a domestic dispute, or his youngster gets in trouble.' And in an article in 1997, Cornwell had similarly speculated that problems could arise as Lee went through the school system.

Barnett never bought into claims that Maher had committed the 'perfect crime'. In various media interviews, he predicted Maher's child was likely to be his 'biggest problem' as years went by.

It was a prediction that would be proved correct.

13

ROAD TO NOWHERE

From 1999 onwards, life on the run in the States got a little bit tougher. Debbie's fake passport in the name of Barbara King expired; since she had no other fake documents, she no longer had any form of official identification. That would restrict what she could do for more than a decade. In her interview for the *Sun*, she told Bob Graham, 'Since 1999, I've been nobody, never had a bank account, no name on leases or anything. That's been kinda hard out here.'

From then on, everything official was done in the name of Mike Maher. Credit cards, rental agreements, utilities … they all had to be in Maher's name, or more correctly, his brother's.

While still in New Hampshire, Maher got a new job. It was to determine his family's movements across the USA for much of the next decade and present the appearance years later that they kept moving to stay one step ahead of the police. While it might have had that effect, it seems Maher and his family set off on a nomadic life across a large swathe of America in order for him to stay in work. And by this time, he needed the money for survival.

The job was with Nielsen Media Research (NMR). Nielsen is a household name in the USA and one of the largest media research companies in the world that has decided the fate of television programmes for decades by providing statistics to networks on viewing figures and trends. The first Nielsen TV Ratings were produced in the 1950s and the company is still best known for providing exactly the same data today. NMR began as a division of marketing research firm AC Nielsen but became an independent company in 1996. It measures audiences for television and radio programmes and newspaper readership.

In previous decades, the firm relied on people keeping a diary of what they watched for its television statistics. Those enlisted to write down their viewing habits were known as 'Nielsen families' and the practice was used to track TV markets for decades. Over the years, more accurate automated systems were introduced, including the use of 'people meters', an electronic device which is attached to the TVs of volunteer families. What the Nielsen bosses did not know in the late 1990s was that they had just hired a convicted criminal who was in their country illegally and whose most recent crime had been to run off with more than £1m belonging to his employer.

Maher's career prospects with Nielsen turned out to be better than he could have imagined. He had found himself a steady job as a technician with a reputable company at a time when he needed cash. In exchange, though, he would have to move his family again and again in coming years.

Just as he had when he lived in Fremantle Close in South Woodham Ferrers, Maher rarely took the time to explain to his neighbours the ins and outs of his life. Jim Coffey's family were left wondering what happened to the Kings when, all of a sudden, their house in Laconia was left empty. He said, 'They were just gone. They were here one day and everything seemed fine ... the next thing I noticed a pawn shop type of truck and they were taking some stuff out of the house. Then they were gone. We wondered if they were in a witness protection plan or something like that. They left quite a bit of stuff if I remember and the people who went in after them didn't want some of it so they just opened the doors and offered the neighbours things.'

When Mark was four, Maher got a promotion at Nielsen's; it involved moving home but it was a good job so was worth the upheaval. This time it was to Anderson in the north-west corner of South Carolina, a journey of more than 1,000 miles that would take them across nine states.

Unlike in New Hampshire, they didn't settle into their new surroundings. Debbie remembered being particularly unhappy in Anderson, which lies midway between Atlanta, Georgia, and Charlotte, North Carolina, and is known as the Electric City due to its claim to fame of being the first city in America's south to have an unlimited supply of electricity. No amount of history or convenient geography was going to win Debbie over though. Remembering her time there, she told Graham, 'I hated it. The racism there was too hard for me to handle.'

Maher and Debbie may have been unhappy in Anderson but he did not want to give up what was turning out to be a successful job with Nielsen. He opted for asking his bosses for a transfer; the firm had a call centre in Florida and that's where he wanted to go. The request was granted and the family was back on the road again. Their destination was Nielsen's headquarters in Dunedin in Pinellas County.

If the police theory about how he escaped from England is correct, Maher was now just 100 miles from the spot where he had first walked on to US soil as a fugitive. Ten years had passed and, seemingly, the money he'd brought with him, or had sent to him, was now gone. Ironically, he was now in the surroundings many people back in England imagined him to be in - overlooking white sandy beaches and the blue waters of the Gulf of Mexico and being bathed in sunshine.

At one stage, the *Daily Mirror* had run a story on the search for Maher switching to Florida after people told of his dream of one day moving to the USA. The paper's headline read: 'HAS FAST EDDIE FLED TO FLORIDA WITH STOLEN £1M?' The subhead continued: 'Sunshine dream of lost guard'.

Despite the picture most people back home had in their minds, there was no life of luxury by the time he reached Florida. If Maher was drinking cocktails, they weren't out of crystal glasses. While it may not have been a life of a millionaire, the Florida sunshine was a big improvement on Anderson. Maher found a small rental house a few minutes from the coast. Debbie later described it as 'absolutely beautiful'.

At one point, Nielsen employed 1,100 people at the Dunedin call centre. Staff there were responsible for recruiting people from around the USA to become participants in its ratings system. The call centre in Virginia Street was a mix of permanent and temporary workers, with the number of temporary staff varying according to the season. Nielsen's ratings system tracked many TV stations seasonally, leading to a fluctuation in workload across the year.

A few years later, Nielsen began cutting jobs from the call centre and eventually closed it altogether, moving 850 workers from Dunedin to its new headquarters in nearby Oldsmar. The move came amid changes at Nielsen aimed at modernising its operations.

Maher's arrival in Dunedin preceded those changes and he avoided the job cuts which would follow. The Rockies must have seemed a world away as he drove to work in Dunedin. Within his reach every day was Florida's breathtaking coastline. A short drive along Virginia Street would have taken Maher toward the coast where, before long, he would have arrived at Dunedin Marina. Turning south, it would have only taken a few minutes for him to reach the spectacular Clearwater beach, with its long stretch of white sand underneath the kind of blue sky most east Londoners can only dream of.

The beach is lined with mansions and luxury apartments – the kind of place where millionaires cool off in heated pools just metres from the crystal-clear ocean, thereby avoiding the annoyance of sand.

While Debbie was apparently happier than she had been in a long time, things were good for Maher, too; his profile within

Nielsen was on the rise. He spent time working in Philadelphia in 2004 and also impressed his bosses enough to win another promotion. Again it involved moving – this time to Wisconsin.

They moved to the area around Green Bay on Lake Michigan in the east of the state, and subsequently Maher got what Debbie would later describe as 'a huge promotion' to become area manager for two states, Wisconsin and Missouri. Debbie would later tell Bob Graham, 'Every time he got a promotion they moved us because of the company policy that you could not boss your peers around, the people you'd been working with. That's why we moved quite a few times, not because of any other reason.'

The new job involved a lot of travelling, so Maher was away from his young family a lot. Gradually, it began to get the better of him. They spent time in Milwaukee, Wisconsin's largest city, in 2005 while Maher worked as the firm's field supervisor before moving a little over 20 miles to Grafton in 2006.

By this time, Maher's boys were growing up. They had lived a childhood on the road, moving from school to school and repeatedly making new friends only to leave them a short time later. It was a lifestyle that would have an impact on any child. There was no wider network they could rely on, no other relations they knew, no family friends allowed into Maher's inner circle. Their only constant was their parents.

Lee was now well into his teens. If the family had stayed in South Woodham Ferrers, he would likely have been midway through his studies at William de Ferrers School with his brother at one of the town's primary schools. Since their dad was a fanatic West Ham supporter, regular trips to Upton Park might not have been out of the question, possibly with the uncles, aunties and cousins who had become total strangers to them.

Football – or soccer as they more likely knew it – would have been all around them at school and a place in the school's team a constant aim for most kids. When the weather turned warm, they may even have strapped on the pads for a season of cricket.

Instead, Maher's sons were all-American boys. The USA was all they knew - indeed, for Mark, it was the country of his birth. As far as they were concerned, the USA was their home.

Lee loved his football, and both he and Mark played baseball. Maher was a regular on the sidelines at their games. He, too, had embraced the American lifestyle, in particular its sports. While West Ham might have been his first love, he got to know plenty of American teams during his tour of the States and would go on to support one of them just as passionately as the Hammers.

14

AVERAGE
JOE

It was a whirlwind high-school romance that began with a prom date. Lee King was the popular baseball and American football player and Kayla Jacoby was the smitten teenager.

Lee had arrived at Grafton High School midway through 2006. It was another nondescript American town where his family would continue with their lies and do their best to fly under the radar. By now, it was a life they were used to. The lies were well rehearsed and his parents had been calling each other by their false names for more than a decade. This would be just another stop on their almost continuous tour of America. Maher would soon discover, however, that things would get more complicated as his boys got older.

Grafton is in the heart of Wisconsin's Ozaukee County, with a population of about 17,000. Sitting on the Finley River and with a backdrop of the rolling hills of the Ozarks, it lies about 20 miles north of Milwaukee and close to the banks of Lake Michigan. It started as a lumber town, populated largely by settlers of German descent and is about 15 minutes south of Springfield, Missouri's third-largest city. Kansas City is about 100 miles to the north. It is one of Missouri's fastest growing cities and its population has tripled since the mid-1990s.

While it was a new town for the Mahers, it was only 100 miles from their previous home in Green Bay. The boys had been enrolled in local schools and Maher was still with Nielsen so life carried on as it had done for a while. By now, they were used to adapting to new surroundings.

Lee was all but an adult now. And with a teenager's hormones pumping through his veins, he was interested in girls in a big way. And his arrival didn't go unnoticed. Kayla was fascinated by the popular 'new boy' at Grafton High and the pair soon went out on their first date. 'He was sweet … he was athletic,' she said. 'He was somebody that came out of nowhere. He seemed nice and outgoing.'

Within a month, Kayla had been introduced to Lee's parents – who were still using the names Michael and Sarah. She also met Lee's younger brother, Mark. 'We'd always either be round his parents' house or mine,' she said. 'It was not like in an adult relationship where you take your time before meeting the parents. It was all virtually straight away. They were obviously very protective of him. I think it took a while for Sarah to accept me. But I was always a nice person, so that helped.

'Michael was the same. They were pretty much the same from the first day I met them. There was not any steady progression. It was very welcoming from the start, which in hindsight surprises me. I guess they didn't think I was going to end up pregnant.'

Lee's arrival at Grafton High School midway through

junior year had seemed unusual to its principal, Ken McCormick, but the family's motives didn't spark any suspicion, the *Milwaukee Journal Sentinel* reported after Maher's arrest. After all, it was true that they were relocating for Maher's work but the rest of their background remained a well-kept secret. 'I remember Lee moving in,' the paper reported McCormick as saying. 'It was an odd time for a kid to move in high school. He was a pleasant kid. He played football. There was nothing about him or his family's behaviour outside the norm.' McCormick also remembered Kayla. 'They were a pleasant couple and they were together a lot. It was always just the two of them together.'

By the time they both graduated in the summer of 2007, the relationship had quickly moved on. Kayla was five months' pregnant and they were already living together in a one-bedroom apartment in Wisconsin. Kayla, who was 18 at the time, said, 'It was pretty quick. It was a typical high-school relationship. You get so serious so fast at high school.'

With Lee now living with Kayla, the family dynamic had shifted. It was no longer the four of them living their lie together. Inevitably, Lee had grown up and wanted his own life. Maher, Debbie and Mark were still a tight unit, but Lee had another focus now. He had thrown himself into the relationship with Kayla with full force and a baby was on the way.

For the first time since the theft in 1993, Maher didn't have total control of the situation. While he was still in contact with Lee, his son was living his own life. What would happen when it came time for the next move? What would the outsider Lee was bringing into the family ask about their lives before

Grafton? The goalposts had been moved and it would have catastrophic consequences for all of them.

Over the next two years, Kayla got to know Lee's parents as a 'loving and caring' couple. Unlike the few others who were granted a glimpse into their lives, she remembers genuine warmth. But she saw that they were not as welcoming with everyone they met. 'They were always very judgmental of people they didn't know and they were on edge when someone they didn't like was around,' said Kayla. 'I had Michael and Sarah's first grandchild so they were around during the pregnancy. Whether they liked it or not, I was part of the family after that.'

The dynamics of the family quickly became apparent to Kayla, with Maher in charge and Debbie (or 'Sarah' as Kayla would have known her) doing everything she could to 'serve him'. She was one of several people to come into contact with the couple who were left with the same impression. It was a family with a clear hierarchy and Maher was well and truly at the top, they would say – he called the shots. 'I think that they loved each other; they definitely cared for each other,' said Kayla. 'Lee's dad had a very quiet control over the family. If you weren't in their lives you wouldn't know he was controlling them. I wouldn't say he was angry or had a temper. Sarah just wanted to serve him. She waited on him hand and foot. She liked to serve the family.'

The family told Kayla that they regularly moved because of Maher's job, never buying any property or committing to long-term leases, and making few friends along their journey. But the lifestyle they had been forced into meant they were largely on their own, always trying to hide their past. 'They would keep themselves to themselves – I never saw them with any friends,' said Kayla. 'They were very nice to anybody and polite. They would say hi to the neighbours but they would never go to talk to the neighbours. They would go to watch Lee play football and baseball but wouldn't get involved. They always seemed more comfortable in their own home.'

The home in Grafton was a two-storey, three-bedroom building known as a town home; it was near a large park in a friendly neighbourhood. And like other places they called home during their journey across the States, the Kings left an impression on their neighbours. One neighbour in Grafton, Betsy Voit, said the woman she knew as Sarah didn't open up about her background often but had told her the family had lived in Pennsylvania. Debbie had produced a photograph of what she said was their old house, which Voit remembered thinking was a 'mansion'. And in a moment of rare openness, Debbie had also told her that the family had guns. They were always locked up, she assured her, so there was no need to worry. Had the neighbour known Maher was also an international fugitive and an ex-soldier, his possession of guns might have weighed more heavily on her mind.

Quoted on the *Huffington Post* website, Voit said she had been aware the Mahers regularly went to a firing range to practice their shooting. The guns would later give the US authorities enough grounds to hold Maher in custody until their British counterparts unravelled the puzzle of the previous 20 years. Voit added that the family spent freely while in Grafton but didn't appear to be flaunting any wealth. She said at one point they bought four expensive mountain bikes, which they used for several months. And she said Debbie had at one point mentioned that her family needed a second vehicle. Not long after, Maher brought home an SUV for her. 'The one thing I remember her saying was that they didn't believe in payments,' Voit said. They preferred to pay in cash.'

Although an apparently tight-knit unit, there was no sign of their wider family within the Grafton house. Mantelpieces were missing the pictures of nieces and nephews and reminders of family gatherings that most homes have. And their possessions were also kept to a minimum, with everything able to be boxed up at short notice. 'They had photos around the house but they only had the four of them in,' said Kayla. 'There weren't any photos of other family members. They were always on the move. They lived month to month. They would never commit to a six-month or a twelve-month lease because they were always moving. They said it was because of Michael's job. They had their packing down to a very tried-and-tested system. They would always have everything ready to go. They didn't seem to have any trouble getting stuff together.'

When it came to what other family they had, Lee's parents rarely revealed anything. Kayla remembers Maher's first son, Terry, being mentioned once, along with Debbie's sisters. But there was never any contact. 'From what I gathered, he had Terry before he was with Sarah but they fell out for some reason and they stopped mentioning him,' said Kayla. 'I knew Sarah had some sisters but I didn't know anything about them. Every once in a while it would come up in conversation but it wasn't very often because they weren't in their lives.'

While Maher was the quiet, controlling husband, with a dry sense of humour, Debbie appeared more nervous, particularly when it came to getting behind the wheel of either of their two cars. Kayla said, 'She did drive but said she really didn't like doing it. I think now it's because she didn't have a licence. She always seemed a little bit stressed – like she wanted to keep Michael happy and calm. Michael could be quite funny sometimes but was mostly quiet.'

And while they never seemed to struggle for money, there was no extravagance. Kayla said, 'During his time with me, they seemed to have money [but] I never noticed them having particularly nice things. They would eat out a lot. They never had any struggles with money and the kids had the things they needed for school but there was nothing extravagant. The only extravagant thing was Michael always had the latest phones. That was it. They never really gave us any money. They helped us with our rent but then I didn't work and Lee couldn't hold down a job so they had to.'

Kayla would spend a lot of time with Lee's family and enjoyed a joint celebration party when they graduated from high school, hosted by Maher and Debbie. But the big event in the Maher household each year was Boxing Day. 'That was their favourite holiday,' said Kayla. 'They would have drinks and really celebrate it.'

Despite news of Kayla's unplanned pregnancy, Maher and Debbie remained supportive of the young couple. 'When Sophie came they took care of her,' said Kayla. 'They seemed to love her. Nobody would wish that on their children but they didn't seem angry.'

Although her relationship with Lee had started well, it became increasingly strained as time went on. 'In the beginning Lee was very good at making people believe what they wanted to believe,' she said. 'He would say what people wanted to hear. He was good at pretending to be the good guy.' But, she says, soon she saw another side of him, a side that involved wild exaggerations and falsehoods. Sometimes she wouldn't believe the things Lee told her, knowing he was capable of being economical with the truth. So when Lee told Kayla that his parents were on the run, his father was an English assassin and the family was living in America illegally, she was not sure whether to believe him.

Kayla said, 'He told me they were all illegal except for Mark. He told me that his dad was an assassin. He told a lot of half-truths and I just assumed this was another one. He was a very big liar. He told me sometime after our high school graduation. It was around the mid-point of our relationship. I don't know if I believed it or not. It was just another one of these things he talked about. He said never tell his parents that I knew because they would be mad. That was it.'

Incredibly, after more than a decade of hiding and learning the art of lying from his parents, Lee had taken the opposite approach. He had ignored the dangers and told someone outside the family's inner circle that his parents were on the run. It was the first time since Maher had evaded British police in 1993 that someone other than his wife and sons knew he was a wanted criminal. Lee had jeopardised everything Maher had worked so hard to protect since he'd fled England. And Lee had taken it a step further – he had concocted a story which presented his dad as a professional killer rather than a thief who had not even thrown a punch when carrying out his crime.

Rather than making the story seem more believable to Kayla, it convinced her every detail was a lie. Not only did she doubt the man who had been so welcoming to her was a British assassin, she also disbelieved the parts of Lee's story that were true. Maher had no idea of the lucky escape he'd had. Lee had come close to tearing down everything he had worked so hard to build. His American dream could have been in tatters. Instead, Kayla didn't think much more of it, until nearly four years later when news broke that Eddie Maher – the person she knew as Michael King – had been arrested.

One week before their second anniversary, Kayla decided to leave Lee. Their relationship had deteriorated rapidly, despite the birth of their daughter in late 2007. 'It was good for the first couple of months and then it got really bad,' said Kayla. 'I decided it was best for my daughter. I left him when she was six months old … I took my stuff and moved out.'

Lee did not take the news well. 'He was a very angry person. He damaged the place we lived in,' Kayla said.

After leaving Lee, Kayla's contact with his family virtually ended there and then, despite her helping Maher and Debbie pack as they moved yet again in the latter part of 2007. This time they went to Minnesota, having lived in Grafton for about a year-and-a-half.

'They literally packed up and moved in the middle of the night,' Betsy Voit said. Voit would find their four mountain bikes abandoned in her backyard.

15

OUTLAWS AND
IN-LAWS

When Amanda Zignego first met Eddie Maher and Debbie Brett in August 2008 she had no reason to suspect they were harbouring a deep, dark secret. She had been seeing her new 'cowboy wannabe' boyfriend Lee King for a month when the pair drove from Wisconsin to Minnesota to meet his parents.

Maher and Debbie – or Sarah and Michael as they would introduce themselves - had arranged to take Lee and the girlfriend they knew little about to a seafood restaurant near the Mall of America. It was a supersize shopping complex in the city of Bloomington, 10 miles south of the centre of Minneapolis. Keen to seem friendly, Debbie made sure the conversation flowed. Maher, on the other hand, displayed the withdrawn, secretive qualities many now remember about him. 'His dad didn't really say that much,' Amanda recalled. 'He was just withdrawn the entire time.'

It took only one meeting for the new high-school graduate, just returned from a foreign exchange in Germany, to decide that Maher was 'rude'. 'It kind of felt he didn't want to meet anybody new,' she said. 'They seemed kind of secretive. His accent was kind of odd. I didn't know anything about Lee's background at that stage.' And for a time the questions about Lee's upbringing would remain.

Amanda – from Hartford, Wisconsin – had met Lee through friends in nearby Saukville where he was living with a friend's family. Sarah and Michael had moved from Wisconsin to St Paul, Minnesota, where Maher was working as Nielsen's regional manager. They had taken Mark with them but left Lee behind.

Amanda was attracted to his bad-boy persona from the outset. 'It was a month after I graduated high school in July 2008,' she said. 'I met him through a bunch of my friends. It was a few of us getting together hanging out with a group of people.' It didn't take long before Lee made an approach and Amanda snapped up the chance to be with the boy with the hard edge.

At first, things were good with Lee; they enjoyed each other's company and talked of the future, with Lee suggesting children, even though he already had his daughter Sophie with his previous partner Kayla. Amanda thought he was joking when he talked of having children with her and she laughed it off. Within weeks, though, she was pregnant. All of a sudden, her life seemed out of control. 'I had just gotten out of high school two months before,' she said. 'I was a wreck … I was very emotional, I was crying a lot. Everyone else was going off to college and I wasn't.'

Soon, things got worse. Not only was she scared about

becoming a mother, but the thrill of having a new tough-boy partner was beginning to wear off. 'I never really wanted to be with him. I only stayed with him for my daughter because I thought it was something a person would do, to stay with the father,' she said.

The cracks that began developing then became fissures that couldn't be filled later. Pregnant, with no job and a boyfriend who couldn't support her, Amanda saw no choice but to agree to Lee's suggestion that they move to be closer to his parents.

In the short time Amanda and Lee had been together, Maher and Debbie had moved from Minnesota to Missouri. Nielsen Media Research had been going through a process of restructuring and they offered Maher the opportunity to take up the regional manager post in Chicago. It represented another big step in Maher's career. Most of his previous postings had been in mid-sized towns; this would have seen him in a senior position in a city of 2.7 million people.

But, in the words of his barrister David Nathan QC, after years of moving from place to place, often at short notice, it was 'one move to far'. Maher did something he hadn't done in years - he told Nielsen he would not move his family for another post with the company. It was a job that had taken him across a large swathe of the USA and had seen him rise through the ranks; it was a job that kept his family in clothes and gave them food. And now he was quitting, tired of a life on the road, or at least the one dictated by his bosses.

So instead of moving to Chicago, Maher, Debbie and Mark moved to Ozark, Missouri. For his last move in the USA,

Maher chose a nondescript Mid-West town. Now unemployed, Maher had to get a new job - he found one as a broadband technician. Nathan would later tell Southwark Crown Court, 'It was a call-out job. He would have to go if someone had problems with their broadband.'

Quite a step down for someone who had been a regional manager for a world-renowned company. But it was work and Maher's movements would once again be on his terms. Soon, Lee and Amanda packed all of their belongings in their house in Saukville and moved to Ozark, where they crammed everything into a one-bedroom apartment Amanda would come to hate. Neither had a job in their new town, nor did they know anyone besides Maher and Debbie and, according to Amanda, Lee's parents were far from welcoming toward her once they found out about her pregnancy.

She said they 'did not want anything to do with me at that time. They were very disappointed in him because he had already had a daughter and they didn't want him to have another child at that age,' she said. 'All of a sudden I was the enemy because I was the one who got pregnant with their son. That's when they stopped talking to me.'

She said of the parents, while Debbie was the most protective of Lee, Maher also took the news hard. 'He never said anything to me but I'm sure he said something to Lee,' she said. 'He just seemed disappointed. I don't think he really wanted that for his son, two children at 18 and 19.'

The 18-year-old had been unsure about the move to Ozark from the beginning. 'I didn't want to move away from my parents [but] I thought it would be a nice change of pace,' she said. 'We got a one-bedroom apartment and it was tiny compared to the house I was in before and we didn't really do much. Lee didn't have a job so we weren't able to afford the apartment. He was asleep all day long. We fought a lot. One time he threw all my stuff out of the apartment and he locked me out with the dog I bought for him.'

After a few months, she convinced him to move back to Wisconsin, with her insistence that she needed health insurance while she was pregnant – it was as much an excuse as a reason. 'I knew he always wanted to be by his parents but it really wasn't feasible for me, so I guess he just went along with it,' she said. 'He was with me for maybe a month-and-a-half or two months and then he joined the Army and he was away in the Army until June 2009. He was probably only in three months. He had always wanted to be in the Army. I was happy to get rid of him, it was a relief.'

Lee called his girlfriend more than she expected while he was away and then, one day, she got a call from him to say he was being discharged. She was later told by another of Lee's ex-partners, Hannah Evans, that he had used the pregnancy as a way of getting out. Amanda said, 'The story that Hannah told me was he told someone I was having a baby with Down's syndrome and they claimed he was under too much stress to be in the Army … but that wasn't the case.'

A healthy baby girl, whom they named Natalie, was born in May 2009 and Lee received his discharge papers soon after. While she had reservations about him coming back to live with her, the idea of having a new family convinced Amanda it could work this time. 'I was excited because he could see

Natalie for the first time. We gave her baths and he held her and he seemed like a good father,' she said.

They lived with her parents who made sure the young couple had everything they needed to raise their baby, from nappies to clothing. But soon they felt the need to get their own place.

Despite her unhappy time in Ozark during her pregnancy, Amanda again agreed to move to be close to Maher and Debbie. So in September 2009, when Natalie was four months old, they returned to Ozark, a town which carried only bad memories for Amanda. 'I wanted to move out of my parents' house but I didn't want to move that far away,' she said. 'It was a long way for my family as well … it was nine hours away.'

This time they rented a two-bedroom apartment in Ozark five minutes from Maher's home. 'Lee never really wanted to be home much. He didn't really do anything with Natalie, he wouldn't ever feed her a bottle or get her to sleep. I had to do everything,' Amanda said. 'He finally found a job but he still didn't make rent every month. He had to ask for money from his parents.'

At this point, Maher and Sarah's finances weren't in the dire straits that they would plummet to later, but they were careful enough with their cash to make sure Lee knew any help they gave wasn't a gift. 'They said he had to pay them back,' Amanda said, and added that Lee's parents were living in a nice enough house in Ozark but it had become clear they were 'spending money more wisely' than when she'd met them before. 'It was a one-storey, two-bedroom house. It was very clean and neat and tidy. It was just the right size for the three of them,' she said.

Soon, Amanda and Lee fell into a comfortable pattern in Ozark, spending three or four nights a week with his parents and Mark. Mostly, Amanda said, they would sit on the couch watching TV. Maher never showed much more interest in her than on that first meeting at the seafood restaurant. She developed a picture of him as hard-working during the day but slovenly around the house. 'He never did anything when he got home from work. He would just sit on the couch and put his feet up. Sarah would bring his food to him, even the TV remote. He was the dominant one. Lee's mom would usually hold Natalie. We never really did anything but sit in the living room watching TV.'

At the time, Lee's family life appeared 'normal'. In reality – as she would later find out – it was anything but.

The fact the house was kept immaculate was solely down to Debbie, she said. She didn't work, neither did she seem to have any interests beyond looking after Mark, keeping the house in good order and doting on the man she had given everything up for so many years before. 'She loved him more than anybody,' Amanda said. 'She was always telling him she loved him ... they would always hug and kiss. She just seemed obsessed with him.'

Debbie played the role of matriarch well. She bonded with Natalie instantly and the ill feeling attached to Amanda's pregnancy during her first stint in Ozark was forgotten. 'She was all nice to me because Natalie was so cute,' Amanda said. 'I think Lee and his mom were really close.'

When Lee and Maher argued, Amanda said, 'His dad would have a face that said, "I want to kick your ass." You could tell if I wasn't there he probably would have snapped.' But when things were going well, the family got on just fine. On a typical evening, Debbie would hold Natalie on her knee while Maher, Lee, Amanda and Mark would sit on the couch watching TV. Mark, Amanda said, adored Natalie and had bought her a number of cuddly toys. That was typical of Mark, she said, who showed a much more tender side than his brother. 'He was a really nice kid; he was the one that was most open to new people. He was definitely a mommy's boy, though. I know they tried to raise him differently ... they didn't want him to grow up like Lee. He was this little outgoing kid but he was struggling at school because he didn't really have any friends because he was always moving.'

So, for a time, Amanda and Lee built a tight bond with his family. To Amanda, who was by this time engaged to Lee, there was nothing exceptional that raised her suspicions or made her think this family was different from any other. Lee and his dad were fanatical about American football, in particular the New England Patriots, to the point where they wore their beloved Patriots jerseys whenever they watched the games on TV. 'It was all they would ever talk about,' Amanda said. They were also into baseball – Lee had played a lot in high school. In fact, their interests were all-American. And in typical American style, the family had a white Mountaineer SUV which they kept 'in pretty good condition'. And the company Maher was working for at the time provided him with a work truck which also sat in the driveway when he was home.

Lee's parents tried to help their son settle back into Ozark, with Amanda claiming that Maher even illegally hooked up cable TV in their apartment. 'Whatever Lee wanted, Lee got,' she said. And she thought that Maher worked 'pretty long days', leaving at about 7.30am and getting home at 6.00pm. While he was at work, Debbie was rarely known to go out or get involved in the community. And, according to Amanda, neither of them ever talked about their family beyond Lee and Mark. That, she says, is where Lee differed from his parents. He regularly spoke of his background and was well known for appearing to embellish the facts.

During their first stint in Ozark, which the *Mail Online* would later describe as a 'semi-rural backwater', he had volunteered at the local fire station in the hope of getting a job as a fireman. And his reason for wanting that career was one of the first times that Amanda heard him talk about the family's link to England. 'He mentioned to me he had an older brother back in England who had died in a fire when he was a fireman,' she said. Lee also told her his father had been a firefighter in England. The first claim about his brother's death was false, although Terry is a fireman, but what he told her about his father's previous occupation was true. 'He told me he had been born there [in England] and he came over when he was two or three and he had to get speech therapy classes so that he could get rid of the accent he picked up over there.'

So by 18, Lee was telling his girlfriends details about his family's past and, according to Amanda, he was telling other friends, too – but some of the stories were too far-fetched for her to believe. During their second stint in Ozark, Lee showed the first sign of harbouring a secret about his father's past, although his account didn't convince Amanda it was true. 'He told me his dad was an assassin and he was wanted in England and that's why they had to move,' she said. 'He had lied so many times before, so I didn't believe anything he said.'

The claim about his father being a professional killer on the run from the authorities has stayed with Amanda ever since. She says she remembers vividly the moment he told her. They were in their car at a stop light in Springfield, near Ozark, with Natalie in the back. She told him she didn't believe him. 'He was upset with me. Every story he told me he wanted me to fully believe him,' she said. It was one argument of many and their increasingly stormy relationship was putting strains on all involved. Amanda, who was now pregnant for a second time, claims Lee had become controlling and jealous and she had considered asking her parents to collect her and take her home.

One day she went to a petrol station where she planned to call home and, without telling Lee, organise to leave. She claims that before she made the call, Lee pulled up in his car and demanded to know who she was ringing before telling her he would stay and listen while she was on the phone. Amanda believes he sensed she planned to leave him. 'He knew I didn't want to be engaged any more but he said, "I'm not going to let you be my roommate."'

Worried about losing Natalie from their lives, Lee's parents urged the pair to sort out their differences. 'They came over one time to the apartment and they were telling us we needed to work it out for Natalie. They were devastated that Natalie was leaving.'

Instead of telling Lee she was leaving him, she again

convinced him that she needed to return to her parents in Wisconsin so that she could get health insurance while she was pregnant. She moved back in November 2009, taking six-month-old Natalie with her and, a week later, she called Lee to say it was over. That was the last time she saw any of his family. They have never met Lee's third child, Jacob, born 11 months after Natalie.

'They haven't contacted me since,' Amanda said.

By the time Hannah Evans met Maher and Debbie in July 2010, their behaviour was not that of a couple with a lot of cash stashed in the loft. Far from it.

From what Hannah could tell, Maher and Debbie – known to her as Mike and Sarah - were living from week to week, barely getting by on Maher's salary with the cable company. Once again, money was dominating their lives, but now it was a lack of it that was consuming their every thought. Once, it must have seemed they would never have another worry about paying bills and coming up with the rent. But it appeared they had plenty of such worries in Ozark and their desperation began to show.

Hannah, a 21-year-old college student, had been dating their son Lee for about four months before she met his parents. They had been invited to a Fourth of July celebration dinner at Maher's duplex home and Hannah wanted to make a good impression. 'I was kind of nervous because I wanted them to like me,' she said. 'She [Sarah] was really nice. I have allergic reactions to shellfish and she had made shrimp wrapped in bacon but she had made me something without shrimp. He

[Maher] came later, probably an hour after I got there. I think he had gone either to get the food or the fireworks.'

While Debbie proved friendly at that first meeting, Maher was less approachable. In fact, according to Hannah, he didn't speak directly to her the entire night. It wasn't the first time she would feel uncomfortable in his presence. But early on in her new relationship she was keen to do everything she could to make her boyfriend's parents like her.

She had met Lee at a friend's house in early March 2010 and they began dating soon after. As with his other girlfriends, Lee, then nearly 21, wasted no time in making his move. 'He was telling me all his war stories and he just seemed really interesting,' Hannah said. 'I think we both liked each other. Maybe a week after that he invited me to hang out with him. We hung out one day and literally the next day he was on Facebook to change his status to say he was in a relationship with me. I had just gotten out of a long-term relationship with someone who was kind of boring. Lee had accomplished all these things. It was interesting to meet somebody who had accomplished so much. He moved quickly; it was just part of his thing. We had been dating for a month before he had moved himself into my house.'

It was once Lee had moved into the house Hannah was renting in Springfield, Missouri, that she began to get to know his parents. She quickly came to know Debbie as a house-proud woman. As it had for the past 17 years, Debbie's life involved mostly staying at home. She rarely drove because she didn't have a US driver's licence, or any legal documentation that would allow her to get one. 'The house seemed very lived-in to me,' Hannah said. 'It was very comfortable. It looked like a very normal house. There were pictures of the family ... there were pictures of Lee and Mark.'

In a rare glimpse into their old life, Hannah said there was a picture of Terry on display in their home. 'The one time I heard Sarah and Mike talk about them was the first time I was over there and Sarah showed me a picture of Terry and I said, "Wow, that looks like Mike," and Sarah said, "Yeah," and started laughing. Lee told me he was in his early thirties and he told me he was a fireman and he had died in a fire.'

Occasionally Debbie would talk to Hannah about England. 'I had a couple of conversations with Sarah about London and what it was like. I had gone to England when I was 13 so I was talking about my experience and I was talking about how I enjoyed being in London. We were talking about how the countryside was prettier than London. One time she told me a story about her father taking her to a soccer game ... I never really heard Mike talk about it but I could never really understand anything he said anyway because of the accent and he mumbled and he used cockney slang sometimes.'

Adding to her image as the homemaker, Debbie had become known for going all out when it came to decorating the house at the holidays. 'She had an incredible amount of decorations for each holiday,' Hannah said. 'Maybe it was the fact she was at home all the time and that's her little area.'

But Hannah came to dread visiting their house in Ozark, which was about a 15-minute drive away. Maher was never very welcoming and things quickly went from bad to worse. Soon, his money worries began putting a strain on all their relationships. Hannah and Lee split in September 2011, five months after getting engaged. When Hannah told Lee it was over she was four months' pregnant. Their baby boy Arlo - Lee's fourth child - was born in February 2012.

16

HOW TO LOSE
A MILLION

When Eddie Maher walked through the doors of the United States Bankruptcy Court in Springfield, Missouri, he could have been forgiven for taking a moment to reflect on how things had changed. Once he must have laughed at the thought of money worries; now he was going before a court to beg to be discharged from his debts – the ultimate shame for a man once too proud to ask his own son for a loan.

Hannah Evans remembers Debbie pleading with her and Lee for a $1,200 loan in September 2010 to tide them over. She remembers that Debbie had to do the pleading because Maher couldn't bring himself to ask his boy for financial help. They were a proud couple, sometimes living in denial and at other times glossing over their problems to avoid making their sons worry.

Even though it was well known that Lee struggled to keep a job, his parents had turned to him for help when their financial situation hit rock bottom. 'I was a little ticked off because the text messages I was reading were basically Sarah saying Lee had already promised he would give them $1,200,' Hannah said. The trouble was, Hannah and Lee were 'always broke'.

Hannah had resorted to working overtime just for tips at her job serving cocktails because her boss would not let her work more than 40 hours per week. She would turn up for extra shifts and not clock in, just taking home whatever tips she could earn during the night. So a loan was out of the question. 'Sarah was asking us [for money] because Mike was too proud to ask us,' she said.

However, by the time Maher's finances reached their lowest point, a small loan from his son was not going to be enough to deter the bailiffs. He had racked up $34,349 in debts and on just $12.43 an hour in his broadband installation job he was never going to be able to pay it back at the rate his creditors would have wanted. The financial nightmare simply couldn't be ignored any longer.

For a long time, Sarah had not been working. She had developed a life where she was holed up at home, keeping her head down, since she didn't have the fake documents that would allow her to con anyone official into believing she was in America legally. So it was up to Maher to bring in the cash. He had done it in style back in 1993 but, since the money had been spent and he had left his job with Nielsen Media Research, all he could manage was a below-average salary working for cable companies.

Moving around the USA had proved a costly business. They had mostly rented accommodation so never made much progress in reducing their living expenses, even though by this stage Maher was in his fifties. When they reached Ozark, things weren't so bad that they could not afford a decent enough place to live. Those who knew them during their time in Ozark said 3914 North 16th Street was a pleasant house, well kept as always by Debbie and a nice home for Mark. But there was seemingly no hidden pile of cash on hand – Maher still drove his 1997 Mercury Mountaineer SUV even though it had more than 250,000 miles on the clock and there was nothing flash about their existence. The tag 'Fast Eddie' would not have seemed quite so apt at this stage in Maher's life.

When the money situation began to worsen, Maher and his family downgraded from their three-bedroom duplex to a two-bed townhouse. Their home at 5117 North 23rd Street was anything but a luxury pad befitting an international fugitive. It was much smaller and characterless. It looked on to a car park and a factory – but it was cheaper. And that's all that Maher could allow himself to think about at this stage. And still they set it out like a home rather than a temporary stop. Unusually, though, they didn't tell Lee where they were going.

'We went to their duplex and they no longer lived there and we had to call them to find out where they were living,' Hannah said. 'I think they purposefully didn't tell us because Lee was using their address for his mail.'

By Christmas, Debbie had started working for the apartment complex cleaning empty townhouses. She would also sit behind the desk in the rental office in the afternoons. It was helping to cover some of the bills but didn't go far.

During their Christmas Day in the townhouse, Maher and

Debbie gave Lee and Hannah $200 cash as a present. 'Sarah came up to me afterwards and said we could either give the money back to them then or we would have to give it back to them in a couple of weeks,' Hannah said.

By all appearances, Maher's stash had been well and truly exhausted and it had got to the point where he couldn't continue to paper over the cracks. That December, he had walked through the doors of the US Bankruptcy Court in the Western District of Missouri and asked for the slate to be wiped clean. Little did the court officers know that the man before them had once had his hands on over £1m.

To them, he must have seemed as ordinary as they came, cruelly similar to many who pass through their workplace with unhappy tales of hardship and financial misery. Balding, overweight, flat broke and apparently completely out of luck, Maher was there with cap in hand.

Hannah said the problems got worse when Maher lost his job with Mediacom. Unemployment benefit wasn't enough to stop the family's situation from becoming desperate. That's when the pleas for a loan from Lee came but went unheard.

Maher managed to get a new job with a St Louis-based firm called Suddenlink Communications, at first receiving $11.50 an hour as a broadband technician Level 1. Papers filed with the US Bankruptcy Court show he was working for the company in August 2010 and, by October, had been upgraded to a broadband technician 2, a move which saw his pay increase to $12.43 per hour.

When he started with Suddenlink, his family had been living at 3914 North 16th Street but by the time he got his pay rise they had moved to the smaller townhouse. Within months, money – or the lack of it – had taken over Maher's life. Lee and Hannah hadn't been able to stump up the $1,200 he needed as a stop-gap and their other bills were mounting.

Among the most pressing of Maher's concerns was $3,148.53 he owed to the tax man – the Internal Revenue Service (IRS). Then there were the credit card bills – these debts to banks and credit agencies offer a window into Maher's movements across America and his increasing dependence on someone else's cash. In February 2004 – 11 years after the Felixstowe job – he applied for and was granted an American Express card. By the end of 2010 he owed $2,424 on it. Three years later, in April 2007, he took out a Capital One credit card and, by the end of 2010, it had $1,034 owing on it. But just a couple of months after he took out the Capital One card, Maher had to resort to getting a loan from Citi Financial based in Baltimore. By the end of 2010, he still owed them $7,122.

Unable to fund his family's lifestyle, albeit an unpretentious one, he had been forced to get himself into debt. The broadband jobs just weren't paying Maher enough to keep him afloat.

In January 2008, he successfully applied for another credit card, this time from the Household Bank, which has a Les Vegas address, and had run up a $1,336 bill by late 2010.

There was also a student loan for one of the boys, taken out in July 2000, which still needed paying back. When the bankruptcy papers were filed in Springfield, Maher also owed $2,960 to the Department of Education.

The debts were stacking up and they were beginning to weigh heavily on Maher and Debbie. Maher's barrister, David

Nathan QC, would later tell the British judge who finally sealed his fate that the strain affected their health as well. Mr Nathan revealed that, as the financial woes increased, the pressure began to get to Debbie. In 2008, she had a heart-attack. It was a sign that the stress was taking its toll.

Fleeing to the USA had not changed their lives after all. Debts were part of their life in England before the theft and, almost 20 years on, they were still ruining what was to be a dream life on the other side of the Pond. Mr Nathan told Southwark Crown Court that the pair had run up debts in the late 1980s and early 1990s and had been subject to county court judgements regarding payments to creditors. While 'none of them were much more than £1,000', he said, 'still there were a number of them'. And he summed up Maher's life in more ways than one when he declared to the court, 'Mr Maher has never been very good with money … It seems, sadly, a persistent feature of his life that he has lived that way,' he said.

Still though, Maher battled to keep things going. His response was only to get himself in deeper in a bid to keep afloat just a little longer. He went to a local loan company in Ozark called The Loan Machine in October 2010 and asked for cash. He got it and still owed $2,300 by the time bankruptcy was unavoidable.

But he didn't stop there – resorting to even more desperate measures, he went online and borrowed money from Mycashnow.com, based in Chattanooga, Tennessee. On its website, the company promises 'We decide faster, so you can relax sooner'. But far from giving him the chance to relax, it just added to his problems. He owed them $595.16 when his borrowing frenzy finally came to an end.

The declarations Maher made before the bankruptcy court reveal a pattern of borrowing and spending that followed him across the country. What is missing is a pattern of repayment. On top of the taxes, credit card bills and loans he owed, there was a string of other creditors with a vested interest in Maher's financial affairs. He owed $262 to a company called Pen Foster, which runs online and distance learning courses, for a school course from April 2010. He also had a stack of medical bills that needed to be paid: there was a $1,119 bill from St John's Hospital in St Louis; another hospital bill from September 2010 for $101; a doctor's bill from St John's Clinic in Springfield for $539.75; and an unpaid dentist's bill of $143.

In short, Maher was out of cash and there was no way his monthly wage of $1,988.80, plus an average of $149 in overtime, was going to be enough to get him out of trouble.

His monthly rent was $499; they spent about $400 on food every month and, with additional costs like the rent of Mark's musical instrument – $34 – Maher was more than struggling to get by. He later declared that, once his outgoings were considered, he was left with $89.34 – not nearly enough to split between all his creditors each month.

The officers at the bankruptcy court could see the desperation of his situation. Case 10–62817–abf7 was listed and Maher signed his voluntary bankruptcy petition on 15 November 2010 under the name Michael Richard Maher. The court tallied up his earnings at $32,464pa. It estimated a median family income at that time was $54,488 – well over what Maher and his family were surviving on. The papers were filed on 17 November and a meeting of creditors was held in the bankruptcy courtroom in Springfield on 14 December.

The day before the hearing, the court had required Maher to complete an Internet course in personal financial management. That was on the back of him receiving credit counselling two months earlier. Little did the counsellor know that Maher had not only got himself into debt but had managed to work his way through a huge pile of stolen cash.

What stands out was how little he had to show for it. The total value of his personal property was $3,655 and his Mountaineer made up a large slice of that, being valued at $1,700. He had no real-estate assets, just a $300 security deposit handed over when he moved into his latest hideout. All his worldly possessions were furniture in the apartment at 5117 North 23rd Street – a computer, three TVs, a computer printer and a DVD player. He was considered to have a 50 per cent share in all of these with Debbie – a share that totted up to $1,150. The family's clothing was estimated by the court – most likely based on a statement from Maher – to be worth just $250. He also told the court he had a digital camera and a rifle, with a combined value of $170.

And, 19 years after being responsible for the disappearance of £1m, he had just $85 in an account at the Regions Bank in West Jackson Street, Ozark. Fast Eddie – the man behind the 'perfect crime' – was down to his last $85.

After an initial application to the court to delay the discharge of his debts, Maher's bankruptcy was confirmed on 2 May 2011. He was now officially bankrupt. The turnaround in fortunes cannot have been something that escaped his attention. His financial demise had been almost as spectacular as his rise to riches.

Maher was a man who, Mr Nathan told Southwark Crown Court, 'spent beyond his means'. Life in the USA, he said, 'wasn't the dream that Mr Maher had expressed to others before he committed this crime'.

17

THE SECRET
IS OUT

In the space of four years, Lee had been involved in three
failed relationships, all of which had produced children. Even
though high school was only a few years behind him, he was
already a father of four. All three women had left him, the last
kicking him out of the house and telling him not to come back.

For Lee, things were definitely not going to plan. His parents
had become dismayed at his behaviour, according to his
ex-fiancées. With each new woman came a new grandchild
and, before long, another unhappy ending. Lee had proved
more than able to charm a woman into going out with him;
what he'd failed to do was keep them.

By September 2011, he had little to show for his life. He was
on his own, couldn't hold down a job, didn't own a car and was
totally broke. One of his first acts after being kicked out by
Hannah was to buy a lottery scratch card. Maybe he figured his
luck had to change.

He purchased a Missouri Lottery Scratchers card and

scratched it. To his amazement, he had won $100,000. In one simple act, he had gone from being flat broke to having more money than he had ever had – and he hadn't had to steal it from anybody. It wasn't long before he was back at Hannah's door.

'He came back to the house and knocked on the door and asked to talk to us and told us he won $100,000. He had the lottery ticket, he put it up to the glass,' Hannah said. 'My mom said, "Meet us back here at 8.00am in the morning and I'll take you to the lottery office in Springfield."' Even a $100,000 lottery win hadn't been enough for Hannah to welcome Lee back inside. It may not have won him his fiancée back, but his immediate cash worries were over.

The next day, he presented the lottery organisers with the winning scratch card. It takes about two weeks for winners of the Missouri Lottery to redeem prizes of more than $35,000. Lee would have had to submit an official winner's claim form along with his scratch card and present photo ID when he visited the lottery office. His name still appears on the Missouri Lottery website as one of the lucky winners from September 2011. That month the lottery handed out more than $5.3m in prizes. Under the heading '$100,000 Scratchers winners' are the names Anthony Hackworth of Annapolis and Lee King of Springfield. Only two scratch cards had delivered $100,000 prizes that month and Lee had bought one of them.

His winnings would have been subject to state and federal taxes, with the federal government taking a hefty slice of prizes of more than $5,000. But he was still left with a handy sum that had come at a time when he really needed it. It's the kind of luck his dad could have done with a few months earlier; Lee's win came just months after Maher was declared bankrupt. The pair's fortunes were on a different trajectory, for the time being.

Hannah said he wasted no time in spending his winnings. One of his first purchases was a new truck; it used up a large slice of the prize money in one go. He also bought Hannah's mother's car for $4,000 and gave it to her. 'Lee spent his $100,000 in a month or two,' she said. 'It was gone very quickly.' So was the truck – Lee lost control of it and crashed, writing it off. Lee's good luck had not lasted long.

To add to his dismay over losing the truck, he had given Hannah's house as his home address when he went to claim his prize and, before long, letters began arriving from Wisconsin child support services. News of his winnings had spread beyond Missouri. They were chasing him for the child support he hadn't paid to Kayla after the birth of his first child. But it would be some time before they had any success.

Despite his temporary good fortune, Lee showed signs of having grown tired with his family's situation. Hannah says he made repeated efforts to get back together with her and even showed signs of wanting Maher's dark secret to come out. 'After I kicked him out, he told me, "I am finally going to come forward to the authorities and I am going to tell them my dad is here and they are going to let me stay in America,"' she said. 'He said, "I'm going to turn my dad in … they're going to let me stay here." He sounded desperate to me. I believed he was desperate.'

But she still didn't believe his story about Maher. The last time Hannah had had any contact with Lee's parents was when they found out she was pregnant with his child. 'My mom was speaking to Sarah and she had no idea I was pregnant. She got very upset … she was crying and she told my mom she would ring back and we have not been able to get in touch with her since.'

Since leaving high school, Lee had now told at least three people about Maher's past, or his own version of it at least. Kayla Jacoby, Amanda Zignego and Hannah Evans had all heard the story about Maher being a fugitive. At times, Lee had claimed his father was an assassin on the run from the British authorities, while at others he actually spoke about Fast Eddie and the theft of the cash. On each occasion, he told them his family was in the USA illegally. All it would have taken was for one of them to accept his stories and his family's life on the run would have come to abrupt end. But the women simply didn't believe him. His past behaviour had caused them to disregard many of his fantasies and this was just another one of them. Maher remained at large simply because those close to his son didn't trust him.

He had spent years carefully creating a fake persona and had sacrificed stability for his family in order to stay out of jail. It had taken careful planning and his family had never been able to let their guard down. Now Lee's actions were flying in the face of all that. Despite everything his father had told him, Lee had let the cat out of the bag.

And Maher had no idea. As far as he was aware, the only people who knew his real identity were his family and the accomplices that have never been found. In reality, a growing number of people had been told the truth – they just didn't know it.

With Hannah refusing to let him back into her life, Lee began to look elsewhere for company. He had just won $100,000 and hadn't kept it a secret; soon word spread.

Jessica Butler already knew Lee; she was the girlfriend of his best friend. But not for much longer.

Soon, Jessica had left Lee's friend and had started seeing him. And as Lee had previously shown, he wasn't one to hang about when it came to relationships, but this time it was quick - even for him. According to Jessica, though, she had got to know Lee before he won the cash. 'Lee had fun stories and seemed to want attention. I wasn't interested in him at first as he seemed young. But he was charming and he swept me off my feet. He didn't have a lot of money but then he won $100,000 on the lottery in September,' she told the *Daily Mirror*. 'He bought a new truck but I don't know where the rest of the money went – it was all gone in a month. I'd moved into his apartment after only a couple of dates and he came home with a little box with a bow on it and a pretty little ring, and he proposed. I thought I would follow my heart and, if it didn't work, then it didn't work.'

The pair married after being together as a couple for just a week and Jessica had the name King tattooed on her wrist. Records held by the Christian County Recorder of Deeds show the pair obtained a marriage licence on 17 October but they returned it on 24 October without using it, instead saying they had married in Arkansas. 'Our wedding was the happiest day of my life ... or so I thought,' Jessica said.

Maher and Debbie could barely have known their new daughter-in-law. Yet the pictures from the sunny day in October 2011 show Maher beaming with happiness as he stood between his newly-married son and the woman he had brought into the family. All sorts of thoughts must have been running through Maher's mind. What implications would a new member of the family have for their life on the run? Could Jessica be trusted with his secret? Would they have to leave Lee behind if another move became necessary?

If he was worried, he hid it for the photos.

Lee wore a three-piece suit for the day, with a green waistcoat and striped green tie. Jessica's traditional, strapless white dress had a green sash around her waist which co-ordinated their colours. Maher stood between them as the proud father in the photos. He hadn't bothered with a tie and instead wore a plain white shirt open at the neck. His large belly hung over his trousers. They were pictures of a happy couple on their wedding day and an apparently approving father.

'At our wedding, he was polite but didn't speak to anyone beyond "please" and "thank you", and "hi" and "bye",' Jessica said. 'Maybe he didn't want to get into conversations with people who might ask awkward questions. I knew they'd moved to the USA from England but I never asked about why or when. It wasn't a big deal to me.'

Jessica's surprising lack of curiosity about her new family wouldn't last long. Neither would the smiles so noticeable in the wedding pictures. Jessica said Lee's behaviour changed in the weeks after their wedding. She said he became controlling and at times aggressive. 'The controlling just started immediately and then following the controlling came the anger and aggression,' she told Missouri news outlet KSPR.

In what became two tumultuous months of marriage, Lee

made a mistake that finally destroyed the fictional world his father had worked so hard to create. After a bout of heavy drinking on Boxing Day 2011, he revealed all to his new wife. Through slurred speech, he told Jessica the Fast Eddie story. He revealed how his father was a fugitive who was wanted in the UK and that there was a reward on offer for his capture. 'He came home drunk and barely able to walk,' she said. 'He was slurring and started rambling about why his parents came to the USA, the robbing of an armoured car and that his name wasn't really King. Lee said he had a fake birth certificate. He was boasting about how cool it was. I kind of just blew it off. I said he had quite an imagination and needed to go to bed. It sounded absolutely ridiculous.

'The next day I asked him about it. He acted shocked and was like, "Oops, I didn't mean to say anything." But then he said it was true. He told me to keep it a secret. I had to make sure I never said anything about it in front of anyone, especially his little brother because he didn't know. He said he had found out last summer. Thinking back, when Lee was telling me, it was almost like a therapy session for him. He probably felt very alone. But I still didn't believe him.'

Initially, she dismissed it as an 'outlandish story'. 'Lee lied about everything … I didn't trust him,' she said. 'He'd lie about the silliest of things. He once got into a 30-minute argument with his mother over a ladder not being able to fit into the trunk of the car. The ladder did fit – he just lied. He would also lie about where money was going or coming from,' she told the *Mirror*.

Despite having strong doubts about the Fast Eddie story, she did an Internet search with some friends and quickly made a shocking discovery. 'I saw a photo and knew it was Lee's father, even though it was almost 20 years old,' she said. 'I felt sick and very scared.'

Two days later, on 28 December, Lee convinced her to return to the family's home. When she arrived, she was confronted by Maher. 'I could see the anger in his face and guessed Lee told him I knew,' she said. 'I was frightened and got up from the sofa to go to the bedroom. But as I tried to walk past his father, he grabbed my arm. He was right in my face. Very calmly and in a very low, evil whisper, he looked right into my eyes and said, "I know that you know ... I will kill you ... I will bloody kill you." He was really mad, really upset and I believed that he meant it. I'm sure he was more mad at his son than me but I took the brunt of it. I felt scared and panicked. I really thought that this was it – this was how the story of my life ends. It's with these horrible people.'

It was nothing new for Lee to go against everything his father had told him about the secret. But this time he had done something he hadn't done before – he had admitted to his father that he had let the secret slip and, according to Jessica, Maher had sought to prevent anyone else from finding out. Needless to say, Jessica and Lee's relationship was in tatters.

A complaint was subsequently filed with the Christian County Circuit Court about Lee's threatening behaviour. The man making the complaint is not identified in the public court records but he wrote that Lee had twice threatened him and his daughter in December. The complaint listed in court records reads: 'He said if he saw me in public he would kill me and take my daughter. Lee has made repeated threats towards me, saying he will do physical harm to me and my daughter and even went as far as to say he would kill me.'

Jessica, who by now was pregnant with Lee's child, had taken Maher's threat seriously. She had convinced Lee she wouldn't tell anyone and then spent five weeks agonising over whether to go to the police or keep quiet about his past. 'It was the longest, hardest time of my life. I had no doubt that he had meant his threat. But it had to finally stop,' she said. Her decision would finally unravel everything Maher had built over the past 19 years. His time on the run was coming to an end.

On 6 February 2012, two days before Lee was due to appear in court over the threatening behaviour complaint, she convinced her new husband to let her use the car to run some errands. It was the kind of thing she had to ask permission for since becoming his wife. Instead of going shopping, though, she paid a visit to the Ozark Police Department. She met an officer called David Overcast and told him everything she knew. 'I really felt like it was my last out, that I was going to die so I might as well die trying,' she told KSPR a few weeks later.

That same day, Lee was arrested after Jessica called police during an argument on their driveway. Lee was taken to the police station and held in custody over traffic warrants. And now, even though he had spent the past 20 years doing his utmost to avoid the police, Maher was forced to travel the five miles from Ozark to Nixa where Lee lived with Jessica to bail him out. While there, he complained to police that Jessica had stolen one of his guns. Maher was now involving the police in his family's problems. It was a risky move for someone who would rather the police didn't dig into his home life.

When asked why she finally decided to go to the police, Jessica told ITV's *Daybreak* programme, 'I was in fear for my life and, to be honest, it's just the right thing to do. When Eddie found out, I knew he threatened my life so it had to be done.' But, she said, she was not motivated by the prospect of a reward. Lee had mentioned the £100,000 offered for Maher's conviction and the return of the money, but she did not know if it was really on offer. 'Lee had gone on a rant about it once or twice but I didn't even know that was actually true until Eddie had actually been arrested,' she told the programme. She said she had no regrets about her decision and that if a reward was forthcoming, it would be 'very welcome'. 'That is in the hands of my lawyer. The money would help … raising a child by yourself is very difficult.'

Maher's barrister presented a different version of events to the judge who would sentence him. David Nathan QC said Jessica was aware of the reward when she went to the police. He told Southwark Crown Court, 'When the money ran out, she did a little research on Google on the name Maher and realised he could not go back to his country. She heard there was a reward and she went to the authorities. That's how the matter was brought to the authorities' attention.'

Events were beginning to move fast. Lee's arrest had come close on the back of Jessica's decision to alert the police.

While he was in custody, Officer Overcast was single-handedly cracking the case. And he was using one of the key tools of modern policing – the Internet.

18

CAUGHT

At first, Officer David Overcast doubted Jessica King's story. He was being told that a man known in his community as a 60-year-old father-of-two, who spent his days fixing problems with people's broadband, was actually an armoured car thief and international fugitive.

The Fast Eddie tale had not penetrated to the depths of Missouri so even the catchy nickname meant nothing to him. 'I've heard a lot of stories over the years and this, right off the bat, was one of the craziest,' he said, quoted in the *New York Times*.

But Jessica's desperation meant he gave her the benefit of the doubt. She had been so concerned about her safety that they had spoken about safe-house options for her. 'At first I didn't think the information I was given was going to pan out. But the reporting party was very sincere,' he said in an interview with KSPR. 'She really wanted me to believe her story and that's pretty much what pushed me to investigate even harder. She appeared scared of the family, of what may happen, when she was talking to me. I had to give her information about maybe getting her to a safe house for her protection. It made me want to look at it a little further and, when I did, the pieces came together. It wasn't until after she left that I dug into it and found who he was, and that the information was true.'

Overcast ran the names Michael Maher and Eddie Maher through the police systems but neither was listed as being wanted in the USA. But he didn't stop there; he put the name Eddie Maher into an Internet search engine and pressed enter. Unlike the police computer systems, the Internet search yielded results. Among details about the Fast Eddie story, he found a picture from around 1993. He compared the picture with the photo on Michael Maher's Missouri driver's licence and was convinced it was the same man. All of a sudden, the officer was sitting on one of the biggest cases in Ozark for some time. This would not be a run-of-the-mill Monday – what he had found was enough to prompt him to call in the FBI.

He contacted the bureau's Springfield office to tell them the story. Special Agent (SA) Jeffrey W Atwood took the details and compared the photo of Maher on the driver's licence to the pictures released by Suffolk Constabulary back in 1993. He, too, was convinced it was the same man. He was younger and thinner then and had more hair, but there was definitely a strong resemblance to Maher. For the first time in nearly two decades, the authorities knew where Maher was. It was the break police in Suffolk had been hoping for for years and, at this stage they, like Maher, had no idea of the shock they were about to receive.

CAUGHT

The Ozark officers set about contacting their colleagues in Martlesham but, according to some reports, came up against a hurdle when they realised that the local police station's phone contract didn't include international calls. Instead, they turned to email. Suffolk Police had waited 19 years to hear the news they were about to receive, but they could never have guessed it would come via the force's police enquiries email address. A Suffolk Police employee sifting through the email folder read the message from Ozark PD and passed it on. It didn't take long for an officer from the force to respond.

The wheels were in motion finally to bring Fast Eddie in. And the false world that Maher had created over 19 years was to come crashing down in the space of three days. But with no outstanding warrants, there was nothing to arrest Maher on just yet. So the FBI and Ozark PD officers launched a surveillance operation to ensure Maher didn't slip through their grasp – that had happened to police once before, and it had taken 19 years to get a second chance. Maher's apartment at 5117 North 23rd Street was kept under watch.

Meanwhile, other events were taking place that saw Maher accelerate his own demise. With Lee in custody in neighbouring Nixa over the motoring offences, Maher was forced to go to the police station to bail him out. He had spent years avoiding the police whenever he could, and now he was voluntarily walking through the doors of a police station. Little did he suspect that the officers there knew his real identity.

It was during this visit to the police station that Maher made the complaint about Jessica stealing one of his guns. He had no idea what was about to hit him like a freight train. The officer he spoke to told him that police suspected he was a fugitive who was wanted in England, and added that officers were not able to arrest him at that time. So in yet another twist in Fast Eddie's long-running saga, the police had just informed the long-time fugitive that they were on to him, but that they couldn't touch him ... so they watched him walk out of the building.

It was an enormous risk taken by an officer working to his own plan, and could have been calamitous. British prosecutors would later describe the officer's decision to tip Maher off as 'misguided'. It is thought the move was designed to gauge Maher's reaction, but would later be seen as a mistake. The officers in the Nixa police station watched Maher's reaction carefully and they later told the FBI he had been furious when he discovered his cover had been blown. An affidavit filed by SA Atwood with the United States District Court for the Western District of Missouri after Maher's arrest, explained the sequence of events:

On or about 2/6/2012, Maher's adult son was arrested by the Nixa Police Department (NPD). Maher responded to the NPD to post bond for his son. While Maher was at NPD, he also made a complaint to the NPD about one of his guns being stolen by his son's wife.

After making the report, an NPD officer allegedly told Maher that he was wanted in England, but that the officer could not arrest him. Maher's son overheard what the NPD officer said, and asked Maher about it after they left the police station.

Maher's son said that Maher was irate. Maher told his son

that they would have to leave again, and threatened to kill the
person who tipped the police off about his identity.

Maher's immediate reaction had been to run. It was the one constant from his life of the past two decades and he turned to it again in an instant. With the anger building inside him, it might have seemed an option. In reality, the officers watching his every move were not going to let him out of their sight. And while their colleagues kept watch, SA Atwood and his colleague Patrick Thomas continued to gather evidence about Fast Eddie's true identity.

On 7 February, the day after Maher was tipped off that the police were on to him, the agents brought Lee in for an interview. In his affidavit to the court, SA Atwood, an agent with a dozen years' experience, said, 'While Maher's son was being interviewed by the FBI on 2/7/2012, OPD officers were conducting surveillance on Maher's residence located at 5117 North 23rd Street, Ozark, Missouri. During the interview, Maher called his son and told him that they had to leave immediately. Maher's son told Maher that he could not go with him.

'Shortly after the interview was concluded, OPD officers observed Maher, a white female and a juvenile white male leave the residence carrying some clothing. Maher and the others then drove away in one of Maher's vehicles.

'OPD officers and FBI agents continued to conduct surveillance on Maher and eventually followed him to a motel in Ozark, Missouri, where he, the female and juvenile male checked into a room.'

Although Maher had taken flight, he hadn't gone far. Along

with Debbie and Mark, he had grabbed a few clothes and was now holed up in a hotel not far from their home. It's not clear why he did not keep driving. One possibility is that he simply didn't have the cash to leave.

So he found himself in a hotel room considering his options. They stayed at the hotel overnight, all the while being watched by the officers outside. It gave Maher some time to think.

By the next day, the conclusion he had reached was that the game was up. His running days were over. Incredibly, he made the first move; he instructed Lee to go to the police, a decision confirmed by SA Atwood's affidavit:

> On 2/8/2012, Maher's son contacted SA Atwood by telephone and said that he had just received a phone call from Maher.
>
> Maher told his son that he checked into the motel because he was afraid that the police were coming to his house to arrest him.
>
> Maher told his son that he had changed his mind about leaving the area and that if the police were coming to arrest him, he would not resist.
>
> Maher told his son that he was going back home. Surveillance confirmed that Maher went back to his residence.

Maher had considered running. In fact, he had taken the first steps in trying to evade the police again. His immediate reaction to hearing that the police were on to him was to pack up his family and get them out of town. But this time he stopped; it's possible he had grown tired of running. It's also possible that he knew the police would be watching him and it was better for him not to run.

Either way, he effectively handed himself in. While he stopped short of actually walking into a police station and giving himself up, he gave the officers the green light to come to his home and arrest him without opposition.

A day earlier, he had driven out of North 23rd Street with his mind on escaping. Now he had returned, knowing that the police wouldn't be far behind him. He had apparently accepted that his time on the run was almost certainly at an end.

He was right. It wasn't long before agents from the FBI and US Immigration and Customs Enforcement (ICE) officers came knocking on his door. SA Atwood's affidavit reports:

Upon contacting Maher, SA Atwood asked Maher what his name was. Maher responded that his name was Michael Maher and then advised that he had a Missouri Driver's Licence with his name on it. Maher then showed agents his Missouri Driver's Licence which was in the name of Michael Maher. Maher was subsequently taken into custody by ICE agents in order to determine his immigration status.

SA Atwood then contacted Maher's wife who was also at the residence. Maher's wife identified herself as Deborah Ann Brett. Maher's wife provided information including the following: Maher has used the aliases Stephen King and primarily Michael Maher and alias date of birth 4/17/1951. Maher used his brother's identification (Michael Maher) to obtain work and other state identification.

Fast Eddie was taken into custody on 8 February 2012 – 6,956 days after fleeing Felixstowe with the cash. And in addition to officers from Ozark PD, the combined forces of the FBI and ICE, the Bureau of Alcohol, Tobacco, Firearms and Explosives and the US Marshalls Service were involved in apprehending him.

But even with the officers in his home, Maher continued to stick to his story and pretend to be his brother. Debbie, though, did not. She had stopped lying and started to tell the truth. In doing so, she would give the authorities the piece of information which would enable them to keep Maher in custody until the British authorities got their ducks in order. She told them that Maher had bought several guns during his time in the USA. The fact that he had done so under a false name and was in the country illegally in the first place posed yet another problem for him.

The court documents filed by SA Atwood state:

While at Brett's residence, Brett advised SA Atwood that several of Maher's firearms were located under their bed. Brett said that she did not want the firearms and she gave OPD officers permission to seize the firearms.

OPD officers looked under the bed and located a black Hi-Point, Model JHP, .45-calibre pistol, serial number 449068 and a black Jennings, Model 48, .380 pistol, serial number 583190. Those firearms were recovered by OPD officers and placed into OPD evidence. Brett also advised that several of Maher's firearms were located at a storage facility in Ozark, Missouri.

Brett accompanied SA Atwood and OPD officers to the storage facility, advised that she did not want the firearms and voluntarily surrendered [them to] the OPD. Those firearms were located in a camper trailer which was inside of the storage facility.

The officers also recovered a Mauser rifle and a black Mossberg .22-calibre rifle from the camper to go with the two pistols from under Maher's bed.

When he was arrested, officers found that Maher also still had his real passport. Incredibly, after all those years on the run, he had kept the passport that identified him as Eddie Maher. And even though he had been using the identity of his brother Michael for well over a decade, he still had his false passport in the name of Stephen King. Both passports would give police clues about his original escape.

They found neither of the passports had been used to get Maher out of the UK. The one in the name of Eddie Maher did not have any immigration stamps from 1993 to indicate he travelled anywhere that year. And the Stephen King passport had no stamps in it whatsoever.

Later on the day of Maher's arrest, SA Patrick Thomas, the agent who had interviewed Lee the previous day, interviewed his father. Maher was advised of his rights and he acknowledged that he understood; he then agreed to talk to the agent without a lawyer present and signed a waiver of his rights. He then did something he hadn't done in 19 years – he began telling the truth.

He admitted his real name was Edward John Maher. He

told officers his actual date of birth was 2 June 1955. And he admitted that he had been using his brother's name since about 1998 when he started working in the USA. He also acknowledged that neither he nor his brother was a US citizen and that he was in the country illegally. He said he got his social security number using the alias Michael Maher and that he used the name as an alias in order to conceal his true identity. And he told them the reason he wanted to conceal his identity was that he was wanted for a crime that he committed in England. After so many lies, the truth had come flooding out in one conversation.

And he didn't stop there. Turning his attention to the guns, Maher told the agent that he owned the .45-calibre and .380-calibre pistols and the two rifles. He said that he kept them at his house but didn't specify where he had bought them, except for saying he had bought one of the rifles at a sporting goods store. It was enough to prompt the FBI to submit to the court the following day the allegation that he had breached US firearms laws.

The UK authorities were keeping track of events closely and they were determined to make sure those charges were only the start.

After 19 years of guarding his secret closely, Maher had been undone by his son's inability to stay quiet. Lee's drunken error had ruined everything for his father … and it was his wife who had sold him out. All it had taken for Maher's lies to be exposed was a family rift.

Jessica said the period between her telling Ozark Police

about Maher's real identity and his arrest had seemed an eternity. 'I don't think people realise how long it is from Monday to Wednesday. It felt like just months right there in those three days,' she told TV station KSPR.

While she knew what was coming, the people of Ozark had been left stunned by the developments in their town. The news that an international fugitive had been living among them spread like wildfire. One after the other, they lined up to tell reporters who flooded into the town how shocked they were. Some said Maher had seemed a shifty character, while others said the opposite.

Since so little was known about Maher's life over the previous two decades, the reporters were keen to hear any details that the neighbours had to offer, no matter how minor. Alison Brookhart, one of Maher's neighbours in the Fremont Hills Townhouses, was quoted as saying, 'I don't think I have ever been more shocked about anything. He seemed nice. He would always say "Hi" when he came home if we were outside playing. I didn't really have big conversations with him but I just figured that an older man wouldn't want to stand outside with a woman and kids playing.'

The *Daily Mirror* reported the reaction from Brendan Morris, the manager of the apartment complex where Maher had been living. He said, 'They were very well loved around here. I would trust them with my life and all my money. They're good friends of mine and I love them dearly.'

Neighbour Brandon Wise said, 'If somebody was going to steal $1m, I wouldn't expect them to be in Ozark, Missouri, right across the street from me. I never really saw the husband, he was just kind of in and out really in the Suddenlink truck. That's all I saw of him.'

And fellow neighbour David Whithey said of Debbie, 'She was kinda quiet and she didn't really say much about where she came from or anything like that.'

Others were devastated by the events. One resident of the apartments, also quoted in the *Mirror*, said, 'It really kills me. I've been crying off and on … it's like I'm mourning the death of someone I thought was a friend.'

KSPR, the local TV station, was all over the story. Its managing editor Dave Stewart had received a tip from a law enforcement contact about the impending arrest shortly before Maher was taken into custody. 'I received a call from somebody who told me to Google "Fast Eddie Maher, Ipswich" and so I said, "OK," and he said, "Just Google that and I'll call you back in a few minutes." It took about a second-and-a-half to realise the gravity of the phone call.'

Soon after, he confirmed the arrest had been made. 'I called the chief of police and I got confirmation he was in custody and was referred to the FBI and was told he was in the back of a law enforcement vehicle headed to their offices for questioning,' he said. It was a development that left his news-room, and others in the area, buzzing with excitement. 'In a sleepy little town like Ozark, it's surprising that a fugitive that has been on the run from another country is found here,' he said. 'We realised pretty quickly that it was going to be a story that was of international interest.'

Stewart immediately contacted the CNN and ABC news networks and they too 'jumped on it'. 'It was the story on everyone's lips. Anytime we had the opportunity to do a story about Eddie Maher or Lee King, we absolutely took it. It's a fascinating story how a guy ends up taking £1m and lives for nearly 20 years as someone else, just like he's living the so-called American dream.'

Lee's role in putting an end to his father's life on the run had made him almost as much of a story as Maher himself. And Stewart said Ozark PD had taken some pleasure in being the force to finally catch Maher. 'They were very happy with it. It was absolutely a notch in their belt and it's something they still talk about today,' he said.

With Maher now in custody, all the media's efforts were aimed at uncovering details of his past. British media ran interviews with their American counterparts and vice versa. Each country wanted to know what the other thought. The British press was lapping up the story and, for Richard Cornwell, it was almost too good to be true. By now a veteran reporter, well known as 'Mr Felixstowe', it was a story he had never forgotten. 'I was really shocked. I had a text message from one of the radio stations over there saying Eddie Maher had been arrested in Springfield. To begin with, I was thinking, "That's a hoax." In Springfield? I knew I had to check it out. I rang my editor, Nigel Pickover, and he immediately rang the chief constable of Suffolk to get a steer. It just seemed so unbelievable that after all these years he had been found.'

Cornwell's initial tip-off and his subsequent off-the-record confirmation of the amount of money involved had put him ahead of the field in 1993 and, just two weeks before Maher's capture, his instincts had again been spot on. In a story published on 23 January 2012, marking the beginning of Maher's 20th year on the run, Cornwell had written, 'After all this time, a mistake by the thief remains the best chance of him being found. That would seem unlikely as the master criminal has survived two decades so far … but it can never be ruled out.' Some would argue the mistake had been Lee's, but others maintained Maher's decision to reveal all to his son in the first place had been the reason for his downfall.

The Press Association, the newswire used by virtually every news organisation in the UK, flashed the news at 10.06am on 9 February. It headlined its piece 'MAN HELD IN US OVER 1993 RAID' and continued, 'A man who has been on the run for 19 years after a £1 million raid on a security van in Suffolk has been arrested in America. Eddie Maher, known as "Fast Eddie", was arrested in the Ozarks, an area of central eastern US which includes Arkansas and Missouri. Maher vanished after the theft from a Securicor van in Felixstowe in 1993. A spokesman for Suffolk Police said, "We are liaising with the US authorities regarding the detention of Eddie Maher, who police wish to speak to in connection with a security van robbery in Felixstowe in 1993."'

The story was used by almost every major organisation in the UK. The *Daily Mirror* shouted '£1M "FAST EDDIE" HELD AFTER 19 YEARS ON THE RUN'. The *Daily Express* headline read

'HELD AFTER 19 YEARS, FUGITIVE "RAIDER" KNOWN AS FAST EDDIE'. And the *Sun* put it simply with '19-YR HUNT BRIT FOUND'.

Fast Eddie was back in the headlines, with most papers focusing on the length of time he had evaded capture. The blanket coverage also attracted the attention of one man with a keen interest in the case. Peter Bunn, the Securicor colleague Maher had left behind at the bank, found himself revisiting that day all over again. 'I think somebody emailed me,' he said. 'I thought, "You are joking!" I must admit I did smirk. It's not that I have been bothered about it. Nobody got hurt. But it was good to know he had been found.'

And Maher's former neighbours in South Woodham Ferrers also sought to find out what they could about his reappearance. Simon Butterworth, one of the neighbours who saw Debbie leaving the street, remembers the moment he heard the words 'Fast Eddie' and 'Ozark, Missouri'. 'It was on the radio. We said, "Oh blimey, that's Eddie ... they've got him!"' he recalled. 'God ... blimey ... you never thought they'd catch him.'

A few days after the news first broke, the story made page 1 of the *New York Times*. Under the headline '19 YEARS AND £1 MILLION LATER, A PAST CATCHES UP', the paper described Maher as 'a balding local cable technician' who 'was actually an international fugitive who had staged one of England's most infamous bank heists'.

The *Ipswich Star*'s story from a fortnight earlier discussing the fact that Maher had been beginning his 20th year on the run was mentioned again and again as proof that the story had never gone away and people in Suffolk had remained curious as to what had happened to him.

Meanwhile, Maher could do little other than sit tight and await his fate. According to those who came into contact with him while in custody, he was far from agitated by his capture. The local officers Stewart spoke to reported him to be a 'jovial guy'. 'He was normally in a good mood, he was joking with police and joking with other inmates and didn't cause any trouble when he was in custody. All around he was a likeable guy. In my talks with police officers he indicated to them he was relieved, that he was ready to have it over,' he added. 'By all accounts of those who dealt with him in custody, Eddie was ready to move back to the UK, he was ready to serve his time and get it over with.'

Seemingly, Maher had taken his capture with remarkable calmness. Yet a few days before when his freedom was under threat, he had reacted with fury and, according to SA Atwood's affidavit, threatened to kill the person who had put his liberty at risk.

KSPR stuck with the story as long as it could, including interviewing a reluctant Overcast who had been unexpectedly thrust into the spotlight. He was praised publically by Lyle Hodges, the Ozark chief of police, and found himself the focus of some of the media attention. Chief Hodges told the *Ipswich Star*, 'I think he did a really good job. He did that extra bit of research and is really responsible for this taking place. Most officers would check for warrants and, if they had found there was no warrant on the national computer, or in our state computer system, or with Interpol, they would probably have dropped it. Officer Overcast did just a little bit more.'

19

THE £1.17M QUESTION

Eddie Maher's arrest created a whirlwind of excitement on both sides of the Atlantic. The US media were in love with the story as soon as they learned the amount of money involved and the international dimension. Stories linked to foreign countries always added an element of intrigue and appeal to a story for a news editor. And TV bulletins and newspapers were full of Fast Eddie for days.

And throughout those first days, reporters, the police and the public had the same few questions on their lips: Where had Maher and his family been for the past 19 years? How did he get away with it for so long? And a question which, in some ways, still lingers today: What happened to the money?

The question about the money has been mulled over time and again, most often by Suffolk Police detectives who battled to uncover where the money went. Did he get to keep the whole £1m himself? If not, who else got a share? How did he get the money out of the country? What sort of lifestyle had it bought him?

From the point of his arrest, the force was focused on securing a conviction, but Maher was telling them little of the facts they needed to know. The Suffolk Police team knew they would have to find evidence of Maher's financial situation over the previous 20 years if they were to prove he benefitted from the crime. That was not going to be an easy task since they didn't actually know where he had been for a large part of his time in the States. Even when they knew the location, the chance of them finding records of Maher's finances was even more remote.

Slowly, though, they began to build a picture of Maher's spending. And it started with the crime itself. Over the years, the people of Suffolk have marvelled at Maher's ability to disappear with almost £1.2m. Many had become convinced that he had escaped to a new life overseas. But, they wondered, how had he got access to the cash?

Suffolk Police and the CPS have come to the conclusion that Maher had help and someone could have sent him the money once he was in the USA. One police theory is that it was sent through an international money transfer company. Their offices are found on many high streets and it would be a simple way to get the cash to him. But would a very large transaction raise suspicions? Or could it have been sent in a number of smaller amounts?

DI David Giles was one of the officers who travelled to the USA in the hope of following Maher's tracks all those years later. He believes one of Maher's accomplices sent him the money after he arrived in the States. That meant that while the police had no idea where he was, at least one person, possibly more, in the UK knew his whereabouts. 'For somebody keeping their head down, he wasn't trying that hard because somebody knew where to send him the money,' he said. 'We've shown that he was given a lot of money and that someone knew where to find him.'

Throughout the case against Maher, Suffolk Constabulary was not able to pinpoint exactly how much he had received; they simply haven't been able to find that out. But they developed a theory which prosecutors would later present to a judge hearing the evidence against Maher.

Their belief was that Maher had at least received a large chunk of the £1.17m. The romantic theory held by many Suffolk residents over the years was that Maher had escaped with all of the £1m. But security experts and those closer to the case always knew it was something Maher could not have carried out on his own. All the planning, transferring the cash from the Securicor van, even getting him out of the country, all of it had to have taken more than just Maher himself. It stood to reason that those who helped him would also get a slice of the takings.

So if he didn't get it all, how much did he get? When Maher was taken into custody in Ozark and questioned by the FBI, he told them he'd only received £40,000 from the theft. It was a claim that would be rejected by police and prosecutors alike and one that Debbie contradicted in interviews with the federal agents. She put the figure at £200,000 – still considerably less than almost everybody had imagined over the years. While

£200,000 was not a paltry sum, it certainly wasn't enough to create the lasting life of luxury that so many people imagined Fast Eddie had secured for himself.

Maher's own defence team admitted he had at first lied about the amount of money he received from the theft. With police, Debbie, Lee and Mark looking on, David Nathan QC told Southwark Crown Court, 'He claimed he had £40,000 out of this. Plainly, that is not true. He had a share. All credit to Deborah for telling the US officers that he had obtained somewhere in the region of £200,000.'

Police had never believed that Maher could have received anything as minimal as £40,000 from the theft. For starters, no one else was in the frame for the theft in the way that Maher was. While the spotlight would later fall on some suspected accomplices, Maher remained the central figure in the case. It was unthinkable to Suffolk Police that he could have received so little from a crime they believe he masterminded. It had also been evident that his early life in the USA suggested the one thing he had while on the run – at least at first – was disposable cash. After all, he bought a four-bedroom home in a comfortable Colorado community with $120,000 – in cash. Maher had clearly suddenly had access to significant funds and the detectives had no doubt where it had come from. They were also aware that he had left debts in England and was far from flush with cash back home. All of a sudden, he had $120,000 in cash to spend just six months after the theft. That represented 10 per cent of the total sum stolen.

Chris McCann, the head of the CPS's complex case unit, was left in little doubt. 'If you were innocent, you wouldn't have a significant amount of money available to you. How would he get 10 per cent of the proceeds?' he said.

Police found most of their clues relating to Maher's new-found wealth in Colorado. It was during his time there that he appears to have had the most money at his disposal. Since that's where he lived in the early years in the USA, that was no surprise to the detectives.

First there was the $120,000 cash payment for the Woodland Park house. Maher came out of that investment with even more than he had started with by making a $17,000 profit on the house. While it will have cost him some of his Securicor cash just keeping his family in food and clothes, the $17,000 profit from the sale would have gone some way to recouping that.

With his $137,000 and whatever he had left from the original stash from the theft, he bought his next property. The 80 acres in El Paso cost him $24,000, then he paid $58,000 to have his new house built and paid another $10,000 for extras on the property. That meant he spent $92,000 on the El Paso property – considerably less than the $137,000 he walked away with from the Woodland Park house.

All the while he would have been eating into the cash to keep his family afloat. There would have been cars and their running costs, restaurant bills, heating and water, phone bills. And if Amanda's memory of Lee's story about the $20,000 couches in Colorado is true, Maher was also spending freely when it came to furnishing his homes. The reality, though, was that every cent spent left him one step closer to the financial woes that would eventually lead to bankruptcy.

When the time came for them to leave Colorado altogether, Maher sold the El Paso property for $108,000 – $16,000 more than he had spent on it. So his finances were going both up and down. His property sales were leaving him with a profit but all the while his cash reserves were inevitably going down. Without a salary bringing money in each month, his family was moving through the Securicor cash at a pace. Mr McCann said he had determined that Maher 'maintained a lifestyle that frittered it away'. That could explain why Maher moved from a more expensive property in Woodland Park to the cheaper, yet more expansive, hideaway in El Paso.

It is thought that the Laconia house was the last Maher owned in the USA. All his years on the run after that were spent in rental properties. That in itself, police believe, is a sign the cash quickly ran out.

In their briefing before Maher was jailed, Suffolk Police told journalists that enquiries 'had shown that all properties Maher bought over the years have been sold on and the money presumed spent'. The force couldn't prove that the money Maher got back from selling the houses he bought in the USA had been spent rather than squirrelled away, but it was their best guess given the hard times his family later endured.

Giles described Maher's habit of changing properties as 'downsizing'. He said, 'It seems the money was running out. He wasn't exactly living the life of Riley out there and had to downgrade in his lifestyle.' But he said police had to focus on specific parts of the case when gathering evidence against Maher and not all of the questions that had emerged over the past 20 years could be answered. 'Because of the time parameters of this job we have had to focus on particular parts of the inquiry. There are many questions I'd love to find the answer to but it wasn't necessary to prove the case,' he said. So Suffolk Police had to be satisfied to answer just some of the questions they had. But for many, the questions still linger.

One person who became an expert on the case was Colin Adwent, 52 , crime reporter at the *Ipswich Star* and *East Anglian Daily Times*. The papers had dominated coverage of the Fast Eddie story since the first hours after the theft in 1993 and their appetite for it had not diminished by 2012. Adwent spent weeks delving into the secret lives of Maher and his family. He was left to conclude that Maher's stash of cash had all but disappeared by the mid-to late 1990s. 'It would seem that Maher had £200,000 from the theft. He'd made $17,000 profit on the first house, he then builds another house that's cheaper and sold it for a profit,' he said. 'He'd been making a profit on the houses so money doesn't seem to be too much of an object at that time. They at least had money to live on. The problem was the years went on. Gradually, the American dream ended up turning into a bit of a nightmare for them. When Maher was arrested, they clearly had no money, they were living in rented premises. Ultimately he was struggling and had been in debt.'

Adwent believes that Maher hit hard times about the time Mark was born in New Hampshire in 1997. That was also about the time he started his job with Nielsen Media Research. 'I wouldn't imagine that he got a job until he needed a job,' he said. 'I'm thinking that somewhere along the mid- to late 1990s, around the time that Mark was born, things went wrong for them. In my opinion, sometime in 1996-97 that's probably when the financial situation took a downturn. That's probably why he got the job with Nielsen. It would appear the money has run out in 1996-97, possibly '98. Something has gone horribly wrong financially and in 1998 he's been more or less compelled to find a job and then he's been Jobbing Joe from then on.'

And over time, things simply got worse. One of Lee's ex-fiancées would later say that Debbie once told her that Maher had earned $80,000 from his Nielsen job at one stage. But Debbie had also claimed, Amanda Zignego said, that they had lost a large sum of money in a retirement fund when the stock market crashed. The claim has never been verified but, if true, the loss would have been a further blow to Maher's already shaky financial situation. 'It seems as if their fortunes both financially and life-wise had spiralled downwards and spiralled out of control,' Adwent said. 'Life became harder for them. I was told they never appeared to have a lot of money.'

Even the proceeds of an internationally famous armoured van theft had not put Maher on a more stable financial footing. He had been unable to manage his money back in England and he'd been unable to do it again in the USA. 'The general picture that has been painted through his time growing up until he got caught in America was that of a chancer,' Adwent said. 'He couldn't really hold any money. He always seemed to have a plan of how to get some but never worked out the detail of keeping it. Misfortune seemed to follow him financially. For a man who took so much money, he doesn't seem to have been very good with it.'

Investigators found bank accounts belonging to Maher and Debbie in the USA. But if they had been hoping they might yield some of the original £1.17m, they were left disappointed. Accounts in the names of Michael Maher and Stephen King were found, as were accounts in Debbie's false names of Anthony and King. Records showed they never had any significant amount of cash in them. There was a small amount of money that sat dormant in the accounts, suggesting in the early days the family lived purely through cash.

Returning to the question of how much Maher really did get from the theft, Giles is simply not sure. The only person who definitely knows is Maher, with others also likely to share that secret. And without any records of international transfers and with so many years passed since the crime itself, police are unlikely to ever find out for sure. Giles explained the difficulty in trying to find the answer. 'Because of the passage of time, the data recovery is not what it is now. A lot of things have not only been archived but destroyed. In particular, detail like banking history is not available,' he said. 'It's been a real challenge to try to work out what went on.'

But while Maher was credited by some as having committed the 'perfect crime' and won respect from others for having lasted on the run for so long, the investigators were left with one conclusion about how he handled having lots of cash. Giles' conclusion is that Maher is simply 'a man who lived beyond his means'.

And while Maher seemingly ended up with nothing in the long run, what happened to the remainder of the cash still remains a mystery. Adwent said, 'Given that he stole £1.2m, if he did only get £200,000 that leaves £1m to be used for expenses and to be shared out amongst any accomplices.'

Who actually benefitted from the lion's share, and how it was spent, remains a tantalising mystery.

20

SECRETS
AND LIES

When the news of Eddie Maher's arrest broke, there was seemingly no one more shocked than his son Lee. But not only was Lee taken aback that the police had finally caught his father, he was also apparently gobsmacked over the reason for the net finally closing in. Even though he had been telling one fiancée after another for several years that his father was an international fugitive, after Maher's arrest Lee said he knew nothing about it. And even though, according to the FBI, Lee had heard his father erupt into a rage when a Nixa policeman tipped him off that the authorities were on to him and was told that the family would have to move again, publically Lee wasn't admitting to any of that.

In a series of media interviews and text messages, he claimed to have only just discovered his father's past, that his real surname was not King, that he was born in England, not the USA, and that he was actually two years older than he had thought. Looking shell-shocked and teary, he agreed to an on-camera interview with Missouri TV station KSPR. As the cameras rolled, he spent several minutes praising Maher as an amazing father and insisting he was not a criminal. KSPR reported that Lee had said it was one phone call from his mother that 'turned his life upside down'. The station said, 'Not only did he find out his dad has allegedly been on the run for two decades, King found out he has a different last name, he's two years older than he thought and he was born in the UK a few years before this alleged crime spree started.'

An emotional Lee added, 'My dad is one of the nicest guys you'll meet. He's only ever done what's good for us. I don't want everybody to see him in a bad light for something he did 20 years ago. There was no way he would do this thing by choice. He wouldn't just do it to do it. He doesn't commit crime. I mean he's the one that gets me out of trouble.'

Just hours after his dad's arrest, Lee was going in to bat for him. He was telling the world that Maher was a good father and certainly not an out-and-out criminal. If Maher had stolen the money, it definitely wouldn't have been done out of choice, according to Lee.

He went on to tell KSPR that his family had moved around a lot but Maher had told him it was because of his job. He was then shown on screen saying, 'It is very hard,' presumably referring to the shock from the revelations from the previous few days. And he added, 'He is a good guy.'

Fugitive or not, he was trying to portray his father in a positive light. KSPR reported that Lee said his family would 'carry on with our lives and try to pick up the pieces'. He then went on to claim that his mother and younger brother had not known his father's secret.

The interview was a scoop for KSPR. Before long, the story would be huge on both sides of the Atlantic and the station had been quick off the mark securing the one member of the family who was both able and willing to speak. Lee's comments would be used in news stories around the world.

With few of the details of Maher's past known at that stage, much of the media took Lee at his word. Maher's family were reported to be as shocked as everyone else about the dark secret harboured by him for so many years.

Dave Stewart, KSPR's managing editor, had sent a reporter to interview Lee. He reviewed the footage before it aired and later gave his assessment of Lee in an interview with the BBC. 'He was very emotional. He found out just hours before that he wasn't a United States citizen like he first thought, he wasn't from New Hampshire like he thought, he was actually two years older than he had been led to believe by his parents,' he said.

At this stage, no one new to the story had any cause to doubt Lee's version of events. But when denying any knowledge of his father's past, he hadn't stopped there. He had gone on to repeat a story which he had told previous partners – that he was a decorated soldier who had seen service in Afghanistan. Some reported that he had claimed to have been injured in service and was even in the Special Forces.

It was a story that the *Daily Mirror* told on 11 February, three days after Maher's arrest. Headlined 'FAST EDDIE MAHER NICKED BY FBI', the paper said 'to neighbours in Missouri he was a perfect dad ... but for 19 years he was wanted in UK over £1m heist. Lee, who has served in the US military and was awarded a Purple Heart for being injured on active service, said the news had "turned his life upside down".' It then quoted Lee as saying, 'He's an amazing dad. He cares for us, provides for us and takes care of us ... he's been to every baseball game, football game. Everything we've ever done in our lives, he's been there for us.'

So while Lee was defending his father, he was also seemingly creating his own fake back-story. The Purple Heart is awarded to members of the US armed forces who have been wounded or killed by enemy action. Others would later claim that Lee told them he had also been awarded the Bronze Star Medal, which is given for acts of heroism. Lee kept to his story for several weeks.

The *Daily Mail* ran what it described as the most in-depth interview to date with Lee on 13 February. During the interview, Lee repeated his claims of only just having found out about his father's past. The paper said that Debbie, Lee and Mark had vowed to join Maher in the UK if he was extradited because their lives in America had been 'frozen' as they were effectively illegal immigrants. It said Lee had 'revealed that the change will be especially hard for him as he is an "all-American male" who served in the US military and only knows Britain through films like *Snatch*.' It continued, 'The 22-year-old also told for the first time of the moment when his father revealed that everything he knew about himself was a lie – and that he was really born in Dagenham, east London.'

Further into the story, it said, 'He said their illusion fell apart on Wednesday night when Maher finally told them the truth – and that he was called Lee Brett, not Lee King as he had always known himself.'

Maher had, the paper said, told Lee he had not been born in New Hampshire and showed him his British birth certificate for the first time with the words, 'This is you.' It then ran a series of comments from Lee in which he continued to suggest he had known nothing of his father's past. He said, 'It blew my mind – I still can't get my head around it. All my life I've been Lee King, that's all I've known. Now it turns out I was born in Britain and I have a second birth certificate. My parents lied to me but they have had their reasons. Of course, I wish it had not happened, but it has. There is nothing I can do about it and there's no point getting angry. What has happened does not change my opinion of my dad. One stupid mistake is not going to change the fact he was always there for me and would do anything for me.'

The paper said Lee, who like his wife has the name King tattooed on his wrist, had told of his father taking him elk hunting and that the two of them shared a love of American football, wrestling and baseball. And Lee was already considering his future. Having been born in Britain, he was aware he would probably have to return. 'I can't work here … my life is frozen and I can't do anything,' the paper quoted him as saying. 'We've decided to move to England as it's the best thing to do. We just want to be with Dad and, as things are, to stay here will be really complicated. I don't know anything about England and all I know is from films like *Snatch* and *The Italian Job*. It's dreary, there is actual history and people drive on the left in England … that's about it, I have no other preconceptions.'

It appeared that the Guy Ritchie film *Snatch*, from 2000, formed a big part of his vision of England. The film focuses on the criminal underworld in the part of London where his father grew up. The *Daily Mail* interview continued, 'I don't know how I'll adjust because I'm an all-American man and I've always thought of myself that way. I've wrestled, played American football, I love baseball and I served in the military. The only time I've been out of the US was when I served in Afghanistan. I've worked as a fireman here, so maybe I can do that in England.'

By now, Lee was speaking openly about the events of the previous week. He was answering the phone to journalists and being interviewed in person. His father had spent the past 19 years avoiding the reporters, who would have trampled over each other to get an interview with him, and now Lee was giving them everything they could hope for and more.

In a story by the Associated Press reporter Maria Sudekum, run by numerous media outlets on 19 February, Lee was holding to his line that he had been in the dark throughout. In a phone interview with the reporter, Lee said, 'I had just found out that my life is ... not anything that I thought it was.' Growing up, he told her, 'nothing ever seemed out of the ordinary ... It's not something I would even consider because everything was so normal. It really kills me for it to be portrayed this way. I had no idea,' he said. From this, anyone reading the stories would have got the impression that Maher kept his past secret from Lee, as he is believed to have done with Mark.

When Lee was interviewed by KSPR he had claimed his mother had also been unaware, yet when it came to the *Daily*

Mail's report, Lee was quoted as saying that his parents had lied to him, suggesting they both knew. By this time though, Lee's version of events was being questioned by some. First of all, it was in direct contradiction to Jessica King's version of events. It was, after all, Lee's revelation that his father was Fast Eddie that prompted her to search the web to see if it was true. And, she said, when he told his father, Maher had threatened her life.

Ultimately, police and prosecutors believed Jessica's version and the FBI based the early case against Maher on her description of how the events unfolded. She described Lee as a controlling husband whose lies left her with 'no idea what to believe'. Lee's claims about his time in Afghanistan, and particularly his Purple Heart, attracted as much scepticism as his suggestion that he didn't know his father's real identity. No one could verify the claim and his ex-fiancées were telling anyone who would listen that it simply wasn't true. They were still reeling from learning that Maher – a man they had once spent a lot of time with – was a major foreign criminal.

Kayla Jacoby, Amanda Zignego and Hannah Evans had all at one stage been due to marry into Maher's family. He was the grandfather of their children and yet they were discovering they had been fed a string of lies. They were stunned to see Lee in the papers and on websites and even more shocked when they heard what he was saying. Amanda put herself forward for interviews; she had been engaged to Lee when he was in the Army and she insisted he had not been in the forces nearly long enough to go through training and be sent on a tour of Afghanistan.

After joining up, he had been sent to the 30th Adjutant General Reception Station at Fort Benning in Georgia. New soldiers are sent there for the first stage of their army career. They get their first army head shave, are given their uniforms, boots, army-issue glasses if needed, and what is known as a 'battle buddy' – a fellow new arrival who will help them through their transition from civilian to soldier.

Surrounded by 120,000 army personnel and civilian employees on a sprawling base, the new soldiers are shown the ropes of life in the armed forces. They are photographed and given their army ID. These are the first basic steps before a soldier goes anywhere near a firing range, let alone a war zone.

When he arrived, Lee would have had to put away his mobile phone and give up any food or drink that was not army issue. It was the start of a long process to becoming a soldier. According to Amanda, his army records show he started his active service on 25 March 2009 following an assessment the previous day. But before she knew it, he was coming out. She said Lee's discharge papers came through in April.

It wasn't until a couple of years later, after Maher's arrest, that she learned of the details of the papers; they cite his mother's heart attack and the likelihood that Amanda would give birth to a child with Down's syndrome as reasons for Lee being discharged from the Army. She says at no stage during her pregnancy was the chance of having a child with Down's syndrome raised as a possibility. Amanda estimated Lee, a private at the lowly rank of E-2, had been in the Army a maximum of three months, but his discharge papers suggested it was even less than that. When he joined up she had been pregnant and he returned just after the birth of their daughter Natalie. And his story about being injured in Afghanistan and being awarded a Purple Heart just wasn't true, according to those who knew him.

One by one, others came out to discredit Lee's account. Kayla was among them. She watched and read various interviews given by her ex-fiancé and was moved to speak out. 'Lee made up that he served in Afghanistan, that he had a Purple Heart,' she said. 'I was furious. That's the thing that upset me more than anything – that Lee was playing dumb. All of these excuses. He was trying to make himself out to be a good person and saying he had no idea what his dad had done.'

Despite believing them at first, KSPR's Dave Stewart soon became suspicious of Lee's claims. He said, 'I see a young man who's had his world turned upside down … and he's heart-broken this has happened to his family. Your heart goes out to him to a certain extent but then you start to read some other things. His separation papers from the military show there were some psychological issues going on. Through his girlfriends, he made claims. I believe he told his girlfriend he was a Navy Seal serving with Special Forces over in Afghanistan. He was simply an enlisted man of very meagre rank.'

Soon, KSPR ran a story with Lee's ex-partners claiming that he was lying about not knowing his father's background, as well as his military career. In it, Hannah Evans said, 'He says he went on three deployments to Afghanistan. He says he has three Purple Hearts and a Bronze Star. Our family friend told us there was absolutely no way a 20-year-old could be an Army Ranger and started getting suspicious.'

KSPR said it had looked through army documents which showed King did serve in the military, but was discharged based on a psychological assessment. It ran with the story, staying, 'KSPR News did contact King about these allegations. He did not want to go on camera, but through text messages told KSPR the allegations aren't true. He says the four women are only speaking out to cash in on his father's arrest.' Lee was sticking to his story. For now.

Colin Adwent, the *Ipswich Star*'s crime reporter, was doing some digging of his own. He, too, was speaking to Lee's ex-partners and hearing a different story from the one that Lee was presenting. He said he found evidence that Lee had not only known about his father's background, but had shared it with his three ex-fiancées and with Jessica King after their marriage. 'Lee certainly shared this secret with at least four women who he had relationships with,' he said. 'Certainly with Hannah he used the nickname "Fast Eddie" and told her the secret. Whether he was a young lad and he was trying to impress or whether he had had a drink or whether he just shoots his mouth off, ultimately he's the architect of Eddie Maher's downfall. Unfortunately for Maher, he was let down by his own son. Without him, the likelihood is Eddie Maher would still be somewhere in America.

'Reports from America suggest there is an element of the Walter Mitty about Lee. His army record doesn't show the things he laid claim to about tours of Afghanistan, being injured in Afghanistan, he claimed to have been awarded the Purple Heart. There's no evidence to suggest he got beyond his basic training. His army record is very different to the story he was telling everyone else about his time in the military. It's very hard to dovetail anything Lee said after his father's arrest with what had gone on in the days, weeks and years leading up to his father's arrest.' He added, 'He seems to have been a loose cannon, ultimately. Why they felt the need to tell him the secret, only they will know.'

On 14 February, the *New York Times* reported that in the hours after he learned his father's secret had been revealed, Lee sent Jessica 'a barrage' of irate text messages accusing her of telling the police. It said he had claimed they were 'things only you know'. And, the paper said, Lee had 'lamented his role in exposing his father'. 'It's my fault,' one of the messages is purported to have said.

Yet still, Lee carried on with his claims. Before long, the freelance journalist Bob Graham wrote to Maher in prison expressing an interest in interviewing him and his family about their lives on the run. Maher agreed to give him access and arranged for Debbie to let Graham into their home and spend time with her and their sons. The arrangement was that while Graham was there Maher would phone from prison and speak to him.

Graham also took the opportunity to interview Lee, hearing in even more detail his claims about his time in the Army. Lee told him, 'I was in the US military, 2nd Battalion 22nd Infantry Regiment, based at Fort Drum, New York. [I'm] no longer in the Army … I broke my back, got mortared just outside the camp in Kandahar Airfield. I got blown off a rock face, got a punctured lung, three broken ribs and a broken back. It was pretty heavy. I spent most of my time in Helmand in the south-west, on surveillance or as a marksman.' He also said, 'I served three tours of Afghanistan, almost a year and really loved it.'

Lee's story didn't ring true with Graham, who checked the

detail. He came to the conclusion Lee was living 'his own fantasy life as a decorated American war hero'. Like Adwent and Stewart, Graham was in no doubt that 'the son of Fast Eddie was equally fast and loose with the truth – and it eventually led to his family's downfall.'

By now, Lee's credibility as an interviewee had been totally eroded. Three months after his father's arrest, he finally admitted publically that he had been the one to let the cat out of the bag. 'It's because of me that Dad's in jail now. I'm the one responsible for this mess,' he said in an interview with the *Sun* on 22 May. 'What makes it so hard now is realising you'll never meet a more selfless man than my dad. All he cares about is us. I don't think that in my entire life he did one thing that was not for our benefit. Maybe that's why I feel so bad, being responsible for this now. But I don't understand why people are getting mad or mean at Dad. It's not like he's a murderer or something. What he did was a victimless crime 20 years ago and he's lived the perfect life ever since.'

After months of denying any role in it, Lee had taken responsibility for his father's capture. He had stood in front of TV cameras and appeared shaken and upset when describing learning of his father's past. And he had been convincing, just as he had wherever he had lived since high school.

Rory Joyce was one of those stung by Lee's apparent lies. The manager of Youngblood's Car Sales in Springfield told Graham, 'He came in here telling us he was a decorated war hero who'd been injured in battle. He told us he'd been awarded the Bronze Star and we put him on a pedestal because I'm from a military background and we admire those young men so much. Even when the cops arrested his dad and the story of Fast Eddie came out, we were going to get a local congressman to fight his case, to help Lee stay in this country. But it all turns out to be a pack of lies ... all of it. We feel cheated and our military dishonoured.'

Lee would not be welcomed back to work. The list of people who felt cheated by him was growing. In the end, there were too many people who knew the truth. The four women he had had serious relationships with one after the other in the preceding years had joined forces and spoken out. One by one, they told their stories and exposed the truth. They had all learned that among Lee's lies about the military and his dad being an assassin he had been telling the truth when he said that Maher was a fugitive.

Back in Britain, investigators also looked into Lee's background but did not find any evidence to verify his claims relating to his military background. Scothern, of the Crown Prosecution Service, said, 'We never found anything to back that up.'

After splitting from Lee, Kayla had started to rebuild her life. She had a new relationship and became a full-time housekeeper. When she saw Lee's face plastered across newspapers and heard him interviewed on news channels, the memories of their relationship came flooding back. One of the few things she had been told about the family that proved to be correct was the fact that they were in the country illegally. That was one of the stories told by Lee that she had dismissed as a lie, along with his claim that his father was an assassin wanted in England. 'It was a massive shock,' Kayla said. 'Of all the lies Lee told me, I would never have picked this one out to be real.'

Now that she knows the truth, it all makes perfect sense to Hannah, who had got engaged to Lee after his split with Amanda. It was Hannah who alerted Amanda to Lee's dad's real identity when she sent her a link to a website article about his arrest. She said, 'I was stunned but in a way I was kind of happy that his family was finally getting what they deserved, for being the kind of people that they are. They didn't welcome me into their home.'

Almost inevitably, she has spent the time since going over old conversations and patterns of behaviour looking for tell-tale signs of their dark secret. But apart from Lee's seemingly fanciful stories, neither Debbie nor Maher ever gave any indication of their past. 'Only Lee told me where they had all lived and he told me it was so his father didn't get caught for being a hit-man,' she said.

It had occasionally occurred to her that it was odd that neither of Lee's parents ever mentioned their families but she hadn't thought much more of it. 'Lee was definitely the one that gave his family away. How else would anybody find out who he was if he hadn't opened up his mouth because no one over here knew the Fast Eddie thing?' Hannah said. 'I think he actually wanted the truth to come out in some kind of sick way. I think he wanted to end this whole running thing. I think he couldn't deal with it any more. I think he wanted it to come out even if he gave up his father for the rest of his life. If someone had believed him, I think he would have been caught a couple of years ago, but since no one believed him, no one turned him in.'

Some of the things that may appear strange now seemed to have logical explanations at the time – such as Lee's parents keeping a close hold on his fake birth certificate and social security number, which they locked away in their house. Somehow, Maher and Debbie had sourced a false birth certificate that gave Lee's place of birth as the Lakes Region General Hospital in Laconia, New Hampshire – quite different to Barking Hospital, east London, which was where he had actually been born. It said Lee Edward King was born on 1 August 1989 and that his father was Michael Richard Maher, whose date of birth was listed as 17 April 1951. His mother's name was listed as Barbara Diane King-Maher, with a date of birth of 29 September 1960. Debbie's maiden name was given as King; the birthplace of both parents was listed as England.

The certificate was purported to have been originally filed on 10 August 1989 and contained the following declaration: 'I hereby certify that this a true abstract issued from the official records on file at this office. Date issued: 9 June 1997.' Rather than being a 'true abstract' from the records, the certificate was filled with falsehoods.

'If he needed it for a job he had to get it from his parents and his mum said, "You have to give it back to me." I just thought she wanted to keep it safe because Lee will lose anything,' Hannah said.

Amanda will one day have to explain to her children who their father is and where he comes from. 'I have no idea how I'm going to explain it to them,' she said.

For Kayla, one of the most devastating discoveries was that her daughter's name was false. Sophie King had been given Lee's surname. 'I really wish he had told me that,' she said. 'There's a lot of awkward conversations to be had with my daughter in years to come. It's the last name, it's the fact that her real dad has never had anything to do with her, it's the family he comes from. I will handle it as it comes and, at an appropriate time, I will tell her what she needs to know.'

All three women got to know each other after Maher's arrest. Between them, they have been able to piece together the family's movements over the years they knew them. 'Basically, Lee went from girl to girl reproducing,' said Kayla. 'The only reason I know anything is because I have been in contact with his other girlfriends.'

It is from this contact that Kayla discovered Lee had told each of the girls his family's secret. She believes if Maher had found out that Lee had revealed his identity before, the truth would have been exposed much sooner. 'That's the difference between Jessica and me and the other girlfriends. Michael found out that Lee's wife knew about it and threatened her,' Kayla said. 'I think he would have done the same with us if he had known. That might have made me believe, if he had done that. He never knew that I knew, and that's the difference.'

Meanwhile, Jessica King's life had been left in tatters. In the weeks after Maher's arrest, her cars were being repossessed and she said their bank account was empty. She vowed to 'try to move on'. 'I've got to,' she said at the time. 'I don't have a choice. I've six months until I have a newborn child. I have got to figure something out.'

21

BEHIND
BARS

Eddie Maher had moved his family across 10 US states in 19 years. Sometimes, they had moved after pausing for breath for just a few weeks, while in other places they had stayed a handful of years.

Most of the time they didn't tell anyone they were leaving and those left behind were left wondering the reason for the sudden departure. Sometimes, they had even abandoned belongings, in too much of a rush to pack everything, or possibly worried that a removal truck would leave police with a breadcrumb trail to their next hideout.

Nearly two decades on the run had taken Maher on a meandering path through the USA. He had travelled thousands of miles, always being careful not to leave any obvious trace of where he had been. And yet here he was, sitting in a cell in Springfield's Greene County Jail, just one of 450 or so inmates either waiting for their day in court or counting the days until their time was up. His luck, it would seem, had finally run out.

If what had happened to him on 8 February hadn't sunk in up to this point, it surely must have done now. His new home, albeit temporary, was a cell and he was a prisoner of the state of Missouri.

Even though the subject on everyone's lips was the missing £1.17m, the initial charges he faced related to his guns. US prosecutors had seized on the fact that he had bought them under a false identity. While all the other details of his past were being established, it had given them an opportunity to hold him. And on 9 February, the day after his arrest, Maher was charged with firearms offences. Beth Phillips, the US Attorney for the Western District of Missouri, announced that he had been charged in federal court with being an illegal alien in possession of firearms. The charge alleged that Maher had been in possession of a Hi-Point .45-calibre pistol, a Jennings .380 pistol, a Mauser 7.62x39 rifle, and a Mossberg .22-calibre rifle. It was announced that Supervisory Assistant US Attorney Michael S Oliver was to prosecute the case.

It was also the first time the court heard from Maher, and the fact that the man who drove away with more than £1m was now pleading poverty. He told the judge hearing the case that he could not afford a lawyer. A spokesman for the United States Attorney's Office later confirmed, 'The court found that he did not have the resources to have a defence attorney so the court appointed a federal public defender. Mr Maher testified on oath in court that he was financially unable to obtain counsel.'

The media – happily devouring every new development in

the story – lapped up the fact that a man accused of driving away with such a large sum of money was now telling a judge he had but a few pennies to his name.

With the formalities completed, Maher's case was deferred and it was then that he was taken to Greene County Jail. He was searched and any personal property he was carrying was taken from him. He was handed a wristband to identify him and given a dark-green prison-issue jumpsuit. He was finally being introduced to prison life; and whether he liked it or not, he was a celebrity prisoner.

Those who were not in court to see him, soon got their own chance to see how his life on the run had changed him. As it does with all its prisoners, Greene County Jail put a picture of Maher on its website with brief details about him and the charges against him. He was now part of the 'active Greene County Jail population'. Listed under 'M' in its alphabetical list of inmates, the jail said Edward J Maher was 5ft 8in tall and weighed 235lb. It also gave his eye colour, hair colour and listed details of the firearms charge.

The photo brought Maher back into the headlines. The *Ipswich Star* proclaimed 'FIRST PHOTO OF FAST EDDIE MAHER'. The *Star*'s Richard Cornwell – the reporter who broke the story about the 1993 theft – wrote, 'This is the first picture the world has seen of former security guard Eddie Maher since he went missing 19 years ago. Apart from putting on a little weight, having less hair and having gone grey, it is unmistakably Maher, who is wanted in connection with the theft of £1 million from a Securicor van in Felixstowe in 1993.'

While he spent more than two weeks waiting for his next hearing, Suffolk Police took it as an opportunity to intensify discussions with the US authorities over his extradition. It was thought the process could take months and the force was under a lot of public pressure, not least from the media, who wanted to know when Maher would face British justice. 'Suffolk Constabulary has engaged with the CPS about the extradition process,' a police spokeswoman said at the time. 'A review of the investigation and the evidence gathered at the time will take place and be submitted to the CPS. Once the CPS has received this, Suffolk Constabulary will seek their approval to get authority through the courts to sanction the extradition process.'

Maher was able to call Debbie regularly from prison; the stress of the preceding few weeks had only served to strengthen their bond, and Debbie's support for him showed no signs of wavering. During his interviews with the family, Debbie told Bob Graham that Maher was unhappy about being held in custody over offences connected to the guns. She told him, 'He's angered by the gun charges against him to keep him in jail. He bought them legitimately, not from a shady character. He took his licence into the shop there and bought them legally. They got him because he was using a false ID.'

And Lee also told of conversations with his father in jail. 'From what he says from prison, he's getting by just fine, he's minding his own, he was in solitary for a time and there was lockdown 23 hours a day and he couldn't stand it. He couldn't watch TV or use the phone without an appointment ... now he phones every night.'

While Suffolk Police back in the UK were preparing their

case against Fast Eddie and the missing £1.17m, the authorities in the States were focusing their energies on the slightly more mundane gun and immigration offences. So after his two-week wait, Maher was brought back before the Springfield court. He was still in his green prison jumpsuit and had been put in handcuffs and ankle shackles for his trip from the jail. Reporters in the court told how as a US Marshal removed the handcuffs, Maher's court-appointed attorney asked how he was doing. Maher replied, 'Good … good,' and smiled. He seemed relaxed.

Maher was being held without bond on an immigration detainer and the facts had been put before the court in the affidavit from FBI special agent Jeffrey Atwood. The hearing was only three minutes long; Judge James C England recognised the affidavit and asked if the prosecution or defence wanted to add anything to it. Neither did. Maher was returned to prison, aware the gun charges were only the beginning.

Six days later, he was back before the court. This time, the prosecutors introduced a three-count indictment to replace the criminal complaint filed on 9 February. The gun charge remained, along with a forfeiture allegation, which would require him to forfeit the weapons to the authorities. In addition, document fraud and identity theft had been added to the list. The court heard that investigators believed Maher used a Social Security card as an identification document for employment verification in Christian County on 25 May 2010. The indictment said they believed the card was not issued lawfully for Maher's use.

He had also been charged with aggravated identity theft.

The charge alleged that Maher possessed and used a means of identification that he knew belonged to another person. It related to his use of a Missouri driver's licence in the name of Michael Maher on 12 October the previous year.

By this stage, there were two legal processes happening at the same time. The Americans were pursuing charges against Maher on the three-pronged indictment, while the UK authorities wanted him back in England so they could proceed with their own case against him. The negotiations would take weeks to resolve but, in the meantime, Maher was back in court on 20 March for an arraignment. He pleaded not guilty to the charges against him and was remanded in custody until another hearing could be arranged. It meant he could theoretically face a trial over the US charges.

In early May, it was announced that a pre-trial conference had been set for later that month to prepare the parties for trial. But it wouldn't be needed ... and it was Maher who intervened. Despite avoiding it for so long, he indicated he would not oppose being sent back to the UK to face charges over the theft of the money.

During his interviews with the family, *Sun* journalist Bob Graham spoke to Maher when he called from prison. Maher told him, 'I'm alive and kicking here ... it's not so bad. All I'm worried about is my family and how they're coping. All I've ever done is for the benefit of the family; they are my number-one worry, I want to make sure they are protected ... they're the most important thing in my life. Yeah, I'm in jail now but I've been in a sort of prison for years.'

It was the first insight into how Maher had viewed his time

on the run. The place he had avoided for nearly 20 years was apparently 'not so bad' after all. Seemingly, he was ready and willing to face his day in a UK court. And by agreeing to be sent back, he had effectively brought the UK proceedings forward and had the US charges put on the back burner.

On 11 May, a magistrate at the federal court in Springfield approved Maher's transfer to US immigration officials for deportation. It was a breakthrough for Suffolk Police, who had avoided the need to push for a formal extradition. They indicated Maher would face charges of conspiracy to rob. The US authorities for their part said that despite Maher's decision to voluntarily head back to the UK, the US charges would remain in place for now. Suffolk Police and the UK media could now sense progress. The media was desperate for Maher to return, keen to find out whether he would admit his guilt or fight the charges in a UK court.

With her husband in a cell in Greene County Jail, Debbie opened up to Bob Graham about their time on the run. In their end-of-terrace townhouse, which was dominated by a huge TV, Debbie said of life in the USA, 'For all these years we just disappeared … and through it all, I never knew who I was. I know that sounds weird but there was no communication with our families. I have no idea how we managed that. I never saw any money. He said I was to know the littlest possible because I wasn't involved whatsoever. He said, like, "It's hard." I said, "How are we going to live?" He said, "We have a little and we'll make it."'

Debbie told Graham she had asked Maher where the money was and he had responded, 'No, no, no …' refusing to tell her about it. 'So I have no idea, absolutely no idea and that's the way he wanted it,' she said. 'It all so bitter-sweet for me, Eddie's not here but I'm talking to my family again for the first time in 19 years. I've been talking to my sisters again for a few weeks since the arrest. I can't believe it.' She told how she was speaking to her sister Louise via Skype every day. 'I'm now rediscovering my family, as I said … it's all so bitter-sweet,' she said. 'I feel guilty for being apart for so long, I've missed them so much. I'm guilty but I am so happy at the same time. I spoke to Eddie about my guilt and he's said I've got nothing to feel guilty about. He feels so awful about me not speaking to my family all these years, especially Louise. We've spoken about it over the years but we stuck to the rules. It's something Eddie thought we could never do, speak to the family, for whatever reason. And I just love Eddie so much, he's my best friend. It all sounds so clichéd but I would do anything for him … I would jump in front of a bullet for him. I love him that much.'

Life on the road had been hard, Debbie said. 'It was always a struggle … he never had a credit card until he became Mike. There were a thousand times I'd scream and shout at him, "I'm going home … get me a plane ticket … I'm going to the consulate … I'm going home." But I never did, I think that's why it's hard for me, because now I feel like I'm betraying him. All these years he's felt the guilt of it. I know he's felt terrible. Yet, he's awesome. I know he's worried about what will happen to me and the family.'

Debbie told how she hadn't seen England since arriving in America in January 1993. 'What has happened is bitter-sweet, it really is … it's wonderful to meet my family again. What Eddie did … well, I can't talk about it now. We're in a prison now and have been for a long time. We just want to go home now.

'When I spoke to my sister for the first time in 19 years she asked what I wanted to eat that's British when I get home. I said fish and chips and mushy peas … I've not had that for 19 years.

'Eddie has a huge family – five brothers and six sisters. Lee and Mark have never had any family but Eddie and myself; they'll find it strange with such a large family. It's also strange when the boys hear me calling him Eddie now because they've always heard me calling him Mike.

'All I've wanted to say about Eddie is he's an awesome father and awesome husband. The moral is money doesn't buy you happiness – that's the one positive thing that has come out of the last 19 years, that we've stayed together as a family. All Eddie's worried about now is what happens to us because now we have no income and Lee has lost his job at the car dealership because of the publicity of the case. Right now I clean the empty townhouses in this housing complex and sit in the rental office in the afternoons. It covers some of our bills but that's what we are down to at the minute and that's Eddie's biggest worry. He keeps saying he's fine and there's nothing else that can be done for him, but he's worried about us. Like getting the money together to get passports, that's a nightmare. Trying to get documents for the passports is awful.'

And she told of the conversations she had been having with her family about her return. 'We used to go to Butlin's in Clacton every year as a family … it was lovely. I've been talking again to my sisters and reminiscing about growing up. Our kids never thought they would experience that, but now they will. We're not rich people, we struggle, even the car we have has 250,000 miles on the clock. My dad has bowel cancer and now, at least, my sons have been able to meet him over the phone and talk to him. We're embarking on a new adventure and we'll come through it.'

While Maher remained in Greene County Jail, the woman who put him there was also thinking about her future. Jessica King had been speaking publically about her ordeal for a number of weeks and had even enlisted the help of a law firm. Soon, it emerged she was investigating whether the £100,000 reward offered in 1993 was still on the table.

Springfield law firm Whiteaker and Wilson announced it was working with Jessica. It said attorneys Brandon C Potter and Damon S Phillips had been retained by Jessica to 'represent her interests in the Eddie Maher matter'. It said, 'The Eddie Maher story is one of the more intriguing events to occur in the Ozarks in recent times. Had it not been for his daughter-in-law Jessica King's courage, Maher would still be at large after nearly 20 years as an international fugitive.'

The law firm added after Jessica gave her interview to the *New York Times*, 'she realized that she wanted legal representation to guide her through the press bombardment and to steer her through other legal matters relating to this amazing story ... Springfield lawyers Brandon Potter and Damon Phillips are assisting with her divorce, all press coverage, media agreements and collection of a reward of £100,000. They have already contacted the UK firm connected to the monetary reward offered years ago in the armoured-car robbery.'

22

HOMEWARD BOUND, LONDON TOWN

Eddie Maher was proud of his cockney roots; so much so that he had the tattoo 'Homeward Bound, London Town' inked on to his body. It was an identifying characteristic circulated among police forces during his time on the run in the hope that it would help track him down.

It never did.

Yet when Maher's winding journey eventually took him 'homeward bound', it was a trip he never wanted to make. Nearly 20 years after speeding out of Suffolk in a getaway car, he found himself back on English soil in July 2012. Instead of leaving the police in his wake, this time he was being given a flashing blue-light police escort. Sat in the back of a marked police transit van, he was destined for Ipswich Magistrates' Court.

News that Maher's return to the UK was 'imminent' had broken the night before. Sources close to the investigation were happy to confirm, off the record, that Maher was 'in the air' on a flight from Chicago bound for London's Heathrow Airport. He was due to arrive in the 'early hours' of 10 July 2012. Security staff at the court had been forewarned of the arrival of the high-profile defendant on 9 July.

But enquiries to the Suffolk Police press office were being met with the same stock response – that officers were continuing to work with their American counterparts on bringing Maher back to the UK. For 'operational reasons', police did not want details of Maher's return to be leaked; they were determined nothing should go wrong in the final handover. Having got this close to nailing their man, the last thing detectives wanted was a last-minute hitch.

The *Ipswich Star* – the newspaper formerly known as the *Evening Star*, which broke news of the heist in 1993 in a special late edition – was confident in its sources that Maher's return was close. 'EDDIE IS BACK', blasted the front-page headline that hit the streets early on 10 July. 'Exclusive: 19 years after he was named as the chief suspect in a daring £1m theft, Eddie Maher will today appear in a Suffolk court,' the *Star* proclaimed.

It was a story other media were also starting to run with. Shortly before 8.00am, the BBC website said Maher was understood to be back in the UK. BBC Radio Suffolk followed suit and led with the news at the top of its 8.00am bulletin. Then, at 8.05am, came official confirmation. The police statement read: 'Suffolk Police can today – Tuesday, 10 July – confirm that a man who has been wanted by Suffolk Police since 1993 in relation to a security van theft has been deported from the United States and is due to appear before Ipswich Magistrates' Court today charged with theft.

'Edward Maher, 57, formerly of Freemantle Close, South Woodham Ferrers, near Chelmsford, in Essex, and who has more recently been living in the United States, was circulated as wanted by Suffolk Police in 1993 following the theft of a security van from outside Lloyds Bank in Hamilton Road, Felixstowe, on 22 January 1993.'

The release ended with a note to editors, which stated: 'Edward Maher will be held in police custody prior to his appearance at Ipswich Magistrates' Court. For operational and security reasons, we will not be disclosing the location.'

Any media who didn't already know about Maher's return did now. By the time the press release was fired out by Lisa Miller in the Suffolk Police press office, Maher had landed safely on British soil. The overnight flight from Chicago had arrived at about 6.00am UK time, and he was accompanied by FBI officers. But once Maher had been handed over to Suffolk Police, the American officers' job was done.

Maher had been officially deported. The immigration and firearms offences he faced in the USA had been dropped. He was officially no longer their problem. But for the detectives in Suffolk who had been leading the hunt for one of the country's best-known fugitives, it was the moment they had been waiting for. Finally, the man 'circulated as wanted' in 1993 was within their grasp.

According to officers who met him at Heathrow, he was 'in good spirits'. After weaving their way through Customs and completing the various pieces of paperwork, it was 9.00am by the time they left Heathrow. The court in Ipswich was being told to expect an 11.00am arrival.

Around the court, on the edge of Ipswich town centre and opposite the town's main police station, there was an air of anticipation ahead of his arrival. Two police officers were on duty at the back of the 1960s court building, while two police community support officers patrolled near the front entrance. For Suffolk, consistently one of the safest counties in the UK, this counted as a heavy police presence. Police cones were placed alongside the kerb preventing any vehicles stopping in the area, and on the corner of Elm Street and Curriers' Lane, two camera crews from local television stations were poised and ready.

Few court appearances attract such attention in Ipswich. Not since serial killer Steve Wright, the so-called Suffolk Strangler, appeared at the court in December 2006 had such a high-profile defendant been in the dock. It was enough to send the local media into a frenzy.

Barrister Richard Atchley, of Three Raymond Buildings Barristers in London's Gray's Inn, was already at the court by about 10.00am. Arrangements had been made with his chambers the previous day for him to represent Maher – even though he had yet to meet his new client. And as solicitors waited in Court Number 3, where Maher was due to appear, there was only one topic of conversation: Would he enter a plea? What would he look like? Would any of his family turn up at court?

At just after 10.50am, the police van carrying him swept along Elm Street and into the back of the court building, where the gates were quickly shut to prevent prying eyes. After a 20-minute conversation with his lawyer, Maher was ready to appear in court. The court usher announced on the speaker system, 'The case of Edward Maher is now being heard in Court 3.'

Five journalists were in court waiting his arrival, including representatives of Anglia Television, BBC Look East and the *Ipswich Star*. Freelance reporter Andrew Young was also among the five. He was in Felixstowe on the day of the crime and in Ipswich 20 years later for Maher's return. He had been placed on order to file copy for most of the country's national newspapers.

Two people, including a police officer, looked on from the public gallery in the dated courtroom cladded with teak wood. Flanked by two security guards, Maher made his entrance into the dock. He was wearing a yellow polo shirt tucked into light-blue jeans, and his tattoos on his left and right forearms were clearly visible. Prison had apparently done little to reduce his waistline, as his gut hung over his jeans. He stood in the dock as the security guard unlocked the handcuffs that attached him to Maher's right arm; once this was complete, the formalities of the hearing could begin.

'Is your full name Edward John Maher?' asked the female court clerk.

'Yes it is,' replied Maher, in a clear and confident voice.

'Is your date of birth 2 June 1955?'

'Yes it is.'

'Do you understand the charge against you?'

'Yes I do,' Maher again responded, confidently. It was

almost possible to detect a slight tinge of an American accent in the answer.

As the clerk asked if there was any indication of a plea, Maher's solicitor interrupted: 'This man has flown straight in from the USA – it's 5.00am in the morning for him,' he said. 'He has not had the chance to take detailed instruction so there will not be any indication of a plea today.'

The clerk accepted the intervention and went on to read the charge, alleging that Maher stole £1,172,500 belonging to Securicor from a van in Felixstowe on 22 January 1993. Once again, the clerk checked that there would be no indication of plea.

'That's correct,' came the reply from the lawyer.

All the time, the unshaven Maher looked ahead at the clerk and bench chairman passively, occasionally snatching a quick glance across the courtroom at the assembled press.

Paul Scothern, from the CPS Complex Casework Unit, then gave a brief outline of the case. 'It's the Crown's submission that this case should not be dealt with at this court due to the facts of the case and the amount of money involved,' he began, before giving some details of the allegations faced by Maher. 'This is a matter that goes back to 22 January 1993. Mr Maher was at that time employed by Securicor as a driver of security vans. He was concerned in making deliveries to various banks in the Ipswich area. On this day, the call to Lloyds Bank, in Hamilton Road, Felixstowe, was the first of a series of planned drops. It was his job to drive up to the bank while his partner went into the bank. On this day, his partner took an amount of cash inside while Mr Maher waited inside the vehicle. When the partner came out of the bank, Mr Maher was not there. Mr Maher was not seen again and neither was the £1,172,500 that was in the van when the partner went into the bank.'

He told the court how Maher had driven the van away before transferring the money into a waiting getaway car – a Toyota Previa Space Cruiser. Another car 'linked to Mr Maher' was found burnt out near Harlow days later, the court heard. Mr Scothern continued, 'He has been resident in the USA almost since the date of the offence. His partner and child flew out to the USA the day before the offence was committed. He has been living there under assumed identities. Through various things that have happened in his life, he came to the attention of the US authorities and was arrested. He has chosen to voluntarily return to the UK.'

Maher's solicitor then rose to address the court. He said there would be no bail application and stated it was 'very early days' in the case. He also said the 'American matters' had now been discontinued.

Bench chairman Bernard Hindes, flanked by two female colleagues, said, 'This matter is not suitable for this court and will be referred to the crown court.'

At this point, the clerk intervened, asking the prosecutor to make his case for Maher to be refused bail. 'The obvious reason is the likelihood of failing to surrender,' said Mr Scothern.

'He obviously has no fixed abode and has not been in contact with any relatives in the UK for many years. He has no ties. Therefore, you cannot be sure that he would attend on the next occasion.'

The bench chairman then resumed his summary, addressing

Maher directly. He told him, 'The bench has been instructed that this matter is not suitable for trial at magistrates'. Eventually, it will go to the crown court. You will be back in this court for committal to the crown court on 24 July. You will also appear in this court via video link on 17 July. You will be remanded in custody. The reason you are remanded in custody is the nature of the offence and likely sentence that would be imposed should you be found guilty.'

With that, the 20-minute court hearing was brought to a close. Maher nodded towards the bench before being placed back in handcuffs and led out of the court. The hearing had been swift and the lawyers representing both sides were reluctant to answer any questions from the waiting media outside court. Asked about Maher's wife, Debbie, prosecutors confirmed she was still in the USA and there were no immediate plans to extradite her. They also conceded police were yet to establish how Maher had pulled off the crime – a possible stumbling block in convincing jurors at any potential trial.

Meanwhile, a prison van arrived ready to take Maher on the next stage of his journey. For the first time in almost 20 years, Maher was set to spend a night on British soil – behind bars in a cell at HMP Norwich. It was to become his home for the next few months.

23

FINAL ROLL
OF THE DICE

Everyone arriving at Ipswich Crown Court on 13 September 2012 expected only one thing – Maher was due in Court No 4 for a plea and case management hearing. It seemed like a routine event: the court clerk would read out the charge to Maher, who would be asked to reply with either 'guilty' or 'not guilty'. That was the plea part of the hearing. The case management part involved setting a trial date in the event of a not-guilty plea, or a date for sentencing if the charge was admitted.

All the journalists who had covered the case and police officers who had investigated it were certain Maher was guilty. After all, he had driven off with the money, vanished for the best part of 20 years and seemingly confessed to the crime during his time on the run. And at every court appearance he had made since returning to the UK two months earlier, there had been a suspicion he might hold his hands up at an early stage. His lawyers would also have advised him that admitting the crime, and thereby avoiding a trial at the taxpayers' expense, would lead to a lesser sentence.

If he entered a guilty plea, his inevitable jail term would be a third less than the sentence imposed after being found guilty following a trial. It is an incentive intended to both speed up the justice system and cut down on costs – for even short hearings the bill normally runs into thousands of pounds. So no one arriving at the airy and modern, glass-fronted court building that day could foresee any other outcome than a guilty plea.

For Maher, it was his fifth court appearance since returning to the UK. He had made one appearance in person at Ipswich Magistrates' Court and three more via video link over four weeks between 10 July and 7 August. Each time, it had been an administrative hearing to ensure all the paperwork was in place ready for the case to be sent to crown court. With the amount of money involved, it would have been far too serious a crime to be dealt with by magistrates, who can only impose a maximum jail term of six months.

After his first court appearance on 10 July, quickly followed by a second on 17 July, Maher was back in front of a court for a third time on 24 July. Each time, a different aspect of the case would emerge.

On the morning of 24 July, it was confirmed for the first time that Maher would receive legal aid from the state to fund his defence costs. It was already widely known that he had been declared bankrupt in 2010 but this was further confirmation of Maher's desperate financial plight.

Another new piece of information that emerged during the hearing was the fact that Maher now had a British residential address. Previously, the court had been told Maher had no home in England; that had now changed. When asked for his address, he replied by giving details of a flat in Wannock Lane, in Eastbourne, East Sussex. 'I'm not sure of the postcode,' he added. It would later transpire that it was the address of his sister, Margaret Francis.

As with each of his UK court appearances, the charge was read to Maher but no plea was ready to be entered. The court was told of delays in getting an appointment to see Maher at Norwich Prison, where he was on remand. This meant the defence team had been unable to receive instructions from their client about any possible plea. The court heard that legal aid had been confirmed in the past 24 hours.

Dino Charalambous, another lawyer from the firm representing Maher, told the court an appointment had been arranged for the following week, 31 July. Paul Scothern, for the CPS, said progress was being made in preparing the case; an initial 210 statements had been cut down to 69.

Maher was told he was being remanded in custody ahead of a further appearance at the court on 7 August, when arrangements would be made to send the case to crown court. Wearing a turquoise T-shirt, Maher responded by saying, 'OK, thank you.' The court then clerk asked him if he had understood what had happened at the 20-minute hearing. 'Yes, I did. Thank you,' he replied.

The next court appearance, on 7 August, was a routine event with the paperwork completed and ready to be sent over to the crown court less than a mile away. There had been no delays and, on a bright autumn day in September, the moment had finally arrived for Maher to face up to the crime for which he had spent so many years trying to evade punishment. But once inside the impressive Ipswich Crown Court, there were whispers of a flaw in the expected plan. Maher's defence team were hinting that he was set to plead not guilty. Ahead of the case being called on at 2.00pm, frantic calls were being made to news desks informing them of the likely development.

It had been thought this was the day that the full story of Maher's audacious crime, his life on the run and then dramatic downfall could finally be told. Pages had been left blank in the next day's newspaper editions and running orders for that night's television news had been left with an empty slot at the top of the programme. But the rumours coming out of Ipswich Crown Court meant all that would have to change. If, as now predicted by those representing him, Maher entered a not-guilty plea, only the most rudimentary details of the case could be reported for legal reasons. It meant the Fast Eddie story would not be able to be told that day.

As news of the likely events was shared between officials and reporters, there was a buzz around the court. Nobody could quite believe it. But then this was perhaps typical of Maher, the archetypical chancer. For him, this was one final roll of the dice.

At 2.00pm, the moment arrived as the court usher announced the case of Edward Maher was being heard in Courtroom 4. Maher was not due to be there; he would appear on a large television screen, via a video link from Belmarsh Prison. As the legal teams, court officials and media took their seats in the court, the screen was switched on to reveal the top half of Maher, sitting in a chair with an 'HMP Belmarsh' sign on the wall behind him. He was wearing a navy-blue, round-neck jumper and seemed relaxed.

When Judge John Devaux arrived in court, the business of the day was ready to begin. The clerk stood, turned to her right and read the charge to Maher, who was watching proceedings via a video link of his own. She explained that Maher was accused of stealing £1,172,500 from a Securicor van in Felixstowe in January 1993. She then asked, 'To that charge, do you plead guilty or not guilty?'

As if to add to the already heightened tension, the technology temporarily failed at that very moment. Everyone in court could still see Maher and he could obviously hear the clerk. He was seen to mouth the words 'not guilty', but nothing was heard. He was asked to repeat his plea and did so, but was again not heard due to the sound problems. Then, at the third attempt, the system kicked back into action. Emphatically, in a confident and unwavering voice, Maher uttered the words, 'Not guilty.'

His representative, Rachel Kapila, then rose to explain the reasons behind the not-guilty plea. 'The defence is going to be one of duress,' she said. 'We say it is very much a follow-the-money type of case. This defendant didn't end up with the profits. They were transferred to others. With that in mind, enquiries we are going to make involve digging out financial records over the past 20 years. We will be instructing a forensic accountant to reconstruct the life that Eddie Maher has been living for the past 20 years, to demonstrate that it is not the life of someone who had over £1m to spend.' She told the court that family members and senior Securicor staff would be called upon to give evidence; witnesses would also be flown over from the United States, she said.

For Paul Scothern and the CPS, it was the first clue they had been given about any possible defence case. Like everyone else, police and prosecutors had expected a guilty plea.

The court heard the trial would be expected to take two weeks and a provisional trial date was set for 18 February 2013. Further discussions would be needed before a decision was made on whether it would be heard in Ipswich or London, with the Old Bailey a possible venue. Maher was told he was being remanded in custody ahead of his trial and, with that, the 22-minute hearing was brought to a close. As Maher was seen to get out of his chair, the television was switched off.

Yet again, the story of Fast Eddie had taken an unexpected twist.

24

UNDER
DURESS

It seemed to have been a terrifying ordeal. Eddie Maher told how in the dead of night three men burst into his rented home in Fremantle Close, South Woodham Ferrers, early in January 1993. One of the men produced a shotgun and waved it around. Maher described how he was then threatened and ordered to comply with their plan. If he refused, he and his family would be harmed, including his three-year-old son. The men also made reference to the firebombing of Maher's pub in September 1991.

In his statement outlining his defence of duress, he said he had not known any of the three raiders and was unable to name them, but he claimed he had been left in no doubt that if he had failed to comply with their demands his family would have faced serious consequences. That, Maher said, was the reason he was forced into driving off with a Securicor van packed with cash on the morning of 22 January 1993. His entire defence was based on the claim of duress – that he was unlawfully pressured into performing an act he would not normally have carried out.

What seemed to be a straightforward open-and-shut case for the prosecution had now become extremely complicated. Maher had been very deliberate in the way he phrased his defence argument, making clear that he had been forced to take part in 'their' plan, rather than anything he had been involved in plotting himself. He was not denying taking the money but he said he had no other choice. The reference to the firebombing of his pub was also a clever ploy.

The fact the attack had happened was not in dispute, and Maher knew that police had never been able to trace the culprits. It was quite conceivable that the same people who held a grudge against Maher in 1991 could have pursued that again less than 18 months later, having learned he now had access to vast sums of money in his new job.

Police had fully expected Maher to enter a guilty plea and little progress had been made on the case in the seven months since his arrest. As far as they had been concerned, there was not much more work that needed to be done. But they had been taken by surprise by Maher's not-guilty plea.

It was slowly dawning on the investigation team that he had an almost plausible explanation that could see him cleared at trial. And just as there were holes in the original inquiry, similar gaps were now emerging in 2012. In 1993, most of the unanswered questions surrounded Maher's whereabouts, but that was now known, as was his financial situation and recent work history. The problem now involved disproving Maher's defence. To do that, prosecutors would have to prove he received a large amount of money and provide evidence of how he spent it.

A man forced into a crime would not be given a significant chunk of the proceeds, so officers knew evidence of any lavish purchases, particularly made using large sums of cash, would be crucial. But the problem faced by prosecutors preparing the case was there was no evidence of Maher's financial history. Bank records dating back that far would be hard to come by and most would have been destroyed or archived. Detectives had not been able to locate the information any sooner because they had not known what name Maher was using during his time on the run until his arrest in 2012.

From the outset, detectives had thought Maher was acting with others in carrying out the crime but they had no idea how much money he had received from it. That was another flaw in the case – the original investigation failed to demonstrate exactly how Maher was working with others. Witnesses had seen up to two people around one of the getaway cars in Felixstowe but there were no names to go on. If the prosecution was to present a case that Maher was assisted they would need to provide some evidence to back up the claim. All of a sudden, a seemingly rock-solid case appeared vulnerable. There was the potential for it to be easily picked apart.

And yet requests from prosecutors for the further evidence needed to firm up the case were falling on deaf ears. When Maher pleaded not guilty on 13 September 2012, his defence lawyers outlined a series of witnesses they planned to call to demonstrate their case, including a forensic financial investigator, and some witnesses would be brought from America. As for the prosecution, a lack of first-hand accounts had always been the Achilles heel of the police investigation. The period from the moment Maher drove off to the point he arrived in the United States was still something of a mystery. He had managed to avoid prying eyes at every turn. Now he had a defence that had a realistic chance of success and the prospect of witnesses to support his case. He knew there was a possibility he could get away with it and so did the team of lawyers tasked with formulating the prosecution case.

With any case that goes to trial, there is always uncertainty about which way the jury will go. In this case, prosecutors were concerned that Maher would be able to take advantage of the wave of support he had received from the British public following the theft. In many people's eyes, he had done nothing wrong. He had simply chanced his arm and struck lucky, gaining a great deal of admiration along the way for the manner in which he'd pulled it off. No one had been harmed and the victims of the theft – a multinational bank and a giant security firm – were unlikely to attract a great deal of public sympathy. Prosecutors knew that some juries, having been told a harrowing story of how Maher and his family had been threatened, would acquit him.

Added to the equation was the man the prosecution were likely to face in court. Whispers within legal circles suggested the highly-respected Trevor Burke QC was being lined up to represent Maher. He worked for the chambers that had acted for Maher since his return to the UK; his record and reputation were formidable. The variety of famous names he has represented include former footballer John Fashanu, disgraced singer Gary Glitter, ex-boxer Nigel Benn and REM guitarist Peter Buck. And his Internet profile included a string of ringing endorsements; indeed, over the past few years, the Chambers UK guide has variously proclaimed his renown as one of the UK's leading defence counsels, saying he is 'one of the most able and razor-sharp barristers practising at the criminal bar today ...'; 'Judges adore and juries admire ...'; 'Trevor Burke is a rock in defence who has represented a number of famous names ... He never puts a foot wrong.'

Obvious questions were being posed about how Maher would be able to afford to pay a QC of Burke's quality using only legal aid. It prompted speculation among lawyers and police that Maher somehow had access to a significant source of funds. All in all, having sized up the opposition, prosecutors were concerned. A meeting was called to discuss the case; it was attended by senior police officers and prosecutors at Suffolk Police's Martlesham Heath headquarters at the end of October. Six weeks had passed since Maher entered his not-guilty plea at Ipswich Crown Court and little progress had been made in the police investigation. Matters were coming to a head and the gauntlet was laid down.

Such was the level of concern about flaws in the case, it was 'within days' of being dropped by prosecutors, sources have revealed. 'There was no reasonable chance of conviction with the evidence as it stood,' the source said. 'The police had assumed Maher would get to the plea and case management hearing and then plead guilty. But that didn't happen. There are then obvious lines of inquiry and questions that immediately needed to be investigated. If there's no reasonable prospect of conviction it doesn't pass the evidential test, with the obvious implications that would have. I think we would have been in very great difficulty as it stood.'

The October meeting carried a blunt message as the facts of the case were laid out. A scenario was presented to those gathered outlining how the prosecution could be pulled apart, particularly by someone with the skill of Maher's barrister. The source said, 'At this stage, there was nothing that would undermine what the defence could say. There was also the added worry that Maher would get a sympathetic jury, given his Robin Hood-esque perception and the fun Fast Eddie tag. The police then saw it was clearly something that had no chance of resulting in a conviction as it stood.'

Another court appearance came and went soon after. Maher, appearing via video link from Belmarsh Prison, made an unsuccessful application to be released on bail in a hearing at Luton Crown Court on 2 November. But the threat that the case could have been dropped unless it was 'moved forward' rapidly had the desired effect. Following the meeting, it was decided Suffolk Police would need to reopen the investigation. Had the case been dropped it would have been hugely embarrassing for both the CPS and Suffolk Police. Maher would have gone down in folklore as the man who stole £1m and got away with it and the media would have a host of damaging questions that would need to be answered. Even so, prosecutors were not prepared to take a case to court that they did not feel had a realistic prospect of resulting in conviction.

The message of the meeting had clearly registered and police sprung into action. Within days, a new investigative team had been formed, led by DI David Giles and assisted by DS Stephen Bunn. The prospect of failure loomed large as the two officers took on the mantle of gathering further evidence. While it was a chance for them to make their names, there was the real possibility that it would not end well unless further evidence could be found. It was a challenge many more senior and experienced officers might have shied away from, aware of the potential reputational damage that could come with the case.

By now, a trial date had been set for 4 March, so police knew their time was limited. An analyst was immediately appointed to examine telephone records gathered in 1993. Although the information had been collected during the original inquiry, more work was needed to link it to other pieces of evidence. A pattern of telephone contact was quickly established, much of it focused on the Ilford house where Maher's mother lived at the time. It was crucial information and resulted in new leads in the investigation.

As the inquiry developed, three more arrests were made in connection with the crime. Real progress was now being made for the first time since Maher was found in February 2012. Evidence was mounting that the theft had been planned over several months.

Co-operation between the police and prosecutors had also dramatically improved as the force granted access to the dozens of boxes packed with material from the initial investigation. Police investigating the theft also now had the advantage of access to interviews Maher and Debbie had given to US investigators following their arrest on immigration offences. In her interview, Debbie said Maher had received about £200,000 as a result of the theft. Separately, he had told the American authorities that he only received about £40,000. Police had never been able to trace any evidence of significant funds linked to the couple, so this was crucial evidence.

Debbie had also been more forthcoming than Maher in relation to their time in America, listing a series of places where the family had spent time. She named the address of the first property in Colorado that they had moved to after arriving in the country. A combination of the renewed progress in the investigation and the information from Debbie gave Suffolk police a good enough reason to authorise a trip to America, knowing that the name of the first property could lead them on a paper trail to further clues in the investigation. Giles and Bunn, therefore, packed their bags and boarded a flight.

In January 2013, they landed on American soil, almost 20 years to the day since the theft. Police had known the link with the United States within two weeks of the crime, yet these two officers had become the first to make the trip as part of the investigation. What they came back with was evidential gold.

25

THE CONVICTION

Eddie Maher knew the game was up. The evidence police had found during their trip to the United States was indisputable. There was now no doubt that he had had access to cash - and a significant amount of cash at that. How else would a man whose debts had spiralled to about £10,000 by January 1993 manage to buy a $119,900 house, mortgage-free, six months later?

Not only was there evidence that he had large amounts of money at his disposal, it was also clear he was being helped. Police now knew passports issued in the UK in April found their way to Maher and Debbie in America, providing them with aliases that would enable them to buy the property. For a man supposedly lying low after being forced to carry out a spectacular theft, somebody knew where to find him. He was receiving assistance and police were now certain it was coming from the UK.

After David Giles and Stephen Bunn returned to Suffolk at

the end of January, Maher's defence team was informed of the new evidence. The effect was almost immediate; on 6 February 2013, four weeks before the trial was due to begin, Maher's lawyers wrote to the prosecution and court indicating he wanted to change his plea to guilty.

By now, Maher had switched his legal team. Trevor Burke QC was no longer due to represent him, having been replaced by David Nathan QC from another London chambers. Now, at the eleventh hour, after nearly two decades of escaping justice, there was nowhere for Maher to run to.

Another hearing was set up, to be heard at Southwark Crown Court, on the bank of the River Thames in central London. The case was listed for 10.00am on Tuesday, 5 March, and a media briefing was hastily arranged at Suffolk Police's headquarters on 1 March. Giles and Detective Chief Inspector Bernie Morgan were joined by Chris McCann and Paul Scothern, both from the CPS's East of England Complex Casework Unit. About 15 journalists attended, representing local and national newspapers, radio stations and television. This type of media briefing only happened when police and prosecutors had something to shout about - a success story they were proud of. Just months earlier, the case was on the verge of being thrown out. Now there was a mood of self-congratulation among the officers involved in investigating it.

On the wall of the room chosen at the police building was a photo gallery of Maher's various homes during his time on the run and copies of the passports he had used to disguise his identity. Over the next three hours, the assembled journalists were told the story of how police and prosecutors had got their man.

From the initial inquiry, police had been able to trace 182 of the 197 witnesses; the other 15 had died. In addition, 60 new witnesses had been spoken to in the USA and UK. Reporters heading to Southwark Crown Court four days later now knew what to expect. This time there was no doubt Maher would plead guilty - he had said so himself.

Case number U20130210 was listed for Courtroom Number 1 at the yellow-brick court. There was an air of anticipation with photographers and camera crews waiting outside the court, which is partially obscured by a row of trees at the front. From windows at the back of the building, off Battlebridge Lane, the impressive *HMS Belfast* warship can be seen close by, overlooked by Tower Bridge. The photographers and TV crews were looking out for any members of Maher's family arriving at court.

By 9.15am, Debbie and Mark were already inside, having made their way through the airport-style security scanners. They were waiting patiently outside Courtroom Number 1. It was the first time they had attended any of Maher's court appearances since his return to the UK. They were in no mood to talk to the journalists who approached them; interview requests were politely declined. The woman who left Britain on a chilly January day 20 years earlier was almost unrecognisable from the 47-year-old who attended court that day. Photographs issued following her disappearance showed a woman in her mid-20s with scraped back hair, while other images from their time in America showed her with a bob and a warm smile. They were from happier days. Now, as she waited for her husband's case to be called into court, the ever-dutiful Debbie was a shadow of her former self. The hair was still scraped back but the grey colouring told its own story. Her face was etched with tension and she was clearly ill at ease in her surroundings.

Mark stood by his mother's side, his deep American accent obvious the few times he spoke. It was clearly an uncomfortable experience for Debbie as she was within a few paces of journalists itching to report on her husband's downfall. Avoiding any eye contact, she gazed into the distance.

At just before 9.30am, the courtroom was unlocked. For a moment, Debbie's tension was released. She could now enter the court and find a seat, out of the way of the assembled media. Along with Mark, and another woman who had joined them, she chose a spot as close as she could get to the three-sided glass dock. She knew that was as near as she could be to her beloved husband.

Reporters took their seats in the large courtroom and it was not long before the press benches were full, forcing other journalists to sit in the public gallery, closer than Debbie and Mark probably would have liked. But the court was not ready to start at 10.00am, as had been scheduled. There had been a delay in transporting Maher from the high-security Belmarsh Prison, where he was being held. When he did arrive, David Nathan QC wanted some time to talk to his client. There was a constant chatter in court as the prosecutors, court officials and reporters awaited the beginning of the case. At the back of the court, in their seats behind the dock, Debbie and Mark sat in silence.

Then, at around 10.10am, Nathan returned to the court. At 10.14am, the case was called. Maher, wearing a blue tie, white shirt and smart grey suit, was led into the dock. As he looked to his left, he saw Debbie and Mark. They exchanged smiles as Maher took his seat in the dock, with a female security guard sitting behind him.

Two knocks on the door leading to the judge's room signalled the case was ready to be heard and everyone inside the court rose to their feet, as is standard procedure for the arrival of a judge. Mr Justice Nicol then entered and took his position. Prosecutor Richard Southern QC asked for the charge to be read out to Maher. The clerk stood up from her seat, positioned in front of the judge on a slightly lower level, and asked Maher to do the same. She read out his name and date of birth, to which he responded with a nod and a 'Yes', before reading the charge on the paper in her hand.

Maher was asked for his plea. Without hesitation and in a calm voice, Maher responded, 'Guilty.'

There had been no last-minute change of heart. Just as predicted, Maher had finally given up the life of lies. He now had to sit back and listen while Southern told the court the full story of the theft and Maher's time on the run. 'This defendant Eddie Maher is now 57. He has for the last 20 years been living in America under an assumed name,' he said. 'He has pleaded guilty to a single count of theft. This concerns an offence which was committed in 1993, shortly before he disappeared and went to the USA.'

The story of Maher's arrest and capture was then told in a British court for the first time. Southern said, 'In 2012, the US

Department of Homeland Security was alerted to his presence in the USA and he was arrested on immigration and firearms offences committed as a result of his use of false identities during his stay in the USA.

'The US authorities were also aware that he was the subject of an Interpol warrant which had been issued following his disappearance in 1993. He therefore falls to be sentenced for an offence of considerable age – although the Crown would say the cause of any delay has been occasioned solely as the result of his own conduct.'

The court was then told the maximum sentence for theft was seven years, before being taken on a journey back to Felixstowe in 1993. Then facts of the theft were read out. 'On 22 January 1993, the defendant was the driver of a Securicor van that was due to make deliveries of cash to various branches of Lloyds Bank and a post office in Suffolk,' Southern said. 'He was accompanied by another Securicor employee, Peter Bunn, who was to act as the leg man, i.e. the person who would physically carry the cash from the van and into the premises to which the delivery was to be made.

'After being loaded with the day's cash deliveries, the defendant's vehicle left the Securicor depot in Chelmsford at about 8.25am on 22 January 1993. The actual vehicle used was not the one that would normally complete the trip. The defendant drove the van to Felixstowe, arriving outside the branch of Lloyds Bank in Hamilton Road, Felixstowe, where the first delivery of cash was to be made, shortly before 9.30am. A number of witnesses saw the vehicle parked immediately outside the bank at about this time.'

As Southern continued to outline the case, three people entered the back of the court. The two women and a man quickly took their seats at the back of the court behind Debbie and Mark. There was no acknowledgement between them and the three immediately sat down to listen to the case. Onlookers speculated as to who might have just walked into court, 20 minutes into the case ... and it became obvious that this was the man who had left the UK as a three-year-old child 20 years earlier. It was Lee King, whose loose tongue had resulted in his father being held in the dock before him, thousands of miles from the place they had called home.

In a black polo shirt and denim jeans, with a large tattoo visible below his sleeve on his left arm, he hunched forward as he listened to the prosecutor. It seemed Debbie and Mark, along with most other people in the court, Maher included, had not even noticed him arrive.

Southern had not even paused as he continued to explain the case. He was still describing the moment Maher and fellow guard Bunn had arrived at the bank. He said, 'Bunn recalls that the bank was not open when he first arrived and he had to wait a few minutes until the doors of the branch were opened. He then collected the cash delivery from the security hatch in the vehicle and went into the bank.

'Once in the bank, he discovered that he was required to collect money from the branch which was to be returned to Chelmsford and then on to Lloyds Bank. He was therefore required to wait whilst the cash was prepared before returning to the Securicor vehicle.' When Bunn stepped outside he saw the van was gone and immediately went back inside to ask bank staff to alert his head office, the court was told. Then Maher's escape was detailed. He sat expressionless in the dock, looking straight ahead towards the prosecutor.

'The defendant had driven to another part of Felixstowe – a quiet side street called Micklegate Road, which was only a few streets away from the bank premises and from where the van was eventually recovered,' the barrister continued. 'There he parked the van and there, so it appears, the cash remaining in the van – apart from some coinage – some £1.17m, was removed. The next sighting of significance was in another part of Felixstowe, Landguard Fort, at a car park close to a viewing area that overlooks the river estuaries. Witnesses describe two or possibly three vehicles parked close together – and quite isolated. One was a Toyota vehicle described by all as a 'space cruiser-type' vehicle; another was described variously as a brown Cavalier or Marina-type vehicle.

'The witnesses vary on precisely what was happening but all agree that items, probably sacks, were being transferred from the Toyota vehicle to the saloon. One of the persons doing this was described as wearing a dark-blue pullover and dark-blue trousers or jeans. One witness describes this person as having the appearance of wearing a uniform. Another [says it was] like an ambulance driver because of the shoulder patches on the pullover.

'Some time later, by the side of the road leading to Landguard Fort, a Securicor tie and epaulettes were recovered. There are discrepancies between the witnesses at Landguard Fort but these relate in particular to the person or persons with this man in the blue clothes. Two witnesses saw only one other person who was helping the first man to transfer the contents of the Toyota saloon. Another witness states that he saw two others with the first man – one of whom was a woman and the other whom he thought may also have been another woman. All witnesses agree, however, that whoever was with the man in blue clothes, they appeared to be assisting him in what he was doing.

'As the witnesses were engaged in their own business, they did not pay further attention to what was going on but each seems to have had a reason to recollect what they saw. Their statements were given within days of the incident. One saw the saloon vehicle driven out of the car park after a short time.'

The prosecutor then sought to put the witness 'in context' with information that emerged during the investigation. He told the court how the Toyota Previa vehicle left abandoned in the car park had been stolen from east London in November 1992. It was being stored on an industrial estate on the edge of London, at which point another person of interest to the inquiry emerged, he said. 'At that stage, a man who is identified as a Paul Muggleton was seen to be showing an interest in the vehicle as he went to the industrial estate and examined and sat in the Toyota.

'Muggleton's potential connection with the offence does not end there. Telephone traffic between Muggleton and the defendant's brother, Michael Maher, leading up to and over the period of the theft from the Securicor van, reveals that he was in regular contact with Michael Maher and with two others,

Terence Bender and Michael Sulsh. The significance of these two will become apparent as the picture unfurls. Perhaps the most significant telephone contact was one made on 20 January 1993, two days before the theft, when Muggleton's phone appears to have contacted that of the defendant.

'Although the saloon car into which sacks were being unloaded at Landguard Fort was described as either a Cavalier or Marina, the defendant's own car was a similarly coloured, although rather elderly, Opel Ascona. It's a vehicle the Crown say that is remarkably similar to a Marina of that age or, in fact, what would have been its cousin effectively, the Vauxhall Cavalier.'

He described how the vehicle was found burnt out in Nazeing, Essex, between 25 and 27 January and then told of the site's significance in relation to Maher's mother's house, where Michael was living at the time, and the home of his sister Margaret Francis.

The court was told none of the cash stolen had been recovered.

With journalists frantically scribbling notes to keep up with the pace of the opening speech and the succession of new pieces of information that were emerging, Southern then painted a picture of events that happened in the lead-up to the theft. On 20 January – the date of the telephone contact with Muggleton – Maher phoned his bosses to ask to be placed on a short run on 22 January to allow him to attend a hospital appointment in the afternoon. The story about the appointment was 'not true', the court heard, but resulted in him being placed on the Felixstowe run.

Maher's statement to his colleague that he had travelled to work in a taxi that morning because his car had broken down was another false claim, the prosecutor said. 'The reason he could not use his car to get to work was that it was going to be used as the vehicle into which the Securicor cash was to be transferred at Landguard Fort,' he said.

The hushed courtroom then heard details of Maher's American dream. 'In the months and years leading up to the theft, the defendant had expressed the intention of moving to the USA,' the prosecutor said. He described how Maher had a 'history of failing to pay debts' and said he was being 'chased by creditors'. Maher got a job with Securicor after neglecting to reveal his previous convictions, he said.

Before the theft, Debbie and Lee had flown from London Gatwick Airport to Boston, where they spent two nights in a hotel before checking out, the court was told. 'The defendant joined Brett in the USA early in 1993,' Southern said. 'What is clear is that whilst in the USA the defendant adopted his brother Michael's identity. He was able to do this because he was in possession of his brother's Green Card. He also used another alias whilst in the USA, that of Stephen King. He was able to do this having obtained a passport in that name. His partner, Debbie Brett, also had a passport in the name of Barbara Anthony. These passports were issued in the UK in April and May. Consequently, these passports would have been obtained whilst the defendant and Brett were in the USA.'

The names which emerged for the first time earlier in the hearing were now mentioned again and a series of statements were read out. 'Michael Sulsh was booked on a flight to New York on 26 January 1993 through a company called Felton Travel,' Southern said. 'This company had been contacted by phone by Muggleton on two occasions on 25 January. Sulsh returned to the UK on a flight from Boston on 29 January. 'Michael Maher and Terence Bender flew to Orlando, Florida, in the USA on 22 February 1993 – Michael Maher on a single ticket and Bender on a return ticket. Michael Maher's ticket was purchased on the credit card account of an A W Francis of Abridge. Margaret Francis – the sister of both Eddie and Michael Maher – lived at Abridge. In March 1993, Margaret Francis entered into a business with her brother Michael and Terence Bender called Exitchange Ltd.'

The court heard that the passenger booking the flight that day was told an American visa would be required unless they had a Green Card. 'The question remains as to how the defendant managed to enter the USA,' the prosecutor said. 'There is no evidence of any flight booked in his name either to the USA or elsewhere and no evidence of any use of his own passport following the theft. Moreover, there is no evidence of how his brother, Michael Maher, returned to the UK after the purchase of the one-way ticket booked in his name on 22 February. Police records show that Michael Maher was in the UK sometime after 22 February.

'The inference that the prosecution ask the court to draw is that it was the defendant who travelled out with Terence Bender on 22 February 1993 and not his brother – using his brother's passport and taking with him his brother's Green Card.'

The court was told of the 'marked' similarity in appearance between Maher and his brother, which was 'clearly sufficiently close' for him to 'pass as the real Michael Maher'. In further support of the theory, Maher told US authorities following his arrest that he had entered the country 'on or about' 22 February 1993. Southern continued, 'The prosecution also suggest it is reasonable to infer that the passports in the name of Stephen King and Barbara Anthony were delivered to the USA by Paul Muggleton.' He added, 'The dates of Muggleton's trips to the USA in March/April 1993 and May 1993 coincide with periods immediately following the issuing of each passport. What is clear is that there was a degree of planning involved in the obtaining of these passports and, as both the defendant and Brett were in the USA, assistance was being provided in the UK.'

The court was then told about Maher's first foray into the property market, purchasing a house in Colorado in the summer of 1993 using cash. 'The vendor, in 2013, purported to recognise a photograph of the defendant as an image of the purchaser,' Southern said. A fingerprint from one of the purchase documents was also found to be Debbie's, the court heard.

Details of Maher's arrest in the USA and subsequent return to the UK were read out, as well as details of his previous convictions. Concluding the prosecution case, Southern made reference to the other names mentioned during his address. 'The man Muggleton has been arrested and interviewed under caution – he is currently on bail,' he said.

'Deborah Brett and Margaret Francis have been arrested and are currently on bail. Michael Maher's whereabouts are unknown save that it is thought that he is in Spain. Enquiries continue with regards to Michael Sulsh, Terence Bender and others.'

26

BEYOND
BELIEF

In his 42 years in the legal profession, David Nathan QC had never known a case like it. It was an 'extraordinary' story with 'extraordinary' detail, he told Southwark Crown Court as he prepared to present Maher's mitigation. For a start, he had never known a case where a security guard had driven off with the money. Then there was the escape, the life on the run, the story of his son's lottery win and then, finally, the way in which Eddie Maher had been brought to justice.

Nathan believed he had seen most things but 'after doing this job for very many years, I have never seen a case like this,' he said. 'I have never seen a case where a security guard drove off with the money in the back.' And while the prosecution had focused on the facts of the case – the crime, the escape, the purchases and the assistance Maher received – Nathan set out to fill in the gaps. As he stood to address the court, he began to tell the full, remarkable story.

He started in February 2012, with the tale of how Maher was arrested.

'It's an extraordinary aspect of an extraordinary story,' he said. 'Mr Maher's daughter-in-law had originally been the girlfriend, or partner, of his son Lee's best friend. Lee won a lot of money on the lottery; she left the friend and married Lee. The money ran out and she went to the authorities. Mr Maher has two sons, Mark and Lee, with Debbie. Lee is 23, Mark is still of school age.'

He rattled through the details rapidly. The judge had a puzzled look and had clearly not followed what had been said. For anyone unfamiliar with the intricacies of the story, it had been a lot of information to digest in a very short space of time. Nathan was then asked to explain what he had just said.

'Lee had a friend,' he began, speaking at a much slower pace. 'The friend had a girlfriend. Lee won a lot of money on the lottery – Mr Maher's son. She left the boyfriend to go to live with Lee. Within a matter of a short space of time, she had become so devoted to Lee she married him. When the money that he won ran out, by that time Lee told her that his parents couldn't go back to this country.

'When the money ran out she did a little research on the Internet and realised that Mr Maher couldn't go back because he was wanted under the Theft Act. She heard that there was a reward and went to the authorities. That's how the matter was brought to the authorities' attention.'

Nathan checked the judge had followed his second explanation; the judge nodded and Nathan continued. 'Just to complete that part of this extraordinary tale, Mr Maher knew that they were coming for him,' said Nathan. 'He knew that because some days before they did his son Lee had been arrested over a motoring matter. He had gone down to the police station to bail his son out and was told by one of the officers that there was a rumour that he was wanted for an offence back in this country.

'That night, he and Debbie – I say Mrs Maher because they were married in the USA shortly after they went to live there – took the children, Lee and Mark, to a hotel, no doubt with the intention of fleeing yet again … but then thought better of it. They took their son Mark to school the following day. He [Maher] was arrested at their home in Ozark on 8 February. When the search was carried out of the premises and he was questioned, he admitted he was living in the USA on a false name, as alleged. They were living together as man and wife; they were man and wife but their names were slightly different to what people believed them to be.'

Nathan described how Maher had been arrested for immigration and firearms offences. Debbie was also held as a suspected 'illegal alien', as the Americans called it. Many of the questions that had been unanswered since 1993 were resolved in the interview Debbie gave to American authorities. She provided 'considerable assistance' and gave a 'very full account' of the couple's movements in the USA. 'No doubt as a result of her co-operation, she was granted bail,' Nathan added. 'When Mr Maher came back to this country, he agreed to come back. She came back as well, with their two sons. She was under no compulsion to do so.'

Nathan then spoke about Maher's initial claim to the FBI

that he had only received £40,000 from the theft, and Debbie's statement that it had actually been £200,000. 'It's a great pity that he chose to invent a story to say he committed this offence under pressure,' he said. 'By his plea of guilty, he accepts that he joined in this enterprise voluntarily. It would seem at least three or four others were involved. For the avoidance of doubt, Debbie could not have been involved because it was agreed that she was in Boston at the time the offence was committed.'

Nathan described how Maher had bought and sold properties in his first few years in America but, by the mid-1990s, was forced to find work. Outlining Maher's financial demise, Nathan told how his sole focus was providing for his family. 'They were obviously a caring and loving family and he was a good, loving father. He endeavoured to give them as good a life as he could. He would take his son shooting; they had an interest in the guns. I appreciate that it wasn't the dream that Mr Maher had expressed to others before he committed this crime. Here is a man who has spent too much, has spent beyond his means and had to work very hard to put it right.'

The court was then given a run-through of Maher's life up until the theft. Nathan mistakenly referred to Maher as one of 15 children before correcting the figure to 12. 'His life is quite remarkable,' he said. 'As a juvenile, he got himself into a bit of trouble; in his late teens he joins the Army; he serves two tours in Northern Ireland with the Royal Green Jackets; three of his brothers had joined the same regiment before him. He did not stay in the Army very long. He came out and he then, after a period of time in which he committed the offence which appears on his record, worked on the markets for a few years.'

Nathan continued by stating that, after being convicted of robbery at the Old Bailey in 1977 for snatching money from a milkman, he went on not only to live a 'blameless life' but one that was of 'some value' to others up until 1993. He joined the fire service, was promoted to sub-officer but was 'pensioned out' in 1991 after suffering a back injury, he said. Then he covered Maher's time at the Gardener's Arms pub and how it had been firebombed. Nathan said, 'No one was ultimately arrested or charged for the bombing. The effect it had on Debbie was immediate – she moved out with Lee. He was still fairly young.'

Maher was constantly juggling debts and had 'never been very good with money', he told the judge. 'He entirely accepts that he had expressed an interest in going to the USA,' he said. 'But it was just a pipe dream at that stage.' Money problems were a 'sadly persistent' problem for Maher; while the individual debts were not huge, there were a number of them.

In appealing for a more lenient sentence than the maximum seven-year jail term, Nathan said the guilty plea had taken a 'degree of courage'. 'It must be very tempting for a man in Mr Maher's position to "give it a go", if you will forgive the description,' he said. 'It does take a degree of courage to admit to something this old, which he knows comes with a significant prison sentence.'

Maher's time in custody had been 'six very unpleasant months' for his family, the court was told. After spending two days in the custody of US Homeland Security, he spent 145 days in federal prison and 235 days in custody in the UK, split between Norwich and Belmarsh Prisons. Indeed, the threat of incarceration in the USA had been a very real possibility – Maher could have faced a maximum jail term of two years in the States if convicted of the immigration and firearm offences he was charged with. 'This man has made a mess of his life. What concerns him more is the mess that he has caused to those he loves – to Deborah and the two children. You can't turn back the clock – Mr Maher accepts that. In the end, it's all turned very sour indeed. His real concern is Deborah and the children. She has nothing in this country; she is living off her wider family.

'Notwithstanding that, their youngest son Mark is doing very well in an English school and will hopefully continue to do well. In what is a very remarkable case, one with a number of very unusual features, I accept the delay in justice being served is entirely the fault of the defendant himself. But the effect of the delay must mean that the sentence you are about to impose will be all the more difficult to bear.'

After 2 hours and 21 minutes of evidence from both sides, Mr Justice Nicol retired to consider his verdict. As Maher got up to leave the dock and return to the cells, he blew a kiss in the direction of Debbie, Mark and Lee. He would now have to wait while the judge considered his fate.

27

SENTENCE SPELLS THE END

After retiring to consider his verdict for just 11 minutes, Mr Justice Nicol returned to court to hand down the sentence. He told Maher to remain seated as he summed up the case: 'You have pleaded guilty to one count of theft. In January 1993, you were working for Securicor. On 22nd January you and a colleague were entrusted with making deliveries of cash to various banks and other places in Suffolk. Over a million pounds in cash was loaded into the van.

'You went to the Lloyds Bank in Felixstowe where your colleague got out and delivered the money which had to be deposited there. He was away for only a short time. When he returned to the van, the remaining cash (about £1.17 million), and you had all disappeared.

'A few streets away the cash was apparently transferred from the van to another vehicle. Access to the rear of the Securicor van must have been gained with your assistance. Another transfer was made a little further still. Parts of a discarded uniform, no doubt yours, were found nearby. It is plain that this theft was well planned and several of you were involved in this joint enterprise. None of the stolen cash has been recovered – you disappeared.

'The week before the theft, your partner and your young son had flown to the United States. Within a short time, you had joined them. You adopted your brother's identity and took advantage of his Green Card. You adopted a second alias. Your partner also took up a false name.

'And there matters rested until February 2012 when you were arrested at the place where you were then living in Missouri, USA. You were originally arrested by the US authorities on suspicion of immigration and firearms offences. For many years there had been a warrant outstanding for your arrest. Your extradition was sought from the USA, although in the end you were returned to the UK voluntarily on 10 July 2012.

'Initially you pleaded not guilty and you served a defence case statement. Your trial was due to start on 4 March. However, on 6 February of this year (and so about a month before the trial was due to commence) your solicitors wrote to the court and said you wished to change your plea to guilty. You have done that this morning.

'You are now 57. Before this crime was committed, you had been convicted of 10 other offences on four previous occasions; three of them were convictions when you were still a juvenile. The last was for robbery, but the sentence of 12 months' suspended imprisonment suggests that it was not of the most serious kind. As importantly, that conviction was in 1977 and so some 16 years before the offence for which I have to sentence you. In all these circumstances, I do not consider that any of these previous convictions significantly aggravates the present offence.

'I am told that in your teenage years you joined the Army and served two tours in Northern Ireland. You were then in the fire service. Both occupations will have involved commendable public service. You then ran a pub in Kent, but the pub was damaged, you had to sell up and debts started to accumulate.

'The temptation to commit the present offence must have been too great. It will be for the confiscation proceedings which will follow in due course to decide quite how much was your benefit from this theft. You told the authorities after your arrest that you only received £40,000. Your wife has said it was about £200,000. If she is right, you made a very substantial gain even if, as you have also said, the money has gone over the intervening period.

'I have heard that you have impressed many who knew you in the USA, but who knew nothing of your past. Your wife or partner has stood by you. She and your two sons will be pained by the sentence that I will have to pass. But it is unfortunately a common occurrence that those who commit crimes cause pain and distress to those who are close to them.

'The maximum sentence for theft is seven years' imprisonment. The Sentencing Council has issued a guideline for theft in breach of trust. Where the amount involved is £125,000 or more, or theft of £20,000 or more in breach of a high degree of trust, the starting point after a trial is three years' custody and the sentencing range of two–six years. In your case, there was a gross breach of trust. The amount involved was very, very substantially more than either of these starting points. There was detailed planning … a group of you were involved. I have considered whether the interests of justice mean that I should go beyond this range because of these aggravating features. I have though, concluded that a starting point after trial at the very top of the range will properly reflect the seriousness of the offence.

'You are entitled to credit for your plea of guilty – not as much as if you had pleaded at the first reasonable opportunity, but more than if you had first indicated your change of plea at the beginning of your trial. Your counsel has suggested that somewhere between 15-20 per cent would be appropriate and I agree that a reduction of a little more than 15 per cent is right.

'Your counsel has submitted that I should make further allowance for the five months or so which you spent in custody in the USA. I have heard what he has had to say, but I do not accept it. You were held in the USA on suspicion of committing offences against US immigration laws (because you entered and lived there under one or two false names) and US firearms legislation (because the licence which you had obtained for them was in a false name). To put it at its lowest, there were reasonable grounds to believe you had committed those offences. I am told that they were matters for which you could have been imprisoned if you had been convicted of them. You were not arrested for the theft until you returned to the UK. In all these circumstances, I make no alteration to my sentence to reflect the time in custody in the USA.

'The time in custody in the UK is different. The present legislation means, as I understand, that this will be credited automatically against your sentence, but if there is any doubt, I make it clear that this period should be set against the time you are required to serve. As will have been explained to you, at the halfway stage of this sentence you will be released on licence. If you then commit any further offence or otherwise breach your licence, you may be re-detained.

'Stand up. Edward Maher, for the offence of theft, I sentence you to five years in prison.'

28

HERO OR ZERO?

'I just thought he was a bloody thief. Hero? I don't think so. There's nothing heroic in theft.'

Peter Bunn did not have a very high opinion of Maher and never understood the public's reaction to the crime. So when justice finally caught up with his ex-colleague, Bunn had little sympathy. Along with other witnesses who gave statements to police, he received a letter of thanks from Suffolk Police following the conviction, which read: 'It is because of people like you that we have been able to build a strong case, which has resulted in Maher entering a guilty plea,' it said.

Bunn has safely filed the letter away. It will probably end up in his loft, along with the pipe he left in the Securicor van that day in 1993. 'I got it back … eventually,' he said. 'It took quite a while. My packed lunch was still in the van as well but by that point I wasn't so bothered about getting that back. But I've still got the pipe. It's in a box somewhere in the loft but don't ask me to find it. I wouldn't know where to start.'

Bunn estimated he would have seen billions of pounds during a career as a cash-in-transit driver that spanned four decades but said he was never tempted to do what Maher had done. 'I used to wonder what on earth he would have done with all the money. It's hard to get rid of as much money as that.'

John Barnett, the detective who pursued Maher throughout most of the 1990s, never bought into the theory had Maher had struck gold after committing the crime. 'If you look at his life, I don't believe it's been particularly nice,' said Barnett, now working part-time for Suffolk Police in a civilian role. 'In fact, I wouldn't swap mine for his. The problem he had was once he had done it. Not only did we know about it, his family and friends knew about it and all those nasty people he knew knew about it. I don't think it was a very clever decision. I haven't got a very high opinion of him at all.

'Even if he had got a million, can you imagine going home to your missus and saying, "We're going to move to America ... you've got to change your name and you can't speak to your friends and family ..."? I know what my missus would've said – "I don't think so!" To me, it was someone who had got themselves into a bit of a mess.'

In many ways, Maher's life never quite lived up to what many people imagined it had become. When he committed the crime, it was in the days before the National Lottery and tales of people becoming millionaires overnight were virtually unheard of. People who remembered the theft with a smile had thoughts of Maher living in the lap of luxury on sun-drenched beaches sipping cocktails without a care in the world. The money, they thought, had been the answer to all his prayers – that he had lived happily ever after.

The reality was very different. Within three years, the majority of the cash had seemingly vanished and Maher was once again working for a living. When it emerged following his arrest in America that he had been declared bankrupt, some were not only surprised but a little disappointed - bankruptcy did not fit with the fantasy lifestyle that they'd imagined he'd be enjoying. Andrew Young, the freelance reporter who has covered the story since the day of the theft, said, 'We all had this picture of him living in luxury some-where rather than the reality of how it turned out for him, flitting from place to place.'

In Felixstowe, Fast Eddie has never been forgotten and there remains a feeling in the town that the heist had been a 'harmless 'crime. Retired Port of Felixstowe police officer Richard Cattermole, now in his seventies, said, 'A lot of the talk around at the time was what a hero he was. He had this admiration in some sort of way. He didn't beat anybody up. Then he managed to keep it secret from his colleagues. It was quite a feat what he managed to pull off.'

Following the conviction, police were as keen as they had been throughout the 20-year inquiry to dispel the 'Robin Hood' myth associated with Maher. David Giles, the detective who flew to the United States as part of 2013 investigation, said, 'Over the years, Edward Maher has almost been portrayed as a Robin Hood character, someone who stole from a bank, where no one was injured. Maher took on a position of significant trust working for a security company, a position he abused, resulting in the theft of over £1m.'

Chris McCann, from the CPS, added, 'I think the public might have sympathy with a real Robin Hood … but not Eddie Maher.'

Maher was being jailed in 2013 for a crime that it is highly unlikely he would have been able to commit today. The Internet, social media and closed-circuit television would all have made it so much harder to get away with. Improved security in banks, security vans and airports would also have conspired against him, as would the increased ease of tracking bank accounts and telephone calls. All these tools would have helped Barnett in the initial 1993 investigation. He said: 'It's totally different now. We didn't have CCTV then, social media. I reckon the last 20 years have got to be the biggest 20 years there have ever been in terms of advances in technology. If Facebook had been about then his picture would have been out within minutes. It's a lot harder to disappear now.'

Colin Adwent, the local crime reporter, said it was certainly 'easier' to vanish in 1993. 'When this happened 20 years ago, things were different, technology was different, communication lines were different,' he said.

Of the three officers originally tasked with tracking down Maher, only Barnett is still alive. David Moss, the senior investigating officer at the start of the 1993 investigation, died in 2001 and Peter Noble in September 1993. Asked what they would have thought of Maher's arrest and subsequent conviction, Barnett said, 'I think they would have been the same as me. I'm sure they would have been pleased he had been caught.'

Maher's time behind bars will be hard for Debbie, Lee and Mark, who have been used to having him around. But for the family Maher left behind two decades ago, it is a slightly different feeling. Terry Maher, the son from his first marriage, feels like he has been reunited with his father, despite the fact he is in jail. Speaking to Bob Graham in America following his father's arrest, the father of two said, 'The one good thing to come out of all of this is I get to have my father back and my kids get to meet their grandfather. I never had any ill-feeling for my dad for the way he disappeared – Dad did what Dad did – what he thought was best for Debbie, Lee and himself. Growing up he was a good dad … he was a bit of a hero for me. He did what he did and what he thought was for the best at the time. It's not always right. I'm just happy I got him back.'

Being back in contact with his father had given Terry the chance to fill him in on all the family news that had bypassed him during the previous two decades. 'I don't think people realise what a close family Dad's from and there's much he's missed over the years … [the death of] his mum, my wedding, births and deaths. Lots of them,' said Terry, speaking to Graham in a second interview in London. 'We never had any contact over the years and it's been more than a prison for him. You can't describe it; you've lost your dad but can't grieve for him.

'Because of what happened, people distance themselves from you. I never had any ill feelings towards him because of it, though. At the time, I was nearly 21 and in the Army, the Royal

Engineers. I joined the London Fire Brigade two years later. It was a bit like Dad – he was in the Green Jackets and did three tours of Northern Ireland before he joined the fire brigade. When I joined, a lot of the people knew about my dad but I always told people, "My dad is Eddie Maher." Always best to get it into the open.'

Like many others, Terry never thought any great harm was done by the actual theft. He called it a 'fantasy crime'. 'No one was ever hurt, most people have said, "Good luck to him," especially with the attitude to banks these days,' he said.

Debbie, Mark and Lee all moved to Eastbourne, on the so-called sunshine coast of East Sussex, following their return to the UK. Immigration authorities in America had already started proceedings to remove Debbie and Lee from the country by the summer of 2012. Debbie, along with Mark, returned to the UK in August 2012, followed by Lee a few weeks later. Although living in the same town, they were at separate addresses. Debbie and Mark were staying with Maher's sister, Margaret Francis, and Lee was with another family member.

Maher's sentencing hearing provided a fascinating insight into the family dynamics. As details of the case were read out by the two barristers, sitting at the back of the court were the principal characters in this long-running saga; it would have been hard for them to listen to. Debbie and Mark sat side by side in one row of seats; Lee, accompanied by two women, sat behind them and slightly to the left. They arrived separately and left separately. Throughout the court hearing, which lasted nearly three hours, they barely made eye contact. There was certainly no attempt to paint a picture of a united family as they left court.

For Mark, the experience of an English courtroom must have been surreal. The day of his father's sentencing was his sixteenth birthday. Most teenagers would have spent the day opening presents and enjoying a party with friends. He had only come to the UK for the first time seven months earlier; now he was in a court looking at his father caged in a glass dock, preparing for a lengthy jail term. It would be a birthday he would never forget, but for all the wrong reasons. He remained at his mother's side throughout the court hearing and displayed a demeanour of someone much older than his years. It was a maturity that was perhaps inevitable with the amount of growing up he would have had to do over the previous 13 months.

During a brief pause in proceedings, Maher turned around and blew a kiss to his family. Debbie, Mark and Lee each replied with the same gesture and a wave. At the end of the hearing, Maher waved and winked at them as he was led into the cells, bound for the top-security Belmarsh Prison in south-east London, where he would join some of Britain's most dangerous criminals. His family filed out of court almost immediately, each refusing to talk to reporters as they left.

Walking as quickly as he could down three flights of stairs, Lee was asked a succession of questions by journalists on his trail. 'Lee, anything to say?' … 'What do you think of the sentence' … 'Did your mother say anything to you?' Every question was met with silence.

Lee's inability to a keep a secret had led to his father being brought before the courts and his family's life being turned upside down. Now, perhaps, he had decided he had said enough. Making his way out of court, Lee quickly joined the busy street and headed towards London Bridge Tube station. Debbie and Mark had gone in a different direction.

As Maher was driven out of court in a prison van, his years of aliases, false passports and secrets were behind him. His luck had long since run out. A television report that night said his guilty plea and jail term marked the final act in an 'incredible drama', one that had begun in Felixstowe on a wintry January day in 1993 had ended just over 20 years later in Courtroom 1 of Southwark Crown Court. In between, Maher had managed to vanish into obscurity, leave police trailing in his wake and, in the process, become one of Britain's most wanted criminals. Now, as he was led to the cells from the central London court, he was facing up to the next few years behind bars as a penniless convict. Not only had he been jailed, he had also been told police would be making a bid to seize the £129,000 pension pot from his time as a London firefighter.

The evidence in court revealed police enquiries in relation to the Securicor theft were continuing - three people were named as wanted and three others were on bail at the time. It suggested further prosecutions could follow. However, nine days later, Suffolk Police put out a press release saying all three people arrested in connection with the theft would not face any action. Debbie, Margaret Francis and Paul Muggleton all had their bail conditions cancelled. A Suffolk Police statement read: 'Three people arrested and released on police bail in connection with the investigation into a security van theft outside Lloyds Bank, Felixstowe, in 1993 will receive no further police action at this stage, and have had their bail cancelled. A decision has been made by the Crown Prosecution Service and senior investigating officers at Suffolk Police that no further action will be taken against them at this stage.'

Similarly, Michael Maher, 62, was also arrested before being freed without charge. He had been traced to Torremolinos, a coastal town on Spain's Costa del Sol that is popular with British ex-pats. He had been arrested on suspicion of assisting an offender when he landed at Luton Airport on 9 June 2013, but was released a day later.

Police confirmed soon after that there were no active lines of investigation in the case.

The day when Maher's last penny was taken came on 20 September 2013, when he appeared at Ipswich Crown Court via a video-link from Belmarsh Prison. After a brief Asset Recovery Hearing under the Criminal Justice Act, judge David Goodin ruled the now 58-year-old Maher's pension should be seized.

The judge told Maher, 'You will have six months to pay and, should you fail to do so, you will serve two and a half years consecutive with your current prison sentence.'

Wearing a grey T-shirt and with a 'HMP Belmarsh' sign in view behind him, Maher was asked if he understood. 'Yes, sir, I understand,' was his reply.

The court ruled £50,000 should be paid to G4S and £79,000 to insurers Equitas. No further information came out during the hearing to contradict the now widely-held belief that Maher had pocketed about £200,000 from the theft.

It was a low-key affair, with none of Maher's family in attendance and even the man himself only appearing on a television screen in the corner of the court. It had been decided it was not worth the time and money it would cost to transport Maher from south-east London to Ipswich. Outside court, police investigator Giles told reporters it was 'pleasing' to know that at least some of the money had been recovered.

Elsewhere, lawyers were continuing to pursue the case on behalf of Jessica King, the ex-daughter-in-law who had done so much to bring Fast Eddie to justice. She believed she was entitled to the £100,000 reward offered in 1993 for information about the crime. Following the case, G4S, the company that had taken over Securicor, appeared to give her hope that an agreement could be reached. 'At the time of Mr Maher's disappearance, Securicor's insurers offered a reward for information which led to the return of the stolen money,' said a company spokesman, who added that the case had never been forgotten, even after the Securicor brand 'disappeared'.

'Maher has been found but the sum he stole has never been recovered and this was the basis on which the reward was offered. Despite this, we acknowledge the important role that Jessica King played in Maher's extradition and conviction and we will be in touch with her legal team in the near future.'

The ongoing legal wrangle has the potential to rumble on for years to come, meaning the final act in the 'incredible drama' may be yet to come. But one person unlikely to be following any future developments is the co-worker Maher abandoned during his Securicor shift on 22 January 1993. Until 2012, Peter Bunn had 'wiped' the case from his memory, but the arrest and subsequent conviction brought it all flooding back. Now Maher has been jailed, he said he did not intend to 'give it a second thought'. Bunn retired in 2006 and now collects two pensions – one from Securicor and another from his time in the Royal Navy. He might not be living the high life that Maher so desperately craved, but he is comfortable, living in a semi-detached house in Chelmsford.

So would he have swapped places with Maher, given the chance? 'Good lord, no!' he replies, without a moment's hesitation in his gravelly Essex accent. 'I've had a happy life. I'm not bothered about money. I've got two pensions coming in … I've got sufficient money and have a very comfortable existence. I play golf twice a week. I'm quite happy, thanks.'

Languishing in Belmarsh Prison, Maher can only dream of the sort of life Peter Bunn now enjoys. But given half the chance, Maher would probably gladly swap places with the fellow guard he abandoned on a pavement in Felixstowe all those years ago.